This book is due to be returned not later than the date and
time stamped above. Fines are charged on overdue books

-5 JUL 2006

Managing in the voluntary sector

Managing in the voluntary sector

A handbook for managers in charitable and non-profit organizations

Edited by
Stephen P Osborne
Aston Business School
Aston University

INTERNATIONAL THOMSON BUSINESS PRESS
I ⓉP An International Thomson Publishing Company

London • Bonn • Boston • Johannesburg • Madrid • Melbourne • Mexico City • New York • Paris
Singapore • Tokyo • Toronto • Albany, NY • Belmont, CA • Cincinnati, OH • Detroit, MI

British Library Cataloguing-in-Publication Data
A catalogue record for this book is available from the British Library

First edition 1996

Typeset in the UK by J&L Composition Ltd, Filey, North Yorkshire
Printed in the UK at the University Press, Cambridge

ISBN 0–412–71840–5

International Thomson Business Press   International Thomson Business Press
Berkshire House   20 Park Plaza
168–173 High Holborn   13th Floor
London WC1V 7AA   Boston MA 02116
UK   USA

http://www.thomson.com/itbp.html

Dedication

For the '*three Ms*':
Marian, Martha and Madeline

Contents

List of figures & tables

FIGURES

TABLES

List of contributors

Tony Bovaird
is senior lecturer in Public Services Management and course director of the MBA in Public Services Management at Aston Business School, Birmingham.

Paul Golder
is lecturer in Computer Science at Aston University in Birmingham.

Margaret Harris
is assistant director of the Centre for Voluntary Organization [CVO] at the London School of Economics, London.

Linda Horner
is divisional training manager of the Midlands Division of Barnardo's, based in Birmingham. She writes here in her personal capacity.

Chris Huxham
is senior lecturer in Management at Strathclyde Business School, Glasgow.

David Johnson
is senior lecturer in Public Services Management and convenor of the Public Services Management Group at Aston Business School in Birmingham.

Richard Kay
is director of the Centre for Voluntary Non-profit Studies at LSU College in Southampton. Until recently, he was director of the Rainer Foundation.

Sarabajaya Kumar
is a research associate of the Voluntary and Non-profit Research Unit [VNRU] at Aston Business School, Birmingham.

Mike Luck
is senior lecturer in Public Services Management at Aston Business School in Birmingham.

Mark Lyons
is director of the Centre for Community Organization Management [CACOM] at the University of Technology, Sydney.

Vic Murray
is former director of the Voluntary Sector Management Program at York University, Toronto.

Marian Osborne
is assistant divisional director of the Midlands Division of Barnardo's, based in Birmingham. She writes here in her personal capacity.

Stephen P. Osborne (Editor)	is lecturer in Public Services Management and joint director of the Voluntary and Non-profit Research Unit [VNRU] at Aston Business School, Birmingham.
Paul Palmer	is director of the Charity & Trusts Research Centre at South Bank University, London.
Colin Rochester	is research and dissemination officer of the CVO at the London School of Economics, London.
Anne Rubienska	is a member of the Development Administration Group at the University of Birmingham, Birmingham.
Jill Schofield	is teaching fellow in Health Services Management at Aston Business School, Birmingham.
Bill Tassie	is lecturer in the Voluntary Sector Management program at York University, Toronto.
Ian Taylor	is lecturer in Public Services Management and course director of the MSc in Public Services Management at Aston Business School, Birmingham.
Siv Vangen	is lecturer in Management at Strathclyde Business School, Glasgow.
Asaf Zohar	is lecturer in Voluntary Sector Management at York University, Toronto.

Acknowledgements

The initial impetus for this book came out of extensive training and consultancy work that my colleagues at Aston Business School and I have carried out with managers from voluntary and non-profit organizations. These managers share the credit for bringing this volume into existence and for providing a wealth of experience and suggestions for its content.

As will be apparent, however, this is not solely an *Aston Productions* volume. It also benefits from chapters from colleagues based elsewhere, both in the UK and beyond. Their forbearance for my increasingly frantic efforts to turn this book from a concept to reality are also appreciated.

The book has also benefited from comments and suggestions from people not directly involved in it. Of particular assistance were Nicholas Deakin of Birmingham University, Colin Myers of Westminster University and Chris Cornforth of the Open University. A special debt of gratitude is owed to two people. They are John Perrin of Exeter University (Series Editor for this book), for his advice and encouragement in the early stages of its birth, and to Sarah Henderson, my Commissioning Editor at International Thompson Business Press (or Chapman & Hall as it was in the dark days long ago when this book was commissioned), for her invaluable advice and assistance.

Chapter fourteen, on performance and quality management, drew upon and adapted material produced elsewhere by the editor of this book. This material is 'The quality dimension', in *British Journal of Social Work*, **22** pp. 437–53; *The Public Sector Management Handbook*, with S. Nutley, Longman, London; and Performance management in complex public programmes, in *Financial Accountability and Management*, **11**,(1) pp. 19–38, with T. Bovaird, S. Martin and M. Tricker.

Jean Elkington and Jane Winder at Aston Business School both provided essential administrative support in turning what seemed like endless chapters-on-disc, in innumerable different software formats, into one seamless volume.

Finally, as always, a thank you to my family for their understanding and compassion during the birth of this book.

Introduction: managing in the voluntary and non-profit sector

Stephen P. Osborne

A BRIEF HISTORICAL PRELUDE

The roles and functions of voluntary and non-profit organizations (VNPOs) in contemporary society have undergone a major transformation over the last thirty years. Many of the early proponents of the welfare state in the UK in the 1950s (though interestingly, not Beveridge himself; see Beveridge 1948) assumed that VNPOs would simply wither away, as the state took on its rightful hegemonic role in society. That they did not 'wither away' was at least in part due to the range of governmental programmes to combat urban, and later rural, deprivation that the Labour government of the 1960s introduced in Britain. These programmes have continued, and indeed multiplied, ever since and have provided a key source of finance for VNPOs. However, if these programmes ensured the survival of the sector, it was at a cost. Many VNPOs became dependent upon such governmental funding for their survival and found that it threatened their independence of action. The era of the **quango**, the 'quasi autonomous non governmental organization' (Pifer 1967) had arrived.

During the 1980s a second societal trend had a similarly profound effect upon the finances of VNPOs. This was the determination of, this time, the then Conservative government to move from unitary public services provided by government toward a plural system. This was where government planned and, at best, part-funded such services but where their provision was largely through the 'independent' sector. This latter sector included both for-profit agencies and VNPOs. The reasons for this political change have been well analysed elsewhere (Mischra 1984; Ascher 1988). What is important here is the profound impact that this had upon the roles and financial structure of the voluntary and non-profit sector.

From being, at best, a marginal partner in the production of the public services, VNPOs now found themselves propelled to the mainstream of service provision. This change had, and is continuing to have, a multitude of impacts upon VNPOs. Three are of particular significance for this book. First, it challenged the traditional characteristics and functions of VNPOs which were said to differentiate them from public organizations. These included flexibility, a non-bureaucratic structure and a capacity for innovation (Knapp *et al.* 1990). However, as they took on increasingly public roles it became harder to maintain such traditional differences from public organizations (Osborne 1994). The poachers were turning, or being turned, game-keepers.

Second, government funding was becoming more and more important as a funding source for VNPOs. One recent study has estimated that such income for the sector increased from 41.4% to 53.7%, between 1975 and 1990 (Osborne and Hems 1995). This change had an impact, not only upon the relationship of the sector to government, but also to its other funders and donors. Individuals and institutions were understandably less willing to donate to the work of VNPOs if this money was going to be used simply to subsidize under-funded governmental, and possibly statutory, services.

Finally, both these developments combined to challenge the traditional independence of VNPOs. On the one hand, they found themselves becoming made increasingly accountable to governmental agencies for their work, often through more or less rigorous service contracts (Meadows 1992). The scope and nature of such contractual agreements varies tremendously (Osborne and Waterston 1994), but they all have implications for the traditional accountability of VNPOs to their governing boards and members/beneficiaries. Some have argued that this trend is likely to make VNPOs become more like the major government agencies that fund them (DiMaggio and Powell 1988; Singh *et al.* 1991). Others have likened the whole process to a game, where what is important is not so much the substantive contract or service concerned, but rather the rules through which it is negotiated and evaluated (Bernstein 1991). On the other hand, other critics have raised concerns over the impact of service contracting upon the ability and/or willingness of VNPOs to act as critics of government and to advocate and campaign upon behalf of disadvantaged groups and individuals, for two reasons. First, because government might find reasons to withdraw funding from groups that were making life unpleasant for them. Second, because of an understandable, if regrettable, fear upon behalf of VNPOs of 'biting the hand that feeds them' (Deakin 1991).

These and many other factors make managing VNPOs an increasingly challenging task. This is true whether one looks at small community groups or at large national and international charities (Osborne 1996). This book is dedicated to helping managers in VNPOs to survive, and hopefully to prosper, in their new more competitive environment. Its inspiration has been the wealth of training, education and consultancy work that its editor and contributors have engaged in with, and on behalf of, VNPOs. This made it clear that there was a pressing need for a book which brought the acquisition of key management skills together with a more measured understanding of their context and meaning. There are many good 'how to do it' books available for managers in VNPOs (many produced in the UK from within the sector, such as by NCVO or the Directory of Social Change). There are also some, though rather less, books which reflect upon the changing nature of management in VNPOs. None have attempted to bring these two elements together. This is important for two reasons. First, skills and/or reflection are of limited use in isolation. What is significant is the active reflection upon management-in-action. This is what this book seeks to provide, by combining practical advice about how to undertake key managerial tasks in VNPOs with discussion of their origins and impact upon VNPOs. Second, such skills/understanding gain greater import by being approached holistically, where inter-relationships can be emphasized, rather than being talked about in isolation. This book is aimed thus at the thinking and reflective managers, who want to increase their range of tools for management, whilst also developing a deeper appreciation of their impact upon their organization.

PLAN OF THE BOOK

This book begins with four introductory chapters. The first gives some essential theoretical background to understanding the roles and functions of VNPOs in modern society. The next two then examine respectively the ethics of management in the sector and the major role played by the relationship between the paid staff of a VNPO and its governing board. This is followed by a chapter which outlines some of the basic cost and budgeting issues that a VNPO faces and which underlie most of the subsequent topics discussed.

These are followed by three chapters which explore different aspects of service planning and the macro-level of organizational management – marketing, strategic management and business planning. Six subsequent chapters then discuss key issues in the operational management of VNPOs. These start off by examining project planning and management, which in many ways forms the link between the strategic and the operational levels, and then goes on to examine the issues of managing change, equal opportunities and anti-discriminatory practice, information management, contracting for services and the management of inter-organizational relationships. The final group of chapters focus upon service evaluation and its link to accountability. These cover performance and quality management, the nature of accountability in general and financial accounting and accountability in particular. Each chapter includes both **references** to texts referred to in its body, and an annotated **guided reading** section. This is intended as a guide into the more specialized literature for those readers wishing to take their reading further.

The contributors to this volume come from varied backgrounds. Some are practising managers in VNPOs; some are specialist trainers and consultants in the field of VNPO management; and others are specialists in a field of management practice but with substantial experience of applying this to the voluntary and non-profit sector. All are committed to raising the standards of managerial practice and performance.

A note on terminology

Throughout this volume, the term 'voluntary and non-profit organization' (VNPO) will be used as a generic term to refer to all voluntary, non-profit and charitable organizations.

REFERENCES

Ascher, K. (1988) *The Politics of Privatisation* Macmillan, London.

Bernstein, S. (1991) *Managing Contractual Services in the Non-profit Agency*, Temple University Press, Philadelphia.

Beveridge, W. (1948) *Voluntary Action*, Allen & Unwin, London.

Deakin, N. (1991) The government and the voluntary sector in the 1990s. *Policy Studies*, **12**, (3), pp. 11–12.

DiMaggio, P. and Powell, W. (1988) The iron cage revisited, in *Community Organizations* (ed C. Milofsky) Oxford University Press, New York.

Knapp, M., Robertson, E. and Thomason, C. (1990) Public money, voluntary action: whose welfare? in *The Third Sector* (eds H. Anheier and W. Seibel) de Gruyter, Berlin.

Meadows, A. (1992) *Reaching Agreement*, NCVO, London.

Mischra, R. (1984) *The Welfare State in Transition*, Wheatsheaf, London.

Osborne, S. (1994) *The Once and Future Pioneers? The Role of Voluntary Organizations in Innovation in Social Care Services*, Joseph Rowntree Foundation/ Aston University, Birmingham.

Osborne, S. (1996) What training does the voluntary sector need? in *Voluntary Agencies* (ed D. Billis and M. Harris) Macmillan, London, pp. 200–21.

Osborne, S. and Hems, L. (1995) The economic structure of the charitable sector in the United Kingdom. *Non-profit and Voluntary Sector Quarterly* **24**, (4), pp. 321–36.

Osborne, S. and Waterson, P. (1994) Defining contracts between the state and charitable organizations in national accounts. *Voluntas* **5**, (3), pp. 291–300.

Pifer, A. (1967) *Quasi Non Governmental Organizations* Carnegie Corporation, New York.

Singh, J., Tucker, D. and Meinhard, A. (1991) Institutional change and ecological dynamics, in *The New Institutionalism in Organizational Analysis* (eds W. Powell and P. DiMaggio), University of Chicago Press, Chicago, pp. 390–422.

GUIDED READING

Prochaska, F. (1988) *The Charitable Impulse*, Faber, London. This is a good introduction to the historical roots of the voluntary sector in the UK, though stronger on the philanthropic tradition than the self-help tradition. For the latter, try Harrison, B. and Deakin, N. (1988) *Voluntary Organisations and Democracy*, NCVO, London – brief and to the point.

Davis Smith, J., Rochester, C. and Hedley, R. (eds) (1995) *Introduction to the Voluntary Sector*, Routledge, London and Billis, D. and Harris, M. (eds) (1996) *Voluntary Agencies* are both good guides to the key managerial issues facing VNPOs at present.

Landry, C. (1985) *What a Way to Run a Rail-road*, Comedia, London offers a humourous and perceptive account of management within the voluntary sector. For a more analytic look at management within the sector, the best book remains Butler, R. and Wilson, D. (1990) *Managing Voluntary and Non-profit Organisations*, Routledge, London.

1 What is 'voluntary' about the voluntary and non-profit sector?

Stephen P. Osborne

INTRODUCTION

The good life is an activity not a receptivity; a doing of things sponta-
neously for the good of the community and the satisfaction of the social
instincts in man. . . . Destroy, even check unnecessarily, instincts for
self expression and self realisation which freedom of speech and freedom of association . . . have made possible and we sap the very life
stream of the community. It is a spiritual issue which is at stake. It is in a
freedom of the spirit that the real energy source lies, in energy, which
can transform the material world as a means to the end of the good
community . . .

Voluntary action is experimental, flexible progressive. It can adjust
more easily than the statutory authority its machinery and methods to
deal with changing conditions and with diversity of cases. This capacity
for experiment, for trial and error, is one of the most valuable qualities
in community life.

(Forward by Dr Adams, written in 1948, to
National Council of Social Service (1970))

This chapter will help the reader to understand the nature of organized
voluntary activity and clarify briefly some definitional issues. It will then
focus more specifically upon organized voluntary activity and will summarize briefly the nature and extent of such organized activity in Britain.
By the end of this chapter, the reader should

- understand the core concepts involved in thinking about voluntary organizations;
- be able to think about their own organization using these concepts; and
- be clear about their import for the management of VNPOs.

At the outset, an important point should be emphasized. In this initial
section, the term **voluntary organization** will be used as shorthand for
organized voluntary effort, without prejudice. The second section of this
chapter will explore this term further and argue for the use of the term

voluntary and non-profit organization (VNPO) as the best generic term for such organizations.

DEVELOPING A TYPOLOGY OF VOLUNTARY ACTIVITY

The quotation prefacing this chapter encapsulated many of the popularly held beliefs – and prejudices – about voluntary action. It draws no distinction between individual and organized voluntary action and assumes an altruism and innovativeness which is contrasted to the vested interests and bureaucracy of the statutory services. This mixture is then posited as 'one of the most valuable qualities in community life'.

It is possible to discern the mixture of three different conceptual strands within this mixture. The first is that of a free society, where individuals act together in common cause and where state action is seen as, at best, a necessary evil to be held in check, and at worst an unnecessary and unnatural block on individual action. The second strand is that of individual voluntary effort to meet identified needs. The final strand is that of organized voluntary effort. This latter strand does incorporate ideas from the first two (in that it is seen as qualitatively better than state action and as based upon individual effort), but it also has its own distinctive features.

Whilst all three of these strands are clearly intertwined and are best understood as a triad of concepts, each is distinctive with its own parameters and background ideas. Previous work by this author (Osborne 1993a) has helped in differentiating these strands. This prior work was based upon developing the initial classification of voluntary effort established by Van Til in *Mapping the Third Sector* (1988). This is one of the major recent contributions to the understanding of voluntary organizations, though the particular concern here is his attempt to separate out the above three strands for analysis. He commences with a statement of the core principle of each of these strands, before offering both an empirical basis and normative conceptualization of it. The full typology is reproduced in Figure 1.1.

This approach to the conceptualization of the voluntary ethic is a useful one. It helps separate out the differing strands of the concept and makes explicit their empirical and normative implications. However the approach is not taken through as far as it might be. The starting point of the typology is 'individual action', and its first two components seek to differentiate two types of such action, before moving on to its organized form. This approach is deficient in that it excludes the concept of **voluntary action**, as a societal principle, from its analysis. Yet this is a conceptualization of the voluntary ethic at its most fundamental and one which is found to run through both of the other strands, of individual and organized voluntary action.

In order to include this fundamental concept, it is therefore necessary to develop further this typology. This is done in Figure 1.2. In addition to

Core Principle	'Individual action not coerced . . .	. . . and deemed beneficial . . .	. . . and organized.'
Empirical Form	voluntary action	volunteering	voluntary associations and non-profit corporations
Normative Concept	freedom	volunteerism	voluntarism

Figure 1.1 Typology of voluntary concepts I (Van Til 1988)

Concept	Voluntaryism	Volunteerism	Voluntarism
Focus of concern	Relationship of individual and society	Individual action in society	Organized action in society
Normative statement	Free ('Active') society	Vountary society	Plural society
Background Theory	de Tocqueville Etzioni	Titmuss Horton-Smith	Berger and Neuhaus Gladstone

Figure 1.2 Typology of voluntary concepts II (Osborne)

clarifying more clearly the concepts involved, the distinctions within the typology have also been refined to better delineate the three strands. This typological development thus allows the specification of the focus of concern of each conceptual strand, its normative goal (or 'ideal state'), and the background theory informing its conceptual construction.

It will be useful here to explore the concepts in Figure 1.2 in more depth. The first, **voluntaryism**, refers to the societal principle of voluntary action as a building block for society. At one level it links back to the voluntaryism of the Church and reminds us that religious inspiration has often formed the basis for early voluntary action. Indeed some, such as Collins and Hickman (1991), argue that this is the basis of the distictive contribution of voluntary activity to society.

At another level, this concept has as its ideal state a society where all action is freely chosen, and can be characterized as the **free**, or **active**, society (the term 'voluntary society' has also been used by some authors in this context, but this is to be reserved here for specific usage, in connection with voluntarism). The actuality of such a free society has been well articulated by Schultz:

> . . . a society which achieves a high level of social integration but does this with minimum reliance on force and money as organizing principles . . . Voluntarism (sic) is one of the goals of such a society as it is also a means which is employed to establish and accomplish societal priorities, and to define and solve societal problems.
>
> *(Schultz 1972: 25–6)*

The origins of voluntaryism as a societal principle can be found in the liberalism of the eighteenth and nineteenth centuries, with its emphasis on individual action and its antipathy to state action. The clearest statements of these roots are found in the writings of de Tocqueville (1835, reprinted 1971) on his experiences in America. He identified the principle of voluntary association as an essential component of a civilized society. This theme has been taken to its logical conclusion in the more recent writings of Etzioni (1961; 1968) who posits a society based upon this principle of voluntaryism.

The second concept, **volunteerism**, combines both of the first two core principles of Van Til – 'individualism not coerced' and 'deemed beneficial'. The focus here is upon the **individual** action involved. It encompasses the reality of individual action in society. In ideal terms, it is the principle of voluntaryism applied to everyday affairs. Thus it can encompass the establishment of a business and the committing of adultery, the joining of a club and the decision about what to have for dinner.

Some, such as Gamwell (1984), see a key link between voluntaryism and volunteerism, the latter being the cornerstone of the 'free society' of the former. Others take a more prosaic view of it, concerned with personal voluntary action aimed at the benefit of others. Darvill and Mundy provide what could be called the archetypal definition of a volunteer, as a person:

> . . . who voluntarily provides an unpaid direct service for one or more other persons to whom the volunteer is not related. The volunteer

normally provides his or her services through some kind of formal scheme rather than through an informal neighbouring arrangement.

(Darvill and Mundy 1984: 3)

The complexities of this concept need not detain us further in this context, but are explored in greater detail in Osborne (1993a).

The final concept of this triumverate is that of **voluntarism**, and this corresponds to the 'organized voluntary action' of Van Til. In moving on to the concept of voluntarism, we are moving to the central concerns of this thesis. With voluntarism, the focus shifts to the organizational and institutional level of analysis. It is necessary at the outset to draw a vital distinction between this and individual voluntary action. Whilst it is true that voluntary organizations may well contain volunteers, it is a mistake to see this as their defining feature. It is also a mistake which is commonly made; for example, the recent study of the funding of voluntary organizations in Britain by central government, carried out by the Home Office (1990), made great play of the cost benefits of volunteer labour and maintains an assumption that voluntary organizations are also organizations deriving a significant amount of their strength from volunteers.

In fact, volunteers can play a full or a minimal role in voluntary organizations but this is not the key determinant of voluntarism. It is not individual action on which this concept focuses, but, upon the voluntary organizational characteristics of the bodies concerned. It is these characteristics which define the voluntariness of an organization or structure. They were well summarized half a century ago by Bourdillon. The essential characteristics of such an organization were not the products of its labour, she contended,

> . . . but of their mode of birth and method of government. A voluntary organisation properly speaking is an organisation which, whether its workers are paid or unpaid, is initiated and governed by its own members without external control. Such a body may well undertake work on behalf of a statutory authority, but if it is to qualify as a voluniary organisation it is essential that it should select or cooperate in selecting what that work shall be and how it shall be done.
>
> *(Bourdillon 1945: 3)*

This formulation of voluntarism also denotes a commitment to self-regulation, as has been identified by many social historians. This is especially to be noted within such 'representative' organizations as trade unions and professional associations. This view was explored in detail at an early stage of this century by Webb and Webb (1911). Voluntarism, as a normative concept, views voluntary organizations as the essential elements of a free society, and harks back to the emphasis of de Tocqueville on the importance of association as the cornerstone of civilization. This conceptualization sees society as a 'rich stew', which the diversity of voluntary organizations reflects (Cornuelle 1983).

Within Western society, such voluntarism is often espoused as an essential component of democracy by allowing sectoral and minority interests to have a voice, by keeping a check on the state, and by adding to diversity in service delivery (see, for example, the report of the Finer Committee – US Department of the Treasury 1977). In its ideal state it posits a wholly plural society, where each sector has a voice and where there are multiple sources of public services. This ideal version of vountarism once again makes explicit the underlying concept of voluntaryism in organized voluntary activity. The key proponents of this argument are Berger and Neuhaus (1977), with their view of voluntary organizations as 'mediating institutions' in society, and Gladstone (1979) with his view of these organizations as providing a diversity and choice in public services not to be found in governmental ones.

This ideal version of voluntarism, with its belief in a plural society, and antipathy to the role of the state in society, has its critics. They have argued that it ignores its 'dark side' (Van Til 1988), and lacks a structural analysis of the distribution of power within society. In its ideal form, pluralism requires an equal distribution of power with society (Brenton 1985), and ignores some of the drawbacks of service delivery in a plural society (Salamon 1987).

In spite of these critiques, voluntarism has become a powerful concept in the late twentieth century in the Western world, as the modern states have been perceived to have failed in their tasks of achieving social justice (it is also gathering an increasing impetus in the developing world and in post-communist Eastern and Central Europe, as a core component of the **civil society**; see, for example, Fisher 1993 and Les 1994). Voluntarism, it seems, may well be an idea whose time has come. This makes the understanding of the parameters of its key organs, voluntary organizations, even more essential. It is to this task that the remainder of this chapter is devoted.

DEFINING ORGANIZED VOLUNTARY ACTIVITY

This chapter began by agreeing to use the term **voluntary organizations** to denote organized voluntary effort but made the point that this term would need to be explored further at a later stage. That stage has now come. There are a number of ways of describing organized voluntary effort in contemporary Western society, both in terms of individual organizations and of the sector as a whole. These include **charities and philanthropic organizations** (Butler and Wilson 1990; Gurin and Van Til 1990), **non-profit organizations** (James 1990; Salamon and Anheier 1994), **non-governmental organizations** and **para-governmental organizations** (Cousins 1982; Hood 1984) and as **quangos** (Pifer 1967; 1975; Barker 1982).

Each of these terms has its strengths and limitations, and again these have been discussed further in Osborne (1993a). However, for this book, it is argued that the term voluntary and non-profit organization (VNPO) is the most useful. It is the one which focuses our attention on the organizational and institutional characteristics of these organizations.

In doing so, however, the contribution of the recent work by Salamon and Anheier (1994) – see also Anheier (1995) – and their colleagues in the Johns Hopkins Comparative Nonprofit Sector Project has to be acknowledged. Although using the term **non-profit**, their focus was upon the organizational characteristics of such organizations. These characteristics were that they:

- were formally constituted organizations;
- were private organizations and separate from government (though they could receive governmental support for their work);
- were non-profit distributing, to their owners or directors;
- were self-governing and 'equipped to control their own activities'; and
- had some meaningful voluntary content, such as voluntary income, volunteer labour or voluntary management.

This is an important approach and one which goes beyond the basic **non-profit** definition to embrace the organizational dimensions.

The approach taken here, therefore, will be to use the term **voluntary and non-profit organization** (VNPO) to denote organized voluntary activity, but to draw upon the insights of the Johns Hopkins project in doing so. By applying these insights it is possible to subdivide the two organizational characteristics of VNPOs described earlier by Bourdillon (1945) into five, to give a more explicit understanding of this phenomenon.

First, VNPOs must be **formally structured**. The extent and nature of this formalization can vary (from having an agreed constitution to having paid staff, for example). Nonetheless it is apparent enough to separate them out from informal gatherings and meetings.

Second, they should be **founded** independent of state control. They exist because a certain group of people want them to, not because there is some legislative requirement for them. The state (at either a local or central level) may have a role in encouraging such organizations to come together but it must not be a prime mover, either by legislating to form such organizations or by being a majority force in its founding membership.

Third, VNPOs should be **governed** by a management committee which is able to decide its own composition, either at the behest of its membership or by its own decisions, and have independent decision-making capacity. Again, they might share this capacity with government but cannot abnegate it entirely.

Fourth, they have a distinctive pattern of **financial management**. VNPOs cannot distribute any surplus accrued by their mission critical activities, but must re-invest it in services. They are also differentiated from statutory organizations by having voluntary income which is not raised through taxation.

Finally, the **motivation** of a VNPO should not be based upon financial gain, but rather should hold some normative **voluntary** value. In this there is a clear echo of the 'public benefit' clause of the legal definition of a charity. However, it is wider than this, in that it includes activity which has an element of self-benefit (such as self-help groups), but which are excluded under charity law. It is important to emphasize that the nature of this voluntary content can vary. It may mean the participation of volunteers in the fund-raising, management or service-delivery activities of an organization, for example, or the presence of voluntary funds for the organization.

Such a definition is broad enough to include the wide range of truly voluntary organizations, whilst excluding those organizations which, although 'non-profit' making or 'non-governmental', do not derive their mainspring from voluntarism. Private hospitals are a good example of the former and many Housing Associations of the latter. Moreover, it does not draw impermeable boundaries between voluntary and other types of organizations, which boundaries have become increasingly blurred. Leat (1995) for example is exploring the similarities between voluntary and for-profit organizations, whilst other authors have questioned their independence from the state, as governmental funding becomes an essential part of their core funding (for example, Pifer 1975). The definition proposed here has the advantage that it allows exploration of some of the inter-sectoral issues raised by the terms 'non-profit' and 'non-governmental organizations', by reference to the four imperatives outlined above. As Anheier (1995) noted above, such an ability to differentiate is needed increasingly, if we are to make sense of contemporary Western society, and the role of organized voluntary activity within it.

As an example of the way that the above overall definition can be used to highlight key commonalities and differences between different types of VNPOs, it is instructive to compare what Kramer *et al.* (1993) – see also Billis 1991 – call voluntary *associations* and voluntary *agencies*. The former is a more informal type of organization, usually relying upon its members for its activity. The latter, by contrast, is

> . . . more formalized, bureaucratic, and employs paid staff to provide a continuing service to a community . . . While these two organizational forms share many values, norms, and interests . . . when voluntary agencies enter into the world of social service provision, they become more subject to the influence of governmental policy, financing, and regulation.
>
> (*Kramer et al. 1993: 173*)

Both these organizational types exist within the overall field of voluntary organizations. However, each has different characteristics, for example, as outlined above, and different issues to confront. These issues and challenges are exposed by use of the definition and its component dimensions outlined above.

THE SCOPE AND CHARACTERISTICS OF VOLUNTARY ORGANIZATIONS

Having decided upon the appropriate terminology, it is now necessary to look at the scope of the activity which we have thus defined. O'Neill (1989) is in no doubt about this in America. He estimated that his 'Third America' actually employs 7% of the American workforce and accounts for 6% of the GNP (in 1986), whilst its total assets amounted to over 506 billion dollars (in 1987).

In contrast, the size of the voluntary sector in the UK is smaller, but no less impressive. A major recent study of the income and expenditure of the voluntary sector in the UK has provided a similar estimate for this country. This study estimated its income to have been £9,094.3 million and its expenditure to have been £8,498.5 million in 1991, or 1.6% of GDP (Osborne and Hems 1995; 1996).

The range of voluntary organizational activity is equally diverse. In America, the National Center for Charitable Statistics (1986) lists twenty-six types of tax exempt activity (based upon the categories of the American IRS), each one of which is itself split down into numerous subdivisions. Even the more limited classification of the British Charity Commission (concerning charitable work alone) lists ten categories of activities (Bennett 1983). Finally the International Classification of Nonprofit Organizations (ICNPO), of the Johns Hopkins Project, differentiates between one hundred and forty five types of activity, across twenty-seven major categories of activity (Salamon and Anheier 1994).

This organizational diversity has led some to question whether it is possible to speak of a cohesive societal sector comprised of voluntary organizations (the 'voluntary sector'). A range of studies have come down against such a sector, on the grounds that it obscures and masks the diversity of the organizations within it, as much as it illuminates any common characteristics (see, for example, Hatch 1980; Brenton 1985; Kramer 1990). Most recently, Leat (1995) has argued also that it fails to recognize the similarities between voluntary organizations and other forms of organizations.

Others have suggested that, if sectoral analysis is to be employed then it is best approached through the concept of a *Third* or *Independent* Sector counterposed to government and business (for example, Seibel and Anheier 1990). However, this approach is problematic in that, on the one hand, it over-emphasizes the independence of voluntary organizations from the other sectors rather than their increasing interdependence. On the other hand it coalesces voluntary organizations together with neighbourhood and informal groups in a way which belies their differentiation; in doing so it risks the distinctive characteristics of both voluntary organizations and community and neighbourhood groups in a way unhelpful to the understanding of both (Abrams *et al.* 1989; Chanan 1991).

Because of these difficulties some analysts have proposed to further differentiate the sectoral analysis, suggesting a five or even seven sector model (see Horton Smith 1991, for the former; Caiden 1982 and Schuppert 1991, for the latter). Such multi-sectoral approaches, however, disaggregate the components of analysis to such an extent as to question whether the effort is really worth it. Thus it returns one to the concept of the separate sector for voluntary organizations.

It is argued here that the concept of a voluntary sector does have its use, though within strictly defined criteria. It is essentially a descriptive rather than analytic term which draws attention to those organizations which possess the distinctive features of voluntary organizations described above. Such a descriptive term is a useful aggregation, in that it describes their joint features, is able to accommodate their inter-dependence with other types of organizations (which is the reality for contemporary voluntary organizations), and does not mask their heterogeneity of their objectives and activities. To pursue more detailed analysis, however, it may well be necessary to differentiate sub-sectors of organizations from this broad category.

CONCLUSIONS

This chapter began by developing a typology of **voluntary** concepts, moving from the conceptualization of voluntary action as an organizing principle in society (volutaryism) to its application to individuals (volunteerism) and organizations (voluntarism). This typology also drew attention to the 'ideal state', toward which each of these conceptual principles would contribute. In the case of voluntarism, it was toward a plural society, where voluntary organizations would reflect the heterogenity of society and represent the diversity of opinions and aspirations within it as well as offering choice in service delivery. This was contrasted with the monolithic and centralist tendencies of the state, which would reduce this diversity to its lowest common denominators and provide an undifferentiated range of services.

From this clear conceptual understanding of organized voluntary effort, this chapter has gone on to argue for the use of the term **VNPO** rather than other alternatives, such as non-profit organization or charity. It has argued that although the analyses behind the other terms do contribute to our wider understanding of organized voluntary effort (for example, by enabling us to understand their role in the allocation of resources), the term VNPO maintains the link between such organizations and their underlying conceptual principle of voluntarism. The key features of such organizations are their formal existence, independent foundation and governance, non-profit distribution, and a meaningful element of voluntary motivation.

Inevitably, it has not been possible to cover the entire literature pertaining to voluntary organizations, though more detailed discussions can be found in Osborne (1993a; 1993b). Rather the intention has been to provide an initial overview about VNPOs for the reader, and which will provide a framework within which to discuss the more practical concerns of the remainder of this book. It is to these concerns that we must now turn.

REFERENCES

Abrams, P., Abrams, S., Humphreys, R. and Snaith, K. (1989) *Neighbourhood Care and Social Policy*, HMSO, London.

Anheier, H. (1995) Theories of the nonprofit sector, in *Nonprofit and Voluntary Sector Quarterly* **24**, (1), pp. 15–24.

Barker, A. (1982) Quango: a word or a campaign, in *Quangos in Britain*, (ed A. Barker) Macmillan, London, pp. 219–31.

Bennett, J. (1983) Classification of charitable purposes, in *Charity Statistics 1982/83*, Charities Aid Foundation p. 77.

Berger, P. and Neuhaus, R. (1977) *To Empower People. The Role of Mediating Structures in Public Policy*, American Enterprise Institute for Public Policy Research, Washington.

Billis, D. (1991) The roots of voluntary agencies, in *Voluntary & Non-profit Sector Quarterly* **20**, (1), pp. 5–24.

Bourdillon, A. (1945) Introduction, in *Voluntary Social Services, Their Place in the Modern State* (ed A. Bourdillon) pp. 1–10.

Brenton, M. (1985) *Voluntary Sector in British Social Services*, Longman, London.

Butler, R. and Wilson, D. (1990) *Managing Voluntary and Non Profit Organizations*, Routledge, London.

Caiden, G. (1982) *Public Administration*, Palisades, California.

Chanan, G. (1991) *Taken for Granted*, Community Development Foundation, London.

Collins, R. and Hickman, N. (1991) Altruism and culture as social products, in *Voluntas* **2**, (2), pp. 1–15.

Cornuelle, R. (1983) *Healing America*, Pitman, New York.

Cousins, P. (1982) Quasi official bodies in local government, in *Quangos in Britain* (ed A. Barker), Macmillan, London, pp. 152–63.

Darvill, G. and Mundy, B. (1984) *Volunteers in the Personal Social Services*, Tavistock, London.

Etzioni, A. (1961) *A Comparative Analysis of Complex Organizations*, Free Press, New York.

Etzioni, A. (1968) *The Active Society. A Theory of Societal and Political Processes*, Free Press, New York.

Fisher, J. (1993) *The Road from Rio. Sustainable Development and the Nongovernmental Movement in the Third World*, Praeger, Westport.

Gamwell, F. (1984) *Beyond Preference. Liberal Theories of Independent Association*, University of Chicago Press, Chicago.

Gladstone, F. (1979) *Voluntary Action in a Changing World*, Bedford Square Press, London.

Gurin, M. and Van Til, J. (1990) Philanthropy in its historical context, in *Critical Issues in American Philanthropy* (ed J. Van Til) pp. 3–18.

Hatch, S. (1980) *Outside the State*, Croom Helm, London.

Home Office (1990) *Efficiency Scrutiny of Government Funding of the Voluntary Sector*, HMSO, London.

Hood, C. (1984) *The Hidden Public Sector. The World of Para Governmental Organizations*, Centre for the Study of Public Policy, University of Strathclyde.

Horton Smith, D. (1991) Four sectors or five? Retaining the member benefit sector. *Non Profit and Voluntary Sector Quarterly* **20**, (2), pp. 137–50.

James, E. (1990) Economic theories of the non profit sector: a comparative perspective, in *The Third Sector* (ed H. Anheier and W. Seibel), pp. 21–9.

Kramer, R. (1990) *Voluntary Organizations in the Welfare State: On the Threshhold of the Nineties*, Centre for Voluntary Organisation Working Paper, London.

Kramer, R., Lorentzen, H., Melief, W. and Pasquinelli, S. (1993) *Privatization in Four European Countries*, M. E. Sharpe, New York.

Leat, D. (1995) *Revising the Non-Profit/For-Profit Rhetoric*, Researching the UK Voluntary Sector Conference, NCVO, London.

Les, E. (1994) The voluntary sector in post-communist East Central Europe: from small circles of freedom to civil society, in *Citizens. Strengthening Global Democracy* (eds M. De Oliveira and R. Tandon) pp. 195–237.

National Center for Charitable Statistics (1986) *National Taxonomy of Exempt Entities*, Independent Sector, Washington DC.

National Council for Social Services (1970) *Voluntary Social Services*, NCSS, London.

O'Neill, M. (1989) *The Third America*, Jossey Bass, San Francisco.

Osborne, S. (1993a) *Understanding Voluntary Organizations in Contemporary Western Society*, Public Sector Management Research Centre Working Paper Number 23, Aston University.

Osborne, S. (1993b) *Toward a Theory of the Voluntary Sector?* Public Sector Management Research Centre Working Paper Number 24, Aston University.

Osborne, S. and Hems, L. (1995) The economic structure of the charitable sector in the UK. *Voluntary & Non-profit Sector Quarerly* **24**, (4), pp. 321–36.

Osborne, S. and Hems, L. (1996) Estimating the income and expenditure of charitable organizations in the UK, in *Non Profit Studies*, 1(1).

Pifer, A. (1967) *Quasi Non Governmental Organizations*, Carnegie Corporation, New York.

Pifer, A. (1975) The non governmental organization at bay, in *Public Policy and Private Interests* (eds D. Hague, W. Mackenzie and A. Barker) Macmillan, London, pp. 395–408.

Salamon, L. (1987) Of market failure, voluntary failure and third party government. Toward a theory of government – non profit relations in the modern welfare state. *Journal of Voluntary Action Research*, pp. 29–49.

Salamon, L. and Anheier, H. (1994) *The Emerging Sector. An Over-View*, Johns Hopkins University, Baltimore.

Schultz, J. (1972) The voluntary sector and its components, in *Voluntary Action Research 1972*, pp. 25–38.

Schuppert, G. (1991) State, market, third sector: problems of organizational choice in the delivery of public services. *Non Profit and Voluntary Sector Quarterly* **20**, (2), pp. 123–36.

Seibel, W. and Anheier, H. (1990) Sociological and political science approaches to the third sector, in *The Third Sector* (eds H. Anheier and W. Seibel) de Gruyter, Berlin, pp. 7–20.

de Tocqueville, A. (1971) *Democracy in America*, Oxford University Press, London.

Van Til, J. (1988) *Mapping the Third Sector. Voluntarism in a Changing Social Economy*, Foundation Center, New York.
Webb, S. and Webb, B. (1911) *Prevention of Destitution*, Longman, London.

GUIDED READING

Many of the detailed texts have already been covered in this chapter, and are contained in the above references. Three texts are worth highlighting.

Kramer, R. (1981) *Voluntary Agencies in the Welfare State*, University of California Press, Berkeley, offers an excellent, if now slightly dated, introduction to the nature of VNPOs.

Powell, W. (ed) (1989) *The Non Profit Sector*, Yale University Press, New Haven and Anheier, H. and Seibel, W. (eds) *The Third Sector*, de Gruyter, Berlin are both good edited collections of material covering most of the issues detailed above, and others directly relevant to the rest of this book. The former text has a more American focus and the latter one a more European one, but the choice is essentially one of preference.

Finally Rathgeb Smith, S. and Lipsky, M. (1993) *Nonprofits for Hire*, Harvard University Press, Boston, is a good study of the changing nature of VNPOs and the challenges that they face, as a result of their increased involvement in contracting for the provision of public services.

2 Ethics and management in the voluntary sector

Ian Taylor

INTRODUCTION

This chapter addresses a number of questions relating to ethical issues and problems in the VNPO sector. It takes a broad perspective, focusing on ethics in the wider context of the activities of VNPOs as well as in their internal organization. For a number of reasons this is an appropriate time to consider ethics, in view of the prominence of VNPOs in the delivery of services and the growth of the contract culture, both linked to the changing role of the state as 'enabler' rather than 'provider'. As VNPOs both take on this enlarged role in the provision of public services and depend, financially, increasingly on the state sector in the contract culture, so there is the need to raise ethical questions about the relationship between the two sectors. This has a direct bearing on the traditional voluntary ethos of VNPOs.

Those who manage or help to manage VNPOs – whether they be trustees, general managers, or managers with professional backgrounds in the particular professions – may well be faced in the future with increasing conflicts of interest over fund-raising, expenditure, organizational principles and practice. This may lead to the need for more ethical guidance for managers to deal with government, business enterprises and the general public, who provide them with funds, as well as with prioritizing objectives in the day-to-day running of their organizations. That is not to say that those involved in managing VNPOs today are unaware of the ethical consequences of their actions. Indeed, there is a case for arguing that many VNPOs by their very nature are ethical. However, where choices have to be made, where change requires adaptation to new principles and practices and where the potential for conflict exists, it is necessary for managers to be aware of the wider context of ethical issues as well as narrower, internal ones.

By the end of this chapter you will:

● be familiar with some elements of ethical theory and ways in which ethical issues are relevant to assessing the role of the VNPO sector;

- be able to consider how ethical problems may arise in your organizational context; and
- be prepared to consider how a code of conduct (incorporating ethics) may be relevant to your own organization.

ETHICS AND THE VNPO SECTOR: AN OVERVIEW AND BACKGROUND TO ETHICAL ISSUES

Ethics is basically the science of morals. It attempts to place moral issues into a coherent consistent form to guide individuals and organizations. There are a number of theoretical approaches to ethics which in themselves reflect moral, religious and sometimes political, social, economic and cultural values, although it is often difficult to separately identify these values. Before outlining these approaches, it is worth trying to identify the roots of ethical behaviour.

Ethics often relates to notions of justice, fairness, rights, freedom and equality. These are often interlinked. For example, the basis for your moral principles may well depend upon what you (personally) consider to be just. This will be related to what you consider to be fair which in turn may depend on issues relating to individual liberty, social equality or equal opportunities. Your ethical stance may reflect an absolute (at all costs) or a relative (under the circumstances) position. Generally the following may be regarded as important elements in ethics:

1 the equal consideration of people's interests and values
2 the need to be honest and truthful
3 the need to promote fairness
4 the necessity to act impartially
5 the importance of applying ethical principles and practice universally and in a consistent manner.

It is important to stress that even within these broad elements or guidelines, different people will have different priorities. For example, your notion of fairness may be to act partially toward a particularly disadvantaged group such as homeless people through the donation of funds, although this would necessarily involve treating another group unfairly or in a discriminatory manner if you chose not to contribute to its cause. You may take the view that the freedom of the individual to act according to his/her perferences is more important than the right to be treated in the same way as someone else, although it must be stressed that the concepts of freedom and equality should not be regarded as incompatible.

However, the ethical motives and consequences of taking a particular stance need to be asserted and balanced out from time to time in order to develop and maintain a sense of perspective and the ability to judge consistently. This is particularly difficult when your own moral position on an issue, such as abortion or euthanasia, may be diametrically opposed to someone else's. Maintaining your stance on a particular issue may be entirely ethical, although if it offends others it may be that it is its expression rather than the view itself that requires modification. The potential for ethical conflict exists in all organizations. However, it is often most apparent in those that provide vital services and in particular when costs have to be weighed against objectives. This is particularly so for VNPOs in providing public services and/or working with, or for, disadvantaged groups.

How do we determine whether or not our thoughts and actions (based on the broad criteria outlined above) are ethical? There are a number of approaches and theories to consider, although these tend to categorize ethics and may not always be adquate in evaluating a situation or informing us about how we ought to behave. The **utilitarian** approach is based on the notion that actions are right if they involve pleasure and wrong if they induce pain. The ultimate end of human (and government) action is to maximize the sum of personal pleasure and minimize pain to promote the greatest happiness of the greatest number. Utilitarianism, which has its origins in the work of Jeremy Bentham (1748–1832) emphasizes the importance of removing obstacles to the pursuit of happiness in order to enable individuals to lead better lives. Its essence lies in the end product rather than the motive, although it is often difficult to determine whether actions are designed to achieve an ultimate good end or merely to proceed in a moral way with no particular expectation of the achievement of a good end. Bentham's central belief that one person's pleasure was as good as another's was compromised by J. S. Mill (1806–1873), who argued that there were higher and lower pleasures and that for certain people and at particular times it was better to be dissatisfied than satisfied, particularly if temporary dissatisfaction led ultimately to a greater good.

Mill's position, which emphasized motives in behaviour, also reflects a **deontological** position. This holds that intention (rather than end) is the basis for morality. The desire or will to do good, even if the outcome does not match the intent is of paramount importance. The **deontological** school, usually associated with the German thinker Immanuel Kant (1724–1804) reflects and encourages altruism – the desire to do good even though there may be no material gain for the individual.

The utilitarian, on the other hand, reflects a more instrumental and certainly more measurable stance. In reality, means and ends are of equal importance. Without the means to achieve a desired end, ethics remains in the purely theoretical realm, whilst what is required is 'practical ethics' to deliver services in a just and equitable way (deontological approach) to as many people as possible (utilitarian).

The activities of VNPOs often incorporate both systems, since they seek to enable as many people as possible to lead more fulfilled lives through protection and provision. That is not to say that self-interest is not important in their management as it is in any organization. Good management practice and successful marketing may generate more income which leads to greater job security and more influence in the policy process as well as promoting greater happiness for more people.

There are a number of other approaches to ethics. For example, the **natural law** approach focuses on universal entitlements to 'natural' rights such as the right to life and liberty. Whether or not such rights are 'natural' and if they are, whether they should never be violated under any circumstances may pose ethical dilemmas. One's 'natural' freedom (to speak or worship) may offend the rights of another, necessitating safeguards such as laws and their means of enforcement. John Rawls approached such ethical dilemmas through principles of justice. In *A Theory of Justice* (1972) he argued that justice should reflect both freedom and equality so that everyone should have the same right to the most extensive basic freedom compared with a similar liberty for others (**liberty principle**), in order that socio-economic inequalities should be arranged to be reasonably expected to be to everyone's advantage and attached to offices and positions open to all (**difference principle**). These views are summarized in Darr (1987: 4–7).

Instrumentalists like the American philosopher John Dewey (1859–1952) take the pragmatic view that what is considered to be good must be reviewed as societies change and discard values which may be deemed to be obsolete (Denhardt 1988: 34). Dewey viewed a commitment to personal development encompassing self-improvement and the increase of one's moral capacity through learning as the only true moral end (Seedhouse 1988: 7).

The debate about whether absolute or instrumental, deontological or utilitarian ethics should inform our actions is an important one because it helps to clarify what is acceptable, if not absolutely desirable, in the context of moral behaviour. We may take decisions that are considered to be not particularly ethical because we are constrained by social norms or work practice, but which are not necessarily unethical in the context of moral behaviour. Acceptability may reflect what is practical under certain circumstances. The gap between value and fact will always be of significance in managerial decisions, but at least it may be partially or temporarily bridged by informed decision-making. When organizations encounter problems involving what is equitable or fair, instrumentalism reflecting a more relativist position becomes an essential tool in determining how far priorities should be modified, or even compromised, and how far decisions should be based on moral absolutes.

For example, the decision to divert more resources to hip replacement operations rather than kidney dialysis has ethical implications since one category of patient may suffer at the expense of another. The key ethical issue is why, and for what purpose, was such a decision taken? If the motive was to increase patient throughput to enable politicians to benefit from favourable statistics then the ethical basis of such an instrumentalist decision should be questioned. If, however, the aim was to spread scarce resources more evenly under difficult circumstances, the motives may be more acceptable. Peter Singer comments that ethical judgements that are no good in practice must suffer a theoretical defect as well because 'the whole point of ethical judgement is to guide practice' (Singer 1993: 6). This is a view that many service managers in the VNPO and public sectors would subscribe to, as well as to the view of De George (1986) that ethical codes must be policeable and policed if they are to be effective and meaningful.

ETHICS AND VNPOs

VNPOs are often thought of as ethical organizations whose ultimate aim according to Carbone is 'to maximize assistance to intended individuals' (1993: 310). Since the intended individuals are often the underprivileged, disabled or frequently under-represented in society, the deontological credentials of the ethical motives of VNPOs are generally undisputed. They generate goodwill and support, even from those who believe that the principle of compulsion rather than voluntarism should guide social provision.

Because VNPOs depend to an extent on donations from business enterprises and individual members of the public, they need to persuade them that through their deeds they are actually living up to their good intentions and also providing value for money in the process. No matter how well-intentioned and efficient in delivering the goods they may be, VNPOs operate in a complex world in which the scope for activities which may compromise good intentions or question the value of their achievements is always prevalent. Although they may seek to help particular groups, they are multidimensional, needing to function at a number of levels. This is particularly true of the larger organizations. For example, the NSPCC tries to prevent the abuse of children, which is a distinctly ethical thing to do. However, the promotion of its interests involves working with a number of agencies from the public, non-profit and private sectors which may, from time to time, raise questions of priorities as well as propriety, particularly in the context of fund-raising, fund allocation and how far the NSPCC should exercise pressure on government to legislate. The objectives of organizations such as Barnardos are not only to 'provide social welfare services for the benefit of children and young people most in need', but also to 'influence social welfare policy' (Barnardos 1994: 1). The ways and means for such organizations to achieve their objectives involve ethical issues.

The complexity of these issues, not to mention legislative requirements, obligations to funders and expectations of clients, requires an approach to ethics that not only takes account of the wider context in which charities operate but reflects what is achievable within each organization. For example, conflicts of objectives over funding and the need to justify performance measurement to employees are two areas in which ethical codes (explored later) may be useful.

The notion that VNPOs operate 'between profit and state' (Ware 1989) is an appropriate one because it sheds light on the scope for ethical dilemmas. In a sense, they belong to neither sector so that ethical principles and codes designed to guide action in public and private sectors may not be relevant to them. In the so-called **mixed economy of care** and contract culture, VNPOs are depending increasingly on government which, as Ware has suggested 'creates relationships of dependence which can intensify efforts at lobbying by individual organizations to secure funds for themselves' (ibid. 235).

It could also be argued that by reducing its role as provider, the state is transferring a key aspect of its legitimizing role to the voluntary sector. If state legitimacy depends in part on government delivering welfare and other key services, the contract culture has undermined this legitimacy and placed new demands upon VNPOs, through a transfer of responsibility away from traditional forms of democratic political control and account-ability. Whilst there is some truth in the belief that 'the voluntary sector is likely to be the principal beneficiary of market pluralism' (Taylor and Lansley 1992: 167), it would also be true to say that market pluralism creates its own problems for this sector.

The removal or transfer of services from direct political control to independent organizations representing the interests of specific or identi-fied groups such as the elderly, children and the physically handicapped raises public interest questions which have ethical overtones. For example, if charities become increasingly dependent on government funding as a result of the contract culture they automatically, if sometimes unwittingly, become involved in the political sphere. Political decisions about the allocation of resources will inevitably single out organizations which are perceived by politicians, civil servants or public sector managers as being more deserving, or which produce the best value for money, or which will create a good impression through which political capital can be made.

The possible need for VNPOs to become more political in order to win the support of ruling parties in local authorities (Prochaska 1988: 5) raises important questions about their independence. Competition for funding creates the need to market services and promote the organization in a pluralistic market consisting of purchasers and providers in a more 'busi-nesslike' way. If, in order to win a contract, a VNPO promotes one aspect of its work above others, then one group of clients may benefit more than another, compromising the principle of utility and raising questions about the motives of the organization in focusing on a particular aspect of its work. On the one hand this can highlight the differences in priorities between the fund-raising and service providing arms of a VNPO (Eayrs and Ellis 1990). On the other hand it can also lead VNPOs into over-dependence upon the state for their financial security, mutilating their independent mission and substituting the, often changing, priorities of government. This has been characterized by Pifer (1967; 1975) as leading to the creation of the **quango**, or 'quasi autonomous non governmental organization'.

The voluntary principle should distinguish VNPOs from the state sector. As Heginbotham has observed, it is 'a truism of the voluntary ethic that it does not *have* to be: it is not coerced or required either through social attitude or legislation' (1990: 5). Indeed, this has historically been seen as *the* distinguishing feature of such organizations, rather than the more periferal issue of the role of volunteers in them (Bourdillon 1945).

Increasingly though, legislation and the social attitude engendered by the contract culture have placed greater ethical demands on the VNPO sector. The more they are compelled to adapt to legislative requirements and the more VNPOs adopt market principles in their fund-raising and marketing activities, the more likely they are to compromise the voluntary principle and be faced with conflict of interest questions and associated ethical dilemmas. Taylor has pointed out that there is a danger that VNPOs may take on mainstream services and become 'increasingly like statutory service providers they were meant to replace' (1992: 158), a position developed theoretically by Di Maggio and Powell (1988).

It should not be forgotten that there remains a central and fundamental question about whether it is ethical to distribute public funds to, and to encourage donations from, private individuals and corporations to VNPOs rather than to statutory authorities. If the voluntary principle is being compromised or overridden, then so, ironically, is the 'compulsory' universalist and collectivist approach to service delivery. As the contract culture turns local authorities and other care providers into purchasers of services, they are likely to be 'looking for packages' (Houghton and Timperly 1992: 46) which will suit their selective interests rather than the distinctive missions of VNPOs. This dilemma poses ethical questions for managers within both the public and VNPO sectors.

ETHICAL ISSUES IN VNPO MANAGEMENT

Having dealt with ethics and VNPOs in a broad context, it is now useful to narrow the discussion down by dealing with more specific issues concerning the management of VNPOs as well as looking at ways in which the public and private business sector address similar questions of ethics. Some VNPOs have codes of practice that reflect their objectives, and many adhere to guidelines set out by the Charities Commission as well as legislation. Moreover, what is considered to be 'good practice' often reflects ethical positions, particularly in relation to clients. However, knowledge of 'good practice' is not sufficient to guide ethical decision-making in the complex environment in which VNPOs function. It can change as perceptions and knowlege of professional practice change.

Further, the trend toward business style management, particularly in the larger organizations, is likely to bring to the fore issues of propriety and accountability which have strong ethical implications.

Different organizations have different approaches to management based on their broad objectives, management structures, fund-raising activities and the client groups they are involved with. Conflicts of interest often create ethical dilemmas and may stem from financial considerations, conflict between good professional conduct and managerial expediency and between the needs of clients and the particular needs of the organization. For VNPOs, this is similar to the public sector, where a common problem relates to the availability of funds. An example of this is in the NHS, where difficult decisions about whom to treat and how much can be afforded raise fundamental ethical questions particularly when matters of life or death are at stake. Clinicians have professional codes, personal values and legal responsibilities. General managers are accountable to fund holders for the allocation of public money.

Similarly, in VNPOs, fund raisers are often driven and assessed by the imperative to maximize organizational income. In such circumstances it is a temptation to emphasize the dependency of the beneficiaries of their organization and evoke sympathy in the potential donor. By contrast, service providers may well be driven by a contradictory impetus, to develop the control over their circumstances of their beneficiary group and to emphasize their empowerment (Eayrs and Ellis 1990). This distinction often creates a key ethical tension within VNPOs. A further ethical dilemma is the accountability of the services provided by a VNPO. Their strength of independence may also be a drawback! The core issue is whose set of ethical precepts should drive the organization: the fund-raiser/donor, the service provider/beneficiary or the government/citizenry.

Generally, ethical issues play a part in issues which have commonality with both the VNPO and public sectors. Waters *et al.* (1986) says that these include working conditions (including equal opportunities), the customer orientation (including honesty about the product), the role of suppliers (respect for their method of operating), and the position of stake holders (protection of interests). Clients of VNPOs are also citizens and as they take on more of the work of the public sector, so managers in VNPOs will need to take account of the rights and expectations of these and other citizens.

The question of accountability is also important, as managers of VNPOs are managing services on behalf of the general public, for groups of workers within the public services as well as on behalf of themselves, given that they too have a vested interest in the system. Therefore personal ethics, professional ethical codes and wider societal ethics (based on notions of natural rights, citizenship rights, democratic rights) enter into the equation. In spite of the complexities involved in managing public services and the scope for ethical problems, very few managers in either the public or VNPO sectors have received ethical training or follow ethical codes, unless they relate to their professional training and conduct. This contrasts to the more pro-active stance taken by the more progressive business organizations. In the USA, over 90% of business organizations have ethical programmes for their employees and many companies have their own code of ethics (McHugh 1988). Such codes are no substitute for an ethical stance by managers themselves, however. In spite of these proliferating codes in the business sector in the USA, managers must 'decide issues and make choices in an atmosphere that encourages, discourages or ignores the moral element in such decisions' (Longenecker 1985: 65).

Ideally, VNPOs should adopt the best elements of public service ethics and good business practice. A code of ethics should address such questions as trust, confidentiality, fairness of treatment and mutality and it should also reflect the nature and objectives of the organization, serving as a standard through which to achieve various goals.

In the USA, the Independent Sector has published a text containing the various codes of ethics of a variety of voluntary organizations (Independent Sector 1991). Typically, the codes emphasize truthfulness, honesty, responsibility to society, to the workforce and the clients. Some cite philanthropy, voluntarism and the traditions of the organization as being important. In the UK, the Association of Charitable Foundations (ACF) has been working on guidelines for the funders of VNPOs and has been examining issues surrounding codes of practice. (ACF 1995; see also Burkeman 1993).

The recommendations of the ACF on funding reflect the observations of Carbone on US practice. This in turn reflects some basic ethical principles including the need to be honest with others, observe generally accepted standards, safeguard the anonymity of others, respect professional ethics and manage gifts for the sole benefit of intended beneficiaries (Carbone 1993: 298).

The scope for ethical misconduct arises also in the area of the contemporary development in the sector of franchising. This has been adopted by a number of VNPOs in order to develop their services in different parts of the country rather than expand their own organization centrally. In theory, the franchiser gains financially through market penetration and the franchisee gains from business support through, for example, marketing and training, (Houghton and Timperly 1992: 20). However, since the franchisee needs to be offered reasonable incentives to take on this role, ethical dilemmas could occur over the need to balance the interests of franchiser and franchisee, as well as those of service beneficiaries and problems may arise if too little managerial control is exercised over the activities of the franchisee.

Financial considerations are important in the ethical stances of the VNPO sector precisely because so many organizations are founded on the principle of trust – that the funds raised will be utilized as far as possible in the interest of the cause or client group represented. The organization is run on this basis and funds are donated on the understanding that the beneficiary will benefit. Suppose this does not happen. Take, for example, a VNPO that obtained the backing of donors on the basis that 20% of funds raised would be allocated to running the organization and 80% would be distributed to organizations providing care. If, in the event, 50% was spent on administration, has the VNPO operated in an unethical way?

The answer is that 'it all depends.' If the motive and expectations were to adhere to the original figures but due to poor management or some unforseen situation a discrepancy occurred, then the VNPO did not act unethically. It acted 'in good faith' – if poorly managed!

If, however, it was known that the 20% figure was likely to be exceeded, then the bodies lending their names to publicize the VNPO and those organizations and individuals funding the charity had the right to be informed that this was the case. If funds had been raised in the certain knowledge that the figures represented a gross distortion, this was an unethical act because it betrayed trust and mutuality. In this case, both deontological and utilitarian principles would have been ignored or overridden. Thus accountability is a key issue, particularly where financial considerations are involved. This complex issue is discussed below in more detail, in the chapters on accountability and financial accounting.

At a more mundane level, the question of whether or not volunteers with collection boxes should position themselves in the doorways of supermarkets raises interesting ethical issues. On the one hand, whilst deontologically the motivation of the organization and fund-raiser may be admirable, the utilitarian consequences may not be. The shopper may feel more pressurized to donate because of the close proximity of the collector or may feel uncomfortable about not donating, particularly if he or she purchases a National Lottery ticket shortly afterwards (though there is some evidence that the former is becoming replaced by the latter). On the other hand, utilitarian ethics is based on the greatest good for the greatest possible number. Arguably, in this instance, the discomfort or guilt of the individual is of less consequence than the possible good stemming from the actions of the collector, indicating a qualitative as well as quantitative dimension.

CONCLUSION: TOWARD A CODE OF ETHICS

An important point to stress is that in the above, as in many other cases, the dividing line between problems created by inadequate management training and inappropriate techniques on the one hand and deliberate unethical behaviour on the other may be very narrow. This is why codes of ethics, or at the very least, codes of conduct which incorporate ethical principles are necessary to guide both the organization and individual manager or employee.

Ideally, a code of ethics should protect the moral integrity of the individual and reflect the principles of the organization. Managers need to be able to exercise discretion and a code may guide, if not direct, managers towards particular decisions. Notwithstanding the different size, structure and culture of organizations, codes of ethics should aim to facilitate the decisions taken by managers, by addressing the following issues:

1 the relationship between the organization and its beneficiaries
2 the relationship between the manager(s) and paid and unpaid staff
3 the relationship between managers and trustees
4 the management of the expectations of funding agencies and of the general public
5 procedures and principles for fund-raising
6 the criteria for the allocation of funds
7 issues of equal opportunities and anti-discriminatory practice
8 the management of personnel matters, including performance appraisal and career progression
9 the dilemma of secrecy-versus-publicizing of the activities of the organization.

At a time when VNPOs are shouldering an ever-increasing responsibility for public services and adopting business practices in their management, it is important for managers to be able to reconcile their own moral position with the demands of the organization when they come into conflict. The trustees of VNPOs should also be able to ensure that the actions of managers conform to good practice and ultimately serve the interests of the clients. The need to 'blow the whistle' on unethical practice, or act ethically in the face of pressure to do otherwise, arises from time to time in management practice in the public, private and VNPO sectors. Although reconciling the needs of competing and sometimes conflicting groups and individuals often comes with practice, through setting up the appropriate systems and through incremental trial and error, in the larger VNPOs where managerial decisions are complex, codes of ethics would probably establish the means of managing ethically or at least, avoiding unethical action. As smaller organizations with shorter hierarchies come to play an increasingly important role in the provision of public services, so codes of ethics may be of value to them also.

REFERENCES

Association of Charitable Foundations (ACF) (1995) *Guidelines for Funders of Voluntary Organizations*, ACF, London.
Barnardos (1994) *Annual Report and Accounts 1994*, Barnardos, London.
Bourdillon, A. (1945) *Voluntary Social Services. Their Place in the Modern State*, Methuen, London.
Burkeman, S. (1993) *The Simple Truth*, ACF, London.
Carbone, R. (1993) Market-place practices and fundraising ethics, in *Non Profit*

Organizations in a Market Economy (eds D. Hammack and D. Young) Jossey Bass, San Francisco, p. 298.

De George, R. (1986) *Business Ethics*, Macmillan Publishing Co., New York.

Denhardt, K. (1988) *The Ethics of Public Service*, Greenwood Press, New York.

Di Maggio, P. and Powell, W. (1988) The iron cage revisited, in *Community Organizations* (ed C. Milofsky) Oxford University Press, New York.

Eayrs, C. and Ellis, N. (1990) Charity advertising: for and against people with a mental handicap. *British Journal of Social Psychology*, **29**.

Heginbotham, C. (1990) *Return To Community*, Bedford Square Press, London.

Houghton, P. and Timperly, P. (1992) *Charity Franchising*, Directory of Social Change, London.

Independent Sector (1991) *Ethics and the Nation's Voluntary and Philanthropic Community*, Independent Sector, Washington DC.

Longenecker, J. G. (1985) Management priorities and management ethics. *Journal of Business Ethics*, **4**, (1).

McHugh, F. P. (1988) *Keyguide to Information Services in Business Ethics*, Mansell, London.

Pifer, A. (1967) *Quasi Non Governmental Organizations*, Carnegie Corporation, New York.

Pifer, A. (1975) The non governmental organization at bay, in *Public Policy and Private Interests* (eds D. Hague, W. Mackenzie and A. Barker) Macmillan, London, pp. 395–408.

Prochaska, F. (1988) *The Voluntary Impulse*, Faber, London.

Rawls, J. (1972) *A Theory of Justice*, Clarendon Press, Oxford.

Seedhouse, D. (1988) *Ethics: The Heart of Health Care*, John Wiley & Sons, London.

Singer, P. (1993) *Practical Ethics*, Cambridge University Press, Cambridge.

Taylor, M. (1992) The changing role of the nonprofit sector in Britain: moving toward the market, in *Government And The Third Sector* (eds B. Gidron, R. M. Kramer and L. M. Salamon) Josey Bass, San Francisco.

Taylor, M. and Lansley, J. (1992) Ideology and welfare. *Voluntas*, **3**, (2).

Ware, A. (1989) *Between Profit and State*, Polity Press, Cambridge.

Waters, J. A., Bard, F. and Chant, P. D. (1986) Everyday moral issues experienced by managers. *Journal of Busines Ethics*, **5**, (5).

GUIDED READING

Denhardt, K. (1988) *The Ethics of Public Service*, Greenwood Press, New York, provides an excellent theoretical and empirical approach to ethical issues in a public service contract.

Independent Sector (1991) *Ethics and the Nation's Voluntary and Philanthropic Community*, Independent Sector, Washington DC., provides concrete examples of approaches to ethical codes in the voluntary sector, though with an American focus.

Seedhouse, D. (1988) *Ethics: The Heart of Health Care*, John Wiley & Sons, London, deals primarily with ethical matters in health care. However, many of the dilemmas raised are of a general nature and can be applied to other services provided by VNPOs.

Singer, P. (1993) *Practical Ethics*, Cambridge University Press, Cambridge, provides a very lively debate about a wide range of ethical questions and is highly recommended as a starting point for the further exploration of the complexity of moral dilemmas.

Warnock, M. (1960) *Ethics Since 1900*, Oxford University Press, Oxford, remains the classic reference work which covers a number of ethical perspectives.

3 Managing relationships with governing bodies

Margaret Harris and Colin Rochester

INTRODUCTION

Working with governing bodies is one of the most difficult challenges of voluntary and non-profit organization management. Whatever term we use – 'the board', 'trustees', 'the management committee', 'the executive', 'the council' – the relationship between them and staff can often be problematic. Yet this is also the area where experience of other sectors and 'how to do it' handbooks are least likely to provide the answers. Not for nothing has the voluntary governing body been described as 'the organizational joker in the pack' (Batsleer *et al.* 1992).

This chapter aims to help VNPO managers to rise to the challenge of managing their relationships with their governing bodies. It draws on the experiences of fifteen years collaborative research by the Centre for Voluntary Organization at the LSE in order to position the governing body within the VNPO management context; identify the major factors that make the relationship complex; provide a tool for moving to a more constructive relationship between governing bodies and staff; and suggest techniques for helping the governing body to do its job.

By the end of the chapter you should be able to:

- distinguish between formal statements of the governing body role and the actual practice in any organization;
- identify the obstacles to successful implementation of the governing body role;
- manage the process of reaching agreement between staff and board members about the most useful and appropriate definition of the governing body role;
- review these arrangements in the light of the development of the agency and changes in its environment;
- conduct an audit of the composition of the governing body as the basis for recruiting members with the skills and knowledge appropriate to its role; and
- plan meetings in order to ensure that the board gives attention to the way in which it goes about its work.

THE VNPO GOVERNING BODY IN CONTEXT

The existence of a governing body is fundamental to an organization's claim to 'voluntary' status. VNPOs vary enormously in their purposes and methods of work, the resources they command, and the way they are constituted but what they have in common is that they have come into existence because groups of people chose freely to set them up for a particular purpose. By the same token, the continued existence of VNPOs depends on the willingness of sufficient volunteers to act as a governing body.

The governing body can be seen as one amongst four key groupings or 'stakeholders' within a VNPO (Harris 1994). In addition to the board itself, there may be:

- staff (paid and unpaid) who carry out the work of the VNPO;
- beneficiaries who are the recipients of services and other activities of the VNPO (they may also be called clients, customers, consumers, patients or members); and
- 'guardians' who are the people, often founders or funders, who have a long-term interest in the continuity and survival of the VNPO.

The actions of people in any one of these groupings may have important impacts on the other groupings. This chapter focuses especially on the interaction between governing bodies and staff.

Handbooks, documents of VNPOs and articles by practitioners suggest that there is widespread agreement about the roles and responsibilities of the governing body in principle (Harris 1996). In general terms it has the ultimate **authority** to make decisions and to approve the actions taken by the organization. By the same token it is **responsible** in law for those decisions and actions and **accountable** for the conduct of paid and voluntary staff and for the management of agency resources. A second general responsibility is to **maintain the values and autonomy** of the organization. In British charity law the key duty of the board is to ensure that the organization pursues the aims for which it was established. The responsibility for financial integrity which has occupied a central place in the debate over the Charities Acts of 1992 and 1993 is an important but secondary duty.

The general responsibilities as the 'point of final authority' and 'maintainer of values' encompasses further, more specific, functions. The governing body is the **employer** of the agency's staff – even if most of the 'hiring and firing' and day to day management are delegated to senior staff. It formulates and determines agency policy. And it is ultimately responsible for securing the resources necessary for the agency's survival.

Although there seems to be consensus about the significance of governing bodies and the nature of their functions, there is also widespread dissatisfaction with the ways in which they carry out their roles in practice.

VNPO staff complain that governing bodies lack commitment to the organization; do not take their responsibilities seriously; have little understanding of the organization's aims and activities; fail to provide staff with the support they need; devote most of their meetings to matters of detail; and meddle with work that the staff should be left to get on with. Board members are also dissatisfied. They are often uncertain about what they are there for; they feel marginalized by the staff's expertise and the grasp of detail which full-time employment provides; and they are drowning in a rising tide of paper which somehow never gives them the key information needed to make strategic decisions.

A case example

In a study of the local management committees of a national voluntary organization Harris (1989 and 1992) found clear written guidelines about what was expected:

- legal responsibility for the **employment** of staff;
- contributing to the making of **policy** at the national level;
- securing **resources** such as grants, premises and equipment; and
- **monitoring** the quality of the service provided.

However, interviews with staff and board members revealed that in practice they worked rather differently. Management committee members took their legal status as employers very seriously but they nevertheless left staffing matters to senior staff and were 'casual' in their approach to contracts of employment and conditions of service. They felt too ill-informed to appoint staff or to evaluate staff performance. In practice, management committee involvement in selection, assessment, development or training of staff was no more than a formality.

A similar pattern could be discerned when the policy-making function of the committee was considered. Management committees were seen as 'detached' from policy-making and priority setting and tended to regard it as something which they should not be involved in, even in a nominal way. Reasons given included lack of expertise, shortage of time and a belief that policy was the preserve of the national body. The result was a process similar to the pattern observed with the employment function; staff who felt that the committee was unable to understand the issues involved in policy-making and planning took the dominant role.

Again, finance and fund-raising and monitoring the organization's work were seen by the committees as purely formal responsibilities. The Honorary Treasurer was no more than a figurehead who left grant applications, financial projections and planning and negotiations with funding bodies to the staff. Board members generally had unconditional confidence in staff and in their ability to provide an acceptable standard of service. Any problems arising from the work were dealt with within the staff team.

Two possible explanations for this gap between prescription and practice emerged in the case study. Sometimes it seemed that committee members were simply unable or unwilling to carry out allotted functions and senior staff stepped in to fill the gap. Conversely, it sometimes appeared that senior staff just assumed responsibility for functions which were formally the preserve of their boards, and board members acquiesced. In both situations, the research identified a self-reinforcing pattern in the relationship between boards and senior staff. Board members were unable to obtain experience and expertise because staff, for whatever reason, were not sharing key information. Staff, in turn, found committee members to be unfamiliar with crucial aspects of the agency and its service and were therefore unwilling to entrust to them the execution of important functions. The impact on management committees seemed to be to reinforce their remoteness from the work of the agency.

The pattern is illustrated in Figure 3.1. If we start at point A we find that staff may not share information, issues, problems and decisions about the work of the agency with the governing body. The effect is that members of the governing body feel distant from the guiding purposes and the practicalities of running the agency and they do not have the opportunity to gain relevant experience in making decisions (point B). As a result, they are liable to behave in a way that reinforces the belief of staff that they cannot cope with important decisions – for example, by asking 'näive' questions at committee meetings or by their failure to ask any questions at all.

The process may be part of a wider cycle. If committee members do not feel they understand the nature and workings of the organization (point B), they will tend to be overawed by the expertise of the staff (point C) and will not expect to challenge staff views or monitor their

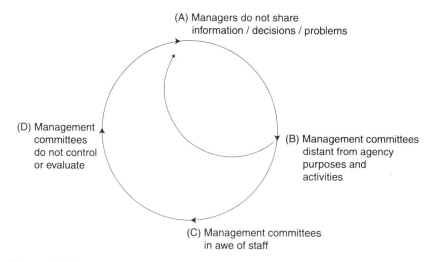

Figure 3.1 Cycles of expectation (Harris 1992: 143)

activities (point D). Staff then are not required, and have no particular reason, to share information and problems with the committee (point A). The circle is closed.

EXPLAINING A COMPLEX RELATIONSHIP

All this is a far cry from the **ideal board** identified by 300 chief executives surveyed by Fletcher (1992) whose members:

- are carefully chosen for the skills and connections they can offer;
- play an active part in long-range strategic planning;
- actively promote the agency in the community and 'open doors to possible funding sources';
- prepare for meetings by reading the material sent to them beforehand; and
- review financial statements carefully, asking questions if there is anything they do not understand.

In practice, even successful managers from the private and statutory sectors seem to suffer from 'stunned rabbit syndrome' (Dartington 1995) and are often unable to apply their expertise and experience to the role of board member in the voluntary sector.

How can we explain the dissatisfaction with the performance of voluntary governing bodies and the chasm between our expectations and the reality? Drawing on our own and other research, several key factors in this difficult and complex relationship between staff and their boards can be discerned.

Ignorance may be part of the problem. Members of governing bodies can be unaware of functions which have been allocated to them in official statements and in law. Research for the '*On Trust*' working party on the governance of charities set up by the National Council for Voluntary Organizations (NCVO) and the Charity Commission found, for example, that only one in three knew they were charity trustees (Ford 1992). Or people can be misled by what has been termed 'the lure of the corporate model' of governance (Hodgkin 1993) into thinking that the paid Director and senior management team can be left to carry out all key functions as is common practice in the corporate sector.

A second element can be the poor organization and presentation of meetings. According to the 1991 National Survey of Volunteering (Lynn and Davis Smith 1991) two-fifths of those who volunteer in Britain on a regular basis serve on governing bodies. A massive 79% of them reported that the experience should have been 'better organized'. Board members may be discouraged if they attend meetings for which they have received little prior information and for which little preparation appears to have been made. Chairpersons who do not encourage full participation, who are unable to keep discussion focused, or who leave doubt about what decisions have been reached, can compound the problem of disillusion and demoralization.

A third explanation may lie in board recruitment practices. In all but the largest and most prestigious national voluntary agencies, finding sufficient numbers of people willing to take on volunteer responsibilities may be a constant battle. Finding people willing to take senior volunteer posts such as Chair and Treasurer are particularly difficult (Harris 1990). There is a temptation to understate the level of responsibility and degree of commitment required and to cajole reluctant people to join boards (Brophy 1994). The common practice of reserving places on boards for 'representatives' of other voluntary and statutory sector organizations is also not conducive to building an active board. The current emphasis on the sanctions to be applied to board members who fail to perform their legal responsibilities under the Charities and Companies Act (Charity Commission 1992; Phillips 1994) is likely to exacerbate the difficulties of recruiting people with a commitment to an agency's goals and a willingness to devote sufficient volunteer time to carry out allotted functions.

A fourth, more comprehensive, explanation, and one suggested by the discovery of 'self-fulfilling cycles' described earlier, emphasizes the interdependent nature of the relationship in practice between governing bodies and staff. It suggests that problems surrounding the implementation of the governing body role can only be solved by seeing that role as interdependent with the implementation of staff roles. For example, the governing body is dependent on the staff for the information and support it needs to meet its responsibilities. Staff may feel responsible for the development of their board or they may effectively prevent it from carrying out its functions. The role of the most senior paid staff person ('Director' or 'Chief Executive') is particularly significant since he or she can use their pivotal position within the communication system of a VNPO, deliberately or unintentionally, to obtain and maintain control. As Fletcher (1992: 291) says, 'much of the professional literature tends to understate . . . the importance of an executive director who takes an active part in making the board work'.

MANAGING THE RELATIONSHIP WITH TOTAL ACTIVITIES ANALYSIS

A practical framework for managing this interdependent relationship between boards and staff, called 'Total Activities Analysis' or TAA, has been developed by staff of the Centre for Voluntary Organization (Harris 1991; 1993). It has been tested and found useful in workshops and projects involving more than a hundred voluntary agencies and appears to have important advantages over other approaches to the roles and functions of voluntary governing bodies.

In the first place, it does not begin with the assumption that there is one 'right' way of doing things and all the manager and the board have to do is to learn how to do it. Instead, TAA provides a means through which staff and board members can explore and analyse what is going on in their organization and negotiate an agreement about the role of the governing body. In the process it avoids exacerbating tensions or further damaging morale. Prescriptive approaches can lead to expressions of blame – 'X is doing it the wrong way' – or guilt – 'I must be doing something wrong'. With TAA, participants are seen as part of the solution rather than as part of the problem.

Second, TAA takes the organization **as a whole** as the focus and looks at the role of the governing body in relation to the roles of other players, rather than considering it in isolation. Third, because the approach is exploratory and analytical rather than prescriptive, it assumes that any definition of the board role that is arrived at is not set in stone but represents no more than the most useful and acceptable set of arrangements that can be devised for the present. What has been negotiated can be re-negotiated in the light of changing circumstances.

How does it work? The first step in TAA is to take one pace backwards to provide a new perspective; the initial focus is not on the governing body's 'job' nor even on the interaction between the board and the staff but on the whole organization. TAA's way of looking at the agency as a whole is to ask committee members and staff to 'brainstorm' answers to a simple question: 'what activities have to be done by this agency if it is to achieve its goals?' This provides the basis for a list of agency functions which is the first stage of the analysis. Over the years this exercise has been repeated in many workshops and projects to the point at which it was possible to distil from the perceptions of the participants a list of ten broad functions which are common to most VNPOs (see Figure 3.2).

Some of these functions cover operational activities like delivering a service, raising funds, pressing for changes in the law, drawing attention to a social problem, monitoring consumer satisfaction, or maintaining contacts with others working in the field. Others are essentially supporting activities which make it possible for the operational tasks to be carried out.

A list of this kind (and each agency needs to develop its own) provides an invaluable framework for exploring the governing body role. Senior staff and committee members can be asked – as individuals – to look at each of the functions in turn and answer a series of questions about the present practice in their agency; not what is *supposed* to happen, nor what they *would like* to happen, but what is *actually* happening. The first two questions may be: *is this function currently being carried out in the agency*; and, if so, *who is doing it?*

In some cases it will be clear that the function is being carried out either by the staff or by the governing body; the provision of services, for example, is commonly carried out by the staff while, for a number of

1. **Providing services** (direct provision and/or advocacy work);

2. **Designing and developing services and structures** (including setting policies and priorities, planning and monitoring);

3. **Developing and maintaining an understanding of need and demand** (for example, in the field of housing, health, human services or the arts);

4. **Maintaining good public relations** (including publicity and making links with key people, groups and agencies in the field);

5. **Fundraising** (from a range of sources and using a variety of arrangements including donations, grants and contracts);

6. **Finance work** (including collection and disbursement of cash, accounting, budgeting and budgetary control);

7. **Staffing and training** (including recruitment, induction and staff welfare work);

8. **Managerial and co-ordinative work** (including selection and induction of staff, prescription of work, co-ordination of work and appraisal);

9. **Logistical work** (including providing premises and equipment, materials and other supporting services); and

10. **Clerical and secretarial work** (including recording and communication of decisions, actions and events).

Figure 3.2 The functions of voluntary organizations (Harris 1993: 272–3)

organizations, fundraising may be the exclusive job of the board. But it is more often the case that the function is shared between staff and board members, leading to a third question: *if the function is being shared between governing body and staff members, what is the relative weight or strength of each contribution?* (In CVO workshops participants are asked to measure this on a four point scale from 'weak role' to 'very strong role'.)

The next stage of the process is for the participants to compare their answers. The results are often very revealing; individual board members and agency staff can have very different perceptions of who is doing what in their organization. In some cases, the uncovering of these important differences of perspective can of itself provide an explanation of the problems the agency has experienced in relations between its board and staff or in defining the role of the governing body. Exploring the reasons why their understandings differ can provide a basis for more successful collaboration in the future.

This is not to argue that there are no problems if perceptions are widely shared. Agencies using the technique have identified areas of concern where they agree either that both governing body and staff are playing very strong roles in some activities (which raises issues about both accountability and effectiveness), or that they both have very weak roles (which suggests that an important function may be being neglected by the organization as a whole).

TAA can also reveal the overall balance of activities as between governing body and staff. If one of the parties appears to be more heavily involved with the work of the agency than the other, this may have practical implications for the agency and it may raise issues of accountability and effectiveness. Some agencies may therefore move on to a final stage of TAA in which staff and governing body members look together at the ways in which the functions of the agency can best be shared between staff and board and how to implement these changes. The whole process can be described as in Figure 3.3:

The analysis of agency functions at stage 1 provides the basis for an exploration of the ways in which these are shared in practice between governing bodies and staff (stage 2). This exploration may lead directly to stage 3 and discussion of the ways in which the sharing of functions

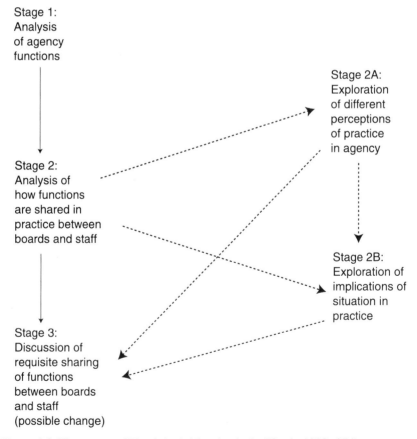

Figure 3.3 The stages of Total Activities Analysis (Harris 1993: 274)

could be differently arranged to the benefit of the organization. The three stages linked by unbroken lines represent the process at its simplest. In many cases, however, stage 2 will lead to further exploration and analysis – either of the reasons why people have different perceptions of current practice in the agency or of the implications of the current arrangements (or, indeed, of both issues) and these in turn may inform the possible changes in practice implied in stage 3.

Another case example

An example illustrates how TAA has been used in practice to help manage the relationship between staff and governing bodies (Harris 1993). A local service-providing agency with a paid staff of twelve and a similar number of volunteers used TAA to explore why its management committee 'wasn't working'. This identified two areas where there were different perceptions about what was actually going on:

- management committee members felt that they had a strong role in fund-raising and public relations but staff felt that the committee's involvement was weak.
- the staff felt that the direct provision of services was their sole responsibility while some committee members expected to work directly with agency users.

It also identified areas where there was agreement but also concern.

- board and staff members agreed that the committee was playing a weak role in 'management' activities.
- board and staff members agreed that neither the committee nor the staff had a strong role in planning and monitoring services.

Discussion of these results of the exercise revealed that:

- management committee members were active in fund-raising and public relations in some areas but left to the staff the job of maintaining the agency's relationship with the local authority which was its principal funder.
- there was considerable friction between staff and committee members over responsibility for service provision; staff felt that committee members were 'interfering' while committee members felt staff were 'obstructive'.
- staff were also unhappy and resentful because they were not being 'managed' by the committee but committee members did not see this kind of management as part of their job.
- nobody in the agency was giving serious attention to the crucial function of planning and monitoring the services it was providing.

The process had thus identified the issues underlying the board's 'failure' to do its job and enabled the agency to address them. It is clear that they are not the kind of issues to which there is only one 'correct' answer. TAA clarified the choices the organization needed to make and left it to make them on the basis of their preferred method of working and their perceptions of the distribution of skills and experience within their staff and committee members.

ADAPTABILITY TO CHANGING CIRCUMSTANCES

TAA has proved to be an invaluable tool for helping agencies to manage the relationship between staff and governing body; for identifying 'who is doing what' and 'who should be doing what'. But the development of an effective board does not stop there. There is a need to recognize the board/staff relationship as dynamic and open to regular re-examination and renegotiation. TAA is not a once-and-for-all tool. It, or some similar exercise, needs to be carried out on a regular basis so that the management of the VNPO can be adapted to changing circumstances; for example, new accountability demands from funders; growth in service provision; or new fundraising techniques.

An important reminder that VNPOs change over time and that appropriate roles for the governing body will vary according to the agency's stage of development is provided by a study by Miriam Wood of twenty-one American non-profit human service organizations (Wood 1992). She suggests that, 'following a non-recurring founding period, a board typically progresses through a sequence of three distinct operating phases and then experiences a crisis that initiates the whole sequence over again'.

During the **non-recurring founding phase** of a new organization, Wood suggests, the ownership of the agency shifts from the board members to an 'owner-director' chief executive. Initially the board members are the agency; they are enthusiastic proponents of the organization's purpose who collectively decide all questions of administration as well as policy. This level of commitment cannot be sustained and, when the board finds a chief executive in whom they can place their full confidence, they are happy to let him or her take over their responsibilities and the ownership of the organization. The founding phase is brought to an end – sooner or later – by some event (possibly the intervention of an external funder) which draws attention to the extent to which the agency is dependent on the chief executive. Galvanized into action, the board looks for a new generation of more active members.

The new recruits tend to be middle-aged professionals who bring a different perspective on management based on the world of business; the language of goals, objects and results replaces the earlier rhetoric of mission and values. The board no longer relies on the chief executive for information, it may ignore his or her advice and overrule his or her decisions. This – the first of Wood's recurrent stages – she calls the **supermanaging phase**.

The new board will eventually replace the chief executive with someone in their own image. This appointment, together with a growing feeling that the crisis that brought the new members on to the board is over, leads to the second phase in the model – the **corporate phase**. Operating along the lines of a business corporation the board and its committees require and receive copious information from the director and staff and make strategic decisions about planning, finance and fund-raising.

Over time the new bureaucratic procedures become fossilized, the board becomes totally dependent on the chief executive for information about the agency and effective ownership passes to the director. The third – **sustaining** – phase will then continue until the board receives an unwelcome surprise that reveals how little they know about what is happening in the organization. Their reaction will then restart the cycle with a new **supermanaging** phase.

To sum up this and the preceding sections, we can say that attempts to manage the relationship between the staff and governing body of a VNPO should take account of three factors: the tensions and turbulence inherent in the relationship; the complex processes involved in the interaction between them; and the changing demands on the relationship at different stages in a VNPO's history and organizational development.

TECHNIQUES FOR EFFECTIVENESS

The collaborative demands of a TAA exercise of the kind we outlined earlier, may, in themselves go a long way towards building senior staff and boards, individually and collectively, into working teams. But some VNPOs have found it helpful to utilize other facilitating techniques – additionally or instead of TAA (Hedley and Rochester 1994).

One such technique is a regular **audit of board composition**. Bearing in mind the expected functions of volunteer governors outlined at the beginning of this chapter, it seems that VNPOs need people on their governing bodies who, between, them, can:

- give the organization stability and a continuity of existence;
- accept responsibility for the work and conduct of the organization if necessary;
- understand the needs the organization exists to address;
- earn and retain the respect of important and influential people with whom the organization has to deal – especially funding bodies; and
- have the time, expertise and skills appropriate to the agency's needs at the particular stage of its organizational development.

The successful recruitment of board members depends in principle on the same considerations as the recruitment of other volunteers. The process is generally seen as reciprocal; attracting volunteers and keeping them involves understanding and meeting their needs and aspirations, as well as ensuring that the experience and expertise they have to offer is what the organization requires (Hedley 1992; Volunteer Centre UK 1992). Matching their skills and motivations to the tasks and functions which a VNPO needs to have performed is just as important in the case of governing bodies.

Some agencies undertake their audit as a group activity – with or without an external facilitator. Using a flip-chart or chalkboard, the members of the governing body and senior staff list all the tasks that the board is expected to undertake during the following year. For each task or group of activities they then discuss:

- the skills or knowledge needed to carry them out and the time commitment involved;
- which – if any – board members have the skills needed and are willing to take on the work, and how the work might be shared and what help might be wanted in the form of support, advice and training.

The final stage of the audit process is to highlight the 'problem areas' – the tasks which no one feels competent to do or no one wants to do – and to identify the additional expertise the board needs to acquire (Hedley and Rochester 1994).

In deciding on which tasks and functions need to be performed, a VNPO can use a list such as that provided in Figure 3.2 above to identify the skills and knowledge needed, the time commitment required and the extent to which existing board members can provide what is wanted. Some agencies have adopted the idea of 'job descriptions' for chairpersons and secretaries and rather fewer have drawn up 'person specifications' for them. The research literature suggests, however, that it is rare for VNPOs to provide potential board members with a clear account of the tasks they will be expected to carry out or the 'terms and conditions of service', such as time commitment or length of service.

But while each VNPO needs to regularly reassess the qualities it needs in its volunteer governors, we do not advocate a variety of characteristics for its own sake. Whereas it is true that most boards need to possess, between them, a range of knowledge, expertise and skills, it is also the case that they have to be able to work together. If the gulf between the values, backgrounds and cultures of different committee volunteers are too wide – or if they lack sensitivity to, and tolerance, of the views of other members – any gain from their special expertise will be more than cancelled out by the threat they pose to the development of a team approach to the governance task. Similarly, if the gap between the values of the board and the values of the staff is too wide, problems of managing that working relationship are likely to become intractable (Kramer 1965).

A second useful technique is to institute an **annual cycle of meetings** (Hedley and Rochester 1994). Planning meetings on an annual basis enables the board to give time and attention to the way in which it conducts its business and has the following advantages:

- the committee can ensure that it discusses major items at the right time: it can, for example, agree the budget for the following year after reviewing priorities and before applying for grant aid;
- it can ensure that there is adequate time to devote to major decisions; and
- it can avoid discussing the same item at meeting after meeting.

One possible model involves:

- devoting the first meeting after the Annual General Meeting to the induction of new members and the discussion and adoption of a programme of meetings for the year (times, dates and agendas);
- taking as a key item of business for other meetings an annual review of specific areas of the organization's work;
- concentrating at another meeting on the adoption of a budget for the appropriate financial year together with fund-raising targets. This would also review the organization's administrative needs and resources, its equipment and premises; and
- taking as a major item of business for another meeting the agreement of the contents of the Annual Report and the arrangements for the Annual General Meeting.

CONCLUSION

That working with governing bodies is one of the most difficult challenges in VNPO management is clear from the wide gap that commonly exists between the formal statements of their responsibilities and their performance. A key explanation of the difficulties is the interdependent nature of the relationship between staff and boards. They are dependent each on the other for the effective performance of organizational tasks and functions. The Chief Executive of a VNPO, as the main link between staff and boards, has a crucial role. He or she can enable or disempower the governing body.

This chapter has provided an analysis and some explanations of the problems and issues that commonly arise in working with governing bodies. It has proposed an organizational tool – Total Activities Analysis – which can help VNPOs to discuss and negotiate a balance of activities between boards and staff. It has suggested that such negotiations need to take place at regular intervals since VNPOs go through different stages of organizational development. Finally, we have suggested techniques which can be used to secure an appropriate board composition and to organize the meetings of the governing body.

REFERENCES

Batsleer, J., Cornforth, C. and Paton, R. (eds) (1992) *Issues in Voluntary and Non-profit Management*, Addison-Wesley, Wokingham.

Brophy, J. (1994) Parent management committees and pre-school playgroups. *Journal of Social Policy* **23**, (2), pp. 161–94.

Charity Commission (1992) *Charities – The New Law: A Trustees' Guide to the Charities Act 1992*, Charity Commissioners for England and Wales, London.

Dartington, T. (1995) Trustees, committees and boards, in *An Introduction to the Voluntary Sector* (eds J. Davis Smith, C. Rochester and R. Hedley) Routledge, London.

Fletcher, K. (1992) Effective boards; how executive directors define and develop them. *Nonprofit Management and Leadership*, **2**, (3), pp. 282–93.

Ford, K. (1992) *Trustee Training and Support Needs*, National Council for Voluntary Organisation, London.

Harris, M. (1989) The governing body role: problems and perceptions in implementation. *Nonprofit and Voluntary Sector Quarterly* **18**, (4), pp. 317–23.

Harris, M. (1990) Voluntary leaders in voluntary welfare agencies. *Social Policy and Administration* **24**, (2), pp. 156–67.

Harris, M. (1991) *Exploring the Role of Voluntary Management Committees: A New Approach*, Working Paper 10, Centre for Voluntary Organisation, London.

Harris, M. (1992) The role of voluntary management committees, in *Issues in Voluntary and Non-profit Management* (eds J. Batsleer, C. Cornforth and R. Paton) Addison-Wesley, Wokingham.

Harris, M. (1993) Exploring the role of boards using total activities analysis. *Nonprofit Management and Leadership*, **3**, (3), pp. 269–81.

Harris, M. (1994) The power of boards in service-providing agencies: three models. *Administration in Social Work*, **18**, (2), pp. 1–15.

Harris, M. (1996) Do we need governing bodies? in *Voluntary Agencies; Challenges of Organisation and Management* (eds D. Billis and M. Harris) Macmillan, London.

Hedley, R. (1992) Organising and managing volunteers, in *Volunteering and Society; Principles and Practice* (eds R. Hedley and J. Davis Smith) Bedford Square Press, London.

Hedley, R. and Rochester, C. (1994) *Volunteers on Management Committees; a Good Practice Guide*, Volunteer Centre UK, Berkhamsted.

Hodgkin, C. (1993) Policy and paper clips: rejecting the lure of the corporate model. *Nonprofit Management and Leadership*, **3**, (4), pp. 415–28.

Kramer, R. (1965) Ideology, status and power in board-executive relationships. *Social Work*, **10**, pp. 107–14.

Lynn, P. and Davis Smith, J. (1991) *The 1991 Survey of Voluntary Activity in the UK*, Volunteer Centre UK, Berkhamsted.

Phillips, A. (1994) *Charitable Status; a Practical Handbook*, Directory of Social Change, London.

Volunteer Centre UK (1992) *Managing Volunteers; A Handbook for Volunteer Organisers*, Volunteer Centre UK, Berkhamsted.

Wood, M. (1992) Is Governing Body behaviour cyclical? *Nonprofit Management and Leadership*, **3**, (2), pp. 139–63.

GUIDED READING

Further details of specific 'tools' and ideas explored in this chapter are given in the references above. From these, we recommend especially:

Dartington (1995) for an up-to-date review of the research and other literature about governing bodies.

Harris (1991) for a more detailed description of the Total Activities Analysis approach.

Harris (1994) which places the governing body of the VNPO in its organizational context.

Hedley and Rochester (1994) which offers practical guidance about the recruitment and retention of volunteer board members.

Phillips (1994) for a clear explanation of the legal complexities and liabilities facing board members who are also charity trustees.

Other useful reading is as follows.

Hedley, R. and Rochester, C. (1992) *Understanding Management Committees*, Volunteer Centre UK, Berkhamsted. The report of a research study of the experience of volunteer committee members which looks at motives and rewards, problems and benefits; and ways in which boards might work more effectively.

Herman, R. (1989) Board functions and board–staff relations in nonprofit organizations: an introduction, in *Nonprofit Boards of Directors* (eds R. Herman and J. Van Til) Transaction, New York. A valuable survey which not only reviews the (mainly US) research on governance but also highlights the importance of the issues with which it is concerned.

Middleton, M. (1987) Nonprofit Boards of Directors: beyond the governance function, in *The Nonprofit Sector: A Research Handbook* (ed W. Powell) Yale University Press, New Haven. Draws together the US literature to place the board in the context of its wider environment including the local community.

Leat, D. (1988) *Voluntary Organisations and Accountability*, NCVO, London. While not specifically about governing bodies this is a very helpful contribution to our understanding of a key concept in discussing the board role.

Smith, D. (1992) Moral responsibilities of trustees : some first thoughts. *Nonprofit Management and Leadership*, **2**, (4), pp. 351–62. This article breaks new ground by setting out to clarify the role of the trustee by adopting a moral definition rather than taking a social science or historical approach.

4 Understanding cost and budget management in the voluntary sector

Stephen P. Osborne

INTRODUCTION

This chapter is concerned with managing the financial flow through VNPOs. In particular it covers the sources of possible funds for VNPOs, the nature of costs inside such organizations, the process and impact of costing a service, and how to use this financial information to construct and understand budgets. The use of this information will then be explored in more detail in later chapters, such as that on business planning.

By the end of this chapter you should:

- understand the different funding sources for a VNPO and their implications;
- be clear about the different types of costs involved in providing a service and how to calculate these;
- know how to use this information to construct a budget for a service; and
- appreciate how to use budgets as part of service management.

All too often, financial management is viewed with dismay by service management in VNPOs, who fear that they may not have the ability to understand and use this information. The intention here is to provide you with the basic 'building blocks' to be able to do precisely this. The guided reading at the end of this chapter will then enable you to explore the issues outlined in more detail and to suit your particular needs.

THE FUNDING SOURCES OF VNPOs

This brief section is intended to outline the possible funding sources of VNPOs and to give some initial consideration to their implications and management. Inevitably, such a brief introduction can do no more than outline the key issues of this important topic. For a more detailed treatment, it is advisable to explore some of the texts in the guided reading at the end of this chapter.

The financial structure of the sector

The financial structure of the sector is diverse indeed. A recent study (Osborne and Hems, 1995; 1996) estimated that the sector included some 143,000 organizations, though this almost certainly underestimates the number of smaller ones. However, the income of these organizations is not distributed evenly. The largest 2.2% of these organizations (with annual income of £1 million or over) account for 73.4% of the income of the sector. By contrast, 88.8% of the organizations have annual income of £100,000 or less, and account for only 7.3% of the total income of the sector. In terms of the income and expenditure of the sector, this is displayed in Tables 4.1 and 4.2. Table 4.1 is of particular concern here, as it emphasizes the range of sources from which VNPOs can glean their funds. This can be simplified to give five main sources:

Government. Overall, this accounts for almost a quarter of the income of VNPOs. Traditionally this has been in the form of grants and donations, but increasingly this is moving towards contract based funding (NCVO 1994), though the difference between the two is not always as clear as it might be supposed to be (Osborne and Waterston 1994). The key issue for managers here is the complex accountability relationships between government and VNPOs and how to manage them – particularly when there are multiple sources of funding (Leat 1988).

Private giving. This is what is usually referred to as the 'voluntary income' of VNPOs. It is, in part, one of the main sources of their voluntary

Table 4.1 The income of VNPOs 1991

	£m	% of total
Sales of goods and services		
To persons	2,049	22.5
To government	1,012	11.1
To for profit organizations	459	5.0
Total	**3,673**	**40.4**
Grants, donations and general funding		
From government	1,198	13.2
From persons	1,049	11.5
From other sources	556	6.1
From other VNPOs	497	5.5
Total	**3,300**	**36.3**
Legacies	600	6.6
Investment	1,398	15.4
Disposal of assets	123	1.4
TOTAL	**9,094**	**100.0**

(*Source*: Adapted from Osborne and Hems, 1995)

Table 4.2 The expenditure of VNPOs 1991

	£m	% of total
Expenditure on goods/services in the UK	3,273	38.6
Staff costs	3,072	36.2
Charitable cash payments to individuals/other VNPOs	1,420	16.7
Financial transactions abroad	472	5.6
Depreciation	222	2.6
Interest payments	39	0.4
TOTAL	**8,498**	**100**

(*Source*: Adapted from Osborne and Hems, 1995)

nature, as was discussed in the first chapter of this book. Fund-raising strategies for VNPOs, especially the larger ones, have become increasingly sophisticated as a range of marketing, direct mail and advertising techniques have been employed (see Gronbjerg 1993). However, there can sometimes be a danger that such strategies and techniques can conflict with the actual mission of the goal. One of the key balancing acts for VNPOs is between obtaining the sympathy of the general public for their beneficiaries, and the impact that such a 'sympathy vote' can have upon those beneficiaries – by emphasizing their inadequacy and dependency, for example (Eayrs and Ellis 1990).

The corporate sector. Corporate donations to VNPOs accounted for only 3.8% of the total income of VNPOs in 1991, though it can be an important one. It can often be used as source of legitimacy by VNPOs, as a way of emphasizing their standing in the local community. This in turn can help them lever money from other organizations, particularly from central government departments, which can place great emphasis upon such corporate funding. However, it is often only the larger and/or more popular causes and organizations which can attract such corporate funding. Moreover, another recent study (PSMRC 1991) found that some VNPOs were actually spending more on seeking out corporate funding than they obtained back in resources. Finally, it is important to emphasize that direct funding is only one form of corporate support. Other forms can often be as, if not more, important and include sponsorship, staff secondments, training, administrative support, and 'in kind' assistance (Passey 1995).

Fees/charges. Fees to individuals and other VNPOs accounted for a sizeable proportion of the income of VNPOs, and are an increasingly important area (Leat 1989). However, whilst they can help an organization gain both control over their resources and commitment from beneficiaries who perceive themselves as customers, it also has its drawbacks. The issue of a pricing strategy is particularly difficult, as is the possible impact upon the intended beneficiary group of fees and charges. (This issue is dealt with in great detail in Gronbjerg 1993.)

Merchandising. Finally, VNPOs are increasingly turning to selling non mission-centred goods as a way to subsidize their mission critical services. These can range from Christmas cards once a year through to the substantial merchandising catalogues of the national charities, such as Barnardos. At its extreme merchandising requires sophisticated financial skills. However, benefit for even the smallest VNPO can derive from it, providing that it is limited and does not take over the entire resource of the organization (Adams and Perlmutter 1991).

Developing a funding strategy should be part of the overall strategic and marketing plans of an organization. These issues have been dealt with in more detail elsewhere in this book. However, five broad issues should be kept to the fore in deciding upon the nature and role of resource acquisition for a VNPO:

- What overall level of funding does your organization require?
- What should be the balance between the different sources of funding for your organization, bearing in mind the different accountability and auditing requirements of each one?
- What impact might your fund-raising strategy have upon your mission-critical activity, and vice-versa?
- What techniques are best suited to your fund-raising needs?
- In what ways are you going to monitor and control the resources that you acquire?

The first four points are dealt with elsewhere in the guided reading at the end of this book. The rest of this chapter is devoted to the last point and, in particular, to the skills of costing and budgeting in VNPOs.

COSTS AND COSTING

It is important at the outset to differentiate between capital and revenue costs. Nutley and Osborne (1994) define capital costs as 'expenditure on things of lasting value (such as land, buildings and major items of equipment)' and revenue costs as 'expenditure on day-to-day running costs (such as salaries, heating and stationery)'. In practice, most managers are concerned with managing their revenue costs and budgets, and this is the focus here. It is important to recognize that capital costs (such as a major piece of equipment, like a minibus) can have revenue implications (such as the interest payments on a loan which might have been taken out to buy it). However, capital budgeting is a specialist topic in its own right. Those managers concerned in particular with this type of cost management are recommended to read Chapters 6–8 of Coombs and Jenkins (1992).

What are costs?

Most simply, costs are the financial value(s) of the resources used to develop a service. At the most simple level, therefore, you need to be clear about the full range of resources which goes into a service and the financial values of these. This is not as simple as it sounds. It may be relatively simple to establish the costs of, say, stationery used in a central office, but not all costs are so straightforward. If you wanted to cost the provision of hot meals in a day centre, for example, you would have to bear in mind a number of factors. Depending upon how you were allocating costs in a service, you might need to include:

● the costs of the food (and its collection/delivery);
● the salaries of those people cooking and serving the food;
● the fuel used in cooking the food, washing up the dishes (assuming a dishwasher is used) and cleaning the kitchen; and
● the lighting/heating rates of the establishment.

The list certainly is not exhaustive, but it does raise the key issues of costings: what are the full range of resources used to provide a service; how much of these resources are devoted to this service alone, if it is shared amongst a number of services; and how to calculate their financial value.

It could be useful at this stage to consider just one part of your own service and try and make a full list of all the resources that go into providing it. Ask yourself which of these you have easily accessible information upon, and which ones you would need to do further research upon.

It is usual when calculating costs to do this across two dimensions. These are the *type* of expenditure incurred and the *site* at which it was incurred. The types of costs of a service are the sort of things that you would have listed above, in terms of your own service. They cover the resources involved in producing a service. A simple example is shown in Table 4.3. Callaghan (1992) offers three simple rules for deciding upon the types of expenditure that you might want to include in your costs:

● be comprehensive – you can always combine types of expenditure at a later date, but it is hard to include new types half-way through a year;
● keep the typology as simple as possible – the more types of costs you include the more time consuming (and costly!) it is to monitor them; and
● ensure the typology suits your purpose – do not assume that the types of resource heading applicable to one service automatically fits another one.

It is also important to make sure that your types of expenditure are exclusive and that you are consistent in how you allocate your costs to them. It is no use including the cost of an external trainer in sessional pay

Table 4.3 Common types of expenditure

Salaries				
Sessional pay				
Training				
Office expenses				
Heating/lighting				
Travel				
Rent				
Other costs				
TOTAL				

one month, and under training the next month. Unless you are consistent you will not be able to monitor and control the changing profile of the costs of your service.

The second dimension that we specified was the site at which costs are incurred. These are usually called **cost centres**. Table 4.4 shows how they would be displayed against the types of expenditure we highlighted above. Again, there is no one definition which should be a cost centre. For a small

Table 4.4 Types of expenditure displayed against cost centres

	Cost Centre A	Cost Centre B	Cost Centre C	Total
Salaries				
Sessional pay				
Training				
Office expenses				
Heating/lighting				
Travel				
Rent				
Other costs				
TOTAL				

VNPO, the organization itself may well be the cost centre, as it would be impracticable or too expensive to split the cost information further. For a larger organization, cost centres might be decided upon the basis of a geographical split (perhaps into the four locations/regions an organization services), organizational functions (such as service provision, training, fund-raising, etc.), or the actual services that comprise the organization (such as a day care centre, a home visiting service, and a 'granny sitting' service for a VNPO working with elderly people).

The use of cost centres is important. It helps you see how costs are spread across your organization and enables you to make decisions about how to spread central costs across a number of services. This decision will probably be made largely upon the structure of your organization – whether it itself is a unitary one, or has a divisional or functional structure. It is important to remember that no one approach is right or wrong, though. Each will often obscure as much as it reveals. To continue with the training example used above, if you were using a service based cost centre, then 'training' would be one of the expenditure types that you would allocate across each cost centre. This would help you to see how training costs compared between services and to make decisions about the appropriate level for each part of your organization. However, it would be harder to compare the costs of training with, for example, administration, which you could do with functionally based cost centres. Then again, these latter cost centres would not help you compare across different services. As with all financial information, the important part is the *use* that you want to make of the information. Once you are clear on this, then it becomes easier to decide both the types of expenditure and the cost centres that will help you most to achieve this aim.

Different types of costs

So far, we have discussed costs in general terms, as if there were only one way in which to present them. This is far from the case. What have been described above are essentially 'unit costs'. In addition, though, there are two other important ways to cost a service. These are through marginal costs and opportunity costs. All three are discussed in more detail below.

Unit costs

This is the simplest and most common way in which to cost a service or organization. It concerns the acknowledged cost of one part, or 'unit', in a service. Depending upon the nature of the work of your VNPO, this could be quite different. It could be the cost per sevice user, cost per service component, or cost per staff member. This information is essential for two reasons. First, it is important in order to be able to gauge the relative efficiency, either of parts of your service or of your service compared to that provided by another organization. For example, imagine you are a counselling service for adults with relationship problems, with three offices in different parts of a county. By comparing the unit costs of each office in terms of the cost of the service per service user, you will get some idea of just how well resources are being used in each office.

You might find that Office A is costing much more than either Office B or Office C. In this case you would need to ask some relevant questions about the utilization of resources in this office and why it is that much more expensive. However, it is important not to assume automatically that a higher unit cost means that a service is being provided inefficiently. It could be because the people using that office have more complex needs than other offices, or because it provides a more specialist (and therefore expensive) service than the other office, or because it is an older building and so more difficult to heat and maintain. Unit cost information does not always give you the answers to the questions about the efficiency of a service, therefore. However, it does help you decide what questions to ask about it.

The second reason that you might need to know the unit costs of a service, is in order both to prepare tenders for government contracts and to decide the appropriate level of fee to charge, if this is one of your sources of income. In both these cases the prices that you charge for the service must be sufficient to at least cover your unit cost, unless you decide intentionally to subsidize the service from other sources of income. This will be a key decision of your funding strategy, as discussed earlier.

Calculating unit costs

Allen and Beecham (1993) offer a useful model for costing the unit costs of a service or organization. This is in four stages:

Stage One is the identification and description of the components of a service. They recommend starting with a detailed description of the service and its component parts. This will then form the basis for your typology of costs, as discussed earlier.

Stage Two is deciding upon the relevant service unit to which a cost is to be attached. It is important that this unit is both meaningful and useful – an appropriate unit for residential care might be a cost per day, whilst for a counselling service it might be more sensible to cost per hour, or even per minute:

> The choice of a unit of measurement for each service and the method by which it is calculated is an integral part of the costing exercise . . . The unit should be relevant to the service and calculated by examining the resource implications of the different activities undertaken by the service. It should also be relevant to the objectives of the (costing) exercise

and take into account the nature of the available data. The unit should remain constant for each type of service, although the elements of the costs may be calculated separately. Thus a home help unit may be costed on the number of minutes but the travel costs may be more easily expressed as cost per visit.

(Allen and Beecham 1993: 30)

Stage Three is the identification and consideration of the key implications of these costs upon the various elements of a service. Different costs will have different implications – employing a member of staff will not only have salary implications for example, there will be the added cost of national insurance payments and also of any training which is provided to enable that person to do their job adequately. This identification is by no means a straightforward task, as you may not have all cost information to hand easily, and so may have to use estimates.

Stage Four is the final calculation of the unit cost for the service. At its simplest, this involves dividing the total cost of a service, as calculated from the above information, by the most appropriate unit of measurement. Again, depending upon the use of the information, this could be the unit cost per service user, per visit, or per member of staff.

Two problems need to be surmounted in developing this final unit cost. The first is the apportionment of the central, or overhead, costs of a service. The second is the costing of difficult items of expenditure.

Overhead costs

These are those costs which might be incurred by your organization as a whole, and which need to be apportioned to the different cost centres – though if your organization is just one cost centre, then of course this will not be a problem to you. The most common approach to these overhead costs is what is called '**absorption costing**'. All the relevant overhead costs are 'absorbed' by the service being costed.

In separating out overheads costs for absorption, it is useful to think of the total costs at each cost centre as comprising four elements. The first is the direct costs of the service. As discussed above, these are those resources actively used to produce a service within the cost centre. The second is the indirect costs which are incurred in support of the actual service and are usually carried out within, or linked to, the service itself.

The third type of costs are the true overhead costs. These comprise those costs of the headquarters and central services of your organization. The final type of cost is capital-related costs, usually consisting of interest repayments or depreciation upon any capital goods in the project. An example of these types of costs for a community transport scheme of a Council for Voluntary Service, is given in Table 4.5.

Table 4.5 Cost classification of a community transport scheme (part of a Council for Voluntary Service)

Direct costs:

- Salary of scheme co-ordinator
- Sessional payments for drivers
- Petrol for minibus
- Maintenance costs of minibus (varies with amount of usage)

Indirect costs:

- Heating/lighting of office for scheme
- Insurance/tax of vehicle (does not vary with amount of usage)
- Training for drivers

Overhead costs:

- Salary of CVS organizer
- Administrative support of CVS
- Contribution to overall costs of any other central CVS officers
- Cleaning of CVS offices

Capital-related costs:

- Interest charge on loan to buy minibus
- Depreciation charge upon minibus

A key issue for any VNPO is therefore the basis upon which to apportion these overhead costs for absorption. Once again, there is no 'right answer'. Each has its own advantages and disadvantages. Common approaches are to allocate the overhead costs:

- equally amongst the services (if there are five services in the organization, then each has to pay 20% of the total overhead costs);
- in the same proportion as the staffing of the organization is distributed amongst services (if your organization employs 100 people and your project uses 10 of these people then you pay 10% of the overhead costs); or
- in the same proportion as the cost of each service in relation to total agency costs (if your service comprises 25% of the total direct costs of the agency then you pay 25% of the overhead costs).

Absorption costing has a number of important benefits for an organization. It makes sure that the full costs of an organization are absorbed at the service level, so that overhead costs are not an on-going drain upon the voluntary income or the reserves of an organization; it ensures that a VNPO can receive the maximum amount of income to cover its costs, especially in relation to contracts with government; and it can lead to greater accountability of the central services of an organization to the service units that are funding them.

However, there are also some problems with absorption costing. Coombs and Jenkins (1992) list the following criticisms:

- absorption costing can lead to inefficiency in central services, as they have no incentive to minimize or control their costs, because they are being met by other parts of the organization;
- if your VNPO is involved in tendering for governmental contracts, it could blunt your competitive edge, either if a competitor has a 'leaner' central organization than your organization, or if they are not working on an absorption model; and
- it can create resentment from service managers, who may feel that they are supporting the central services of the organization, to the detriment of the resources of their own service.

Two alternative models of dealing with overhead costs have evolved. The first is 'workload charging', where central services charge a fee for their services directly to the other parts of their organization. This sort of 'internal market' can lead to more efficient cost allocation and recovery. However, it can also become immensely bureaucratic and time consuming.

The second approach is through 'service level agreements', where a given level of service is agreed between parts of an organization, at a predetermined price. This approach is potentially far less bureaucratic than workload charging, but does require a level of trust between the different parties to the agreement.

Ultimately, there is no one right way forward, as has been emphasized above. The key is to decide which approach provides the best balance between its sophistication and flexibility and its own cost and ease of use.

To return to the central issue of **unit costs**, even if these issues above are resolved, unit costs have their own limitations as a way in which to analyze organizational costs. It is dangerous, for example, to compare the different services and/or cost centres of a VNPO solely upon the basis of their unit costs. Amongst other things, this can obscure differences in:

- the complexity of the needs being met and in the quality of the services being provided;
- the accommodation that a service is operating from, which could affect its costs;
- significant regional differences in salaries or costs, for a national organization; and
- how different services may be treating their costs.

Whilst they are useful, therefore, unit costs should never be looked at in isolation but always with other data, whether the overriding concern is the management of organizational performance or its financial probity.

Difficult costs

A particular problem for VNPOs can be that some of their costs are much more difficult to estimate than for other types of organizations. This is particularly so in the case of volunteers, where most of the costs are actually indirect, and so difficult to estimate. Another problem can be that service users can also be providers in their own right, or bear indirect and/or hidden costs, rather than direct ones. A good example of this latter problem is with carers groups.

Detailed examination of these issues is impossible here. However, they have received attention elsewhere, and particularly from Knapp (1990) in relation to volunteers, and Netten and Beecham (1993) in relation to informal care.

Marginal costs

Marginal costs concern the behaviour of costs at levels of service. At the most simplest, they are concerned with how much more (or less) one additional unit of service will cost, for any one service. To be more concrete, if your organization provides a relief foster care service for autistically disturbed children you might want to know either how much more it is going to cost you to provide a service for one more child, or how much more it is going to cost to provide one more foster home. This sort of information is essential if you need to make a decision about whether to expand, or reduce, your service. The difficulty with marginal costs is that, although extremely useful, they are much more difficult to calculate than unit costs, and one often requires information to be available from a number of years. The general approach is outlined here, but is dealt within in more detail in Knapp (1984).

In the previous section, we discussed how to assess the total costs of your service or organization and the subsequent unit costs. With any service, unit costs will reduce as you increase the number of service users. This is called 'economy of scale', because the costs of a service are spread over a larger number of people. However, there comes a point when these unit costs being to increase again, as you increase numbers (perhaps because your staff group can only cope with a certain number of staff users, or when you need to employ extra staff). This is called 'diseconomy of scale'. A key management decision is, therefore, at what level is service working most efficiently? In order to decide this, you need to decide the cost of an additional unit of service, or its marginal cost.

In theoretical terms, the optimum level of service for an organization is where its unit cost curve and its marginal cost curve intersect – see Figure 4.1. At levels of output below this, unit costs are still falling, whilst the marginal cost of additional units of service is below its unit cost. It is therefore financially worthwhile expanding the service, in order to continue to reduce unit costs. At levels of output above this intersection, though, it is not economical to expand output any further, for the marginal cost of additional units of service is greater than the unit costs, so that the latter cost will start to rise again.

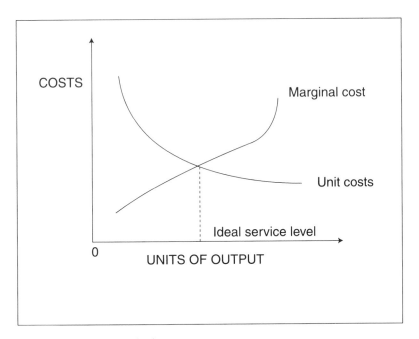

Figure 4.1 Unit and marginal costs

In order to calculate marginal costs, you need financial information of two types, on the **fixed** and **variable** costs of your service. Fixed costs do not change with the level of a service. These include staff salaries and the like. The key issue here is whether the cost of that item of expenditure remains the same whatever the level of service. Returning to our community transport scheme, earlier, you would still have to pay the same amount of road tax for the minibus, irrespective of whether it serves twenty or two hundred people. By contrast, variable costs are those costs which vary in direct relationship to the level of service. With our community transport scheme, this would include the petrol and oil and servicing, which would vary depending upon how much the minibus was used.

In practice, of course, the distinction is more blurred than this. The salary of the organizer of the community transport scheme is fixed, in the sense that it does not vary with usage. However, if your community transport scheme expands so much that you had to employ a second co-ordinator, then this too would become a variable cost. Despite this, the distinction is a useful one and reasonably clear in most circumstances.

Let us take the example of a VNPO providing domiciliary cleaning for elderly people. In simple terms, the fixed costs of this service would be:

- the wages of the (half time) service organizer and domiciliary staff (£10,000).
- overhead costs (£2,000).

The variable costs of this service, for one hundred people would be:

● transport (£200, or £2 per client serviced)
● Cleaning materials (£400, or £4 per client serviced)

The total cost of this service is the sum of its fixed and variable costs, or £12,600.

Let us first imagine that it is possible to expand this service to serve one hundred and twenty people, without any extra staff. In this case the fixed costs would stay the same, whilst the variable costs increased to £240 and £480 respectively. The total cost of the service would therefore rise to £12,720. In such an example, a 20% increase in service led to only a 1% increase in costs. However, if the additional twenty service users meant employing additional domiciliary care staff, then fixed costs would also rise. If we imaginged that the increase in service led to an increase in this wage level of £2,500 then the total cost of the service would become £15,220. In this case, the 20% increase in service would increase the total cost by 21%.

The relationship between your fixed and variable components of your costs is thus the significant factor in determining the marginal costs of your service, and the impact upon your overall costs of expanding or contracting your service level.

Opportunity costs

This concept of cost derives from economic theory. The commonplace is that economics is about the allocation of scarce resources. Opportunity costs concern the effect of these allocative decisions, in terms of service options foregone. They can be defined as the cost of providing a service, not in terms of the financial cost of the resources used but rather from the alternative uses foregone by choosing a specific form of service. More concretely, let us consider a VNPO whose mission is to enable elderly people to live in their own homes for as long as possible. If it chooses to do this by providing a day centre for daytime companionship and stimulation, it will do this by not choosing other options – such as a domiciliary care service, or a respite care service for carers.

A second example could be a child care charity which decides to use a building for a residential home. The opportunity costs have to include not only the alternative uses of such a building (perhaps as a community resource centre for young people) but also the opportunities foregone by not disposing of that building and using the income generated for an alternative form of service delivery.

The most usual way in which opportunity costs are applied to a service is through Cost Benefit Analysis (CBA). Knapp (1984) specifies six stages in this approach:

1 The separation and classifications of the alternatives for a service.
2 Listing of the costs and benefits of each alternative.
3 The valuation and/or quantification of costs and benefits.
4 A comparison of these costs and benefits.
5 Evaluation of these comparisons in the light of changing or uncertain circumstances (i.e. generating alternative scenarios for evaluation).
6 Making a decision upon the above information.

A variation to CBA is Cost Effectiveness Analysis (CEA). In this case, no attempt is made to put a monetary value on the outputs of a service (Sugden and Williams, 1978).

Both these approaches are too sophisticated to deal with in detail here, and reference should be made to the specialist texts referred to above. Two points should be emphasized. First, that 'opportunity cost' is an important approach for the service manager, in that it concentrates his or her attention upon the full range of alternatives for a VNPO and their implications in terms of opportunities foregone.

Second, that opportunity costing and CBA, is not a mechanistic substitute for decision-making, but rather a tool and framework to aid it. Judgements still have to be made about the monetary and mission-related value of a service. Opportunity costing explores and exposes those judgements, it does not replace them.

BUDGETS AND BUDGETING

The budget

CIPFA (1991) has defined five key stages to the process of effective financial management:

- planning
- budget setting
- service activity and expenditure
- budget monitoring and control
- review

An essential component of this process is the budget. Put most simply, a budget is a, usually, short-term plan of action described in financial terms. It gives an overview of the financial ramifications of how an organization delivers its services. Typically, the process of budgeting comprises three distinctive managerial functions: the financial planning, co-ordination and controlling of service delivery.

Coombs and Jenkins (1992) list seven reasons for organizations to have budgets:

- to establish the required level of income for an organization;
- to plan service expenditure levels, and to relate this to income;

- to authorize expenditure with the organization and at different levels;
- to limit and control expenditure
- to communicate to staff the levels of service and of resources required;
- to focus the attention of managers upon the future and upon the need to co-ordinate resources to produce services; and
- to motivate managers to be efficient and effective in service delivery.

It might be useful to consider the budgeting process of your own organization and the extent to which these rationales are built into this process. If some are missing, then consider how they might be integrated in to it or if they are not relevant issues for your organization.

In most except the smallest VNPOs, there will probably be a number of different budgets and as with costs, these can be constructed differently. There might be a budget, for example, for an area office of a large charity, or a functional component of it (such as fund-raising) or for a specific service. Whatever the structure of budgeting, these components need to be capable of aggregation into the overall budget of an organization.

A key issue is the balance between flexibility, accountability and control in budgeting. On the one hand, devolution to the lowest possible level of an organization will produce the greatest flexibility and responsiveness to service users, but it may also result in less financial control of the organization, in relation to its overall mission. By contrast, centralized budgeting will certainly assist this latter point, but at the possible cost of the motivation and autonomy of your service managers. Sound budgeting practice, hence, is no substitute for good organizational management, but rather a core component of it.

Table 4.6 shows the budget of a community care project for children with learning disabilities. The first column displays the items of expenditure in this budget (such as salaries, training or transport). The second and third columns then give the expenditure from last year and the budget for this year. This is the sum that the project manager will have devolved to him or her. In theory, this is the total amount that the manager can spend in that financial year. Indeed, in some larger organizations performance related pay may be linked to remaining within that budget.

However, in the example given here, the organization has recognized that the budget is only an estimate for the year to come, rather than a cap on expenditure. The fourth column therefore gives a forecast of actual expenditure for the year. This allows the organization to track changing financial expenditure over the year and plan how to deal with it. In this case, the project is half-way through the financial year and is facing an overspend of 3.9%.

Having this information enables the management team to do two things. First, it can seek out the reason(s) for the expected overspend. If it is split over a number of item heads then it is likely that the original budget was underestimated, and a case would have to be made for its adjustment

Table 4.6 Example of project budget for communty care project for children with a severe learning disability, of a national charity (half-way through financial year)

Item	Last year expenditure £	This year budget £	This year forecast £	Forecast + inflation £	Next year budget request £
Salaries	73,818	80,441	86,335	102,013	135,197
Training	213	584	584	677	677
Advertising	495	1,000	1,000	1,159	1,159
Security	131	93	93	108	108
Insurance	272	349	349	404	404
Food	157	288	188	334	334
Holidays	829	1,378	1,378	1,596	1,590
Foster parent fees	47,972	61,912	61,912	71,727	61,689
Volunteers	170	295	295	342	342
Rates	216	250	150	174	174
Services	650	720	732	890	890
Stationery/office	1,198	2,013	1,713	1,985	2,094
Transport	7,720	8,695	9,200	9,900	9,900
Others	1,250	1,440	1,672	1,800	1,800
Total	**135,091**	**159,458**	**165,701**	**193,109**	**216,358**
% increase/ decrease		+18.0%	+3.9%	+16.5%	+12.0%

upward. Alternatively, the overspend may be able to be pinned down to one or two specific items, such as travel. This information could then be used to explore the reasons for this (for example, is it because of an increased workload or inefficient use of public transport?) and decisions made about how to manage this issue for the rest of the year. Second, it also gives the manager the basis upon which to seek additional funding from the host organization (or an external funder, depending upon how decentralized fund-raising is) or to take action to reduce spending over the remainder of the year.

A key concept here is that of **virement**. This is the facility to switch money between the item, (or budget) heads. Thus, for example, in this project the manager could switch money from the 'holidays' to the 'food' budget, as long as the overall budget profile was maintained. Similarly, the senior management team of the parent organization could 'vire' money from another project to this one, to cover the overspend. However, such action can be immensely unpopular, as staff can often see no reason to seek cost efficiency in their work, if the saving is to go to another project. Such a process needs to be approached with caution, therefore.

Returning to Table 4.6, column five gives forecasted expenditure for this year, with the addition of an allowance for inflation. This is used as a basis for planning column six, which is the budget request for the next financial year. In this case, we can see that the project is heading for expansion, because its bid for next year is 12% above what it would have received simply allowing for forecasted expenditure and inflation.

Such a financial tool is essential in helping a manager to plan the financial implications of service delivery. However, budgeting rarely exists in a perfect world and it is important for both middle and senior managers to realize the limitations of the real world upon budget management. Nutley and Osborne (1994) list six common problems that budget holders can face:

- they may not know their total budget and/or its breakdown until after the start of the financial year, making it difficult to plan;
- changed circumstances can sometimes force budget cuts upon an organization part of the way through the year, and as expenditure was planned on the basis of the initial budget it can be hard to revise this downward;
- the budget items may not be sufficiently detailed or disaggregated for the budget holder to pinpoint areas of poor financial control, or may include items which are outside the control of the budget holder;
- the level of budget may simply be unrealistic in order to provide a service – this can be a real problem where a VNPO has bid for a service contract from the government and the parent organization has been unrealistic about the actual costs of service delivery (another problem may also be the underestimation of inflation);
- the budget holder may not always be given power to 'vire' funds between item heads, limiting their freedom to act; and
- the lack of regular budgeting information upon which to plan, either because information takes too long to process or because it has been incorrectly coded in the budget, or because it is not in an easily usable format for the budget holder.

There is no easy resolution of these difficulties. Rather, it is important to recognize which ones affect your own organization and/or service, and plan to minimize their impact.

Models of budgeting

The process described above is called **incremental** budgeting, because it builds up incrementally upon what an organization already provides. This increment needs to take account of both inflation and planned growth for a service. It has been the traditional approach to budgeting in both public and voluntary organizations for many years. It has the advantage of being quite easy and inexpensive to manage, does not over-complicate budgeting for items of expenditure which will continue from year to year and is inherently cautious, so avoiding possible costly mistakes. Against that, it can be quite a 'blind' process, in that much of the higher expenditure of an organization is never questioned, it focuses attention upon financial inputs rather than the service outputs and tends to encourage spending up to the budget (especially where savings cannot be carried forward into the next year) rather than service efficiency.

Because of these drawbacks, two alternatives to incremental budgeting have developed. Although not widespread in their usage, it is important to know about them. **Zero based budgeting** (ZBB) requires that the whole of a budget be reviewed and approved each year, with no assumption of an increment upon top of a basic (unquestioned) 'base' budget. It was developed with the American governmental system in the 1970s as a way to try and control rapidly increasing costs. In theory this can focus attention upon the relationship between the expenditure of a project/organization and its mission critical goals. However, it can be extremely expensive and time consuming and so has been adopted only rarely.

The other alternative is **Planning programming budgeting systems** (PPBS). Again, this was developed with the American government system and is a highly rational approach to budgeting. The idea is to identify the key programmes of an organization, as they relate to its objectives and to match the budget to these, even if they cut across a number of project bases or cost centres. Despite its attractiveness in linking budget to mission-centred goals, however, PPBS has proved difficult to implement, particularly because of the complexity of organization structures in relation to particular goals and because of what is called the 'bounded rationality' of organizational life. That is, that organizations usually exist in states of uncertainty, ambiguity and often downright irrationality associated with the interpersonal behaviour of human beings. Rational systems, therefore, can never capture or predict the actual behaviour of an organization.

The human element

Finally in this section on budgeting, it is important to recognize that, even if incremental budgeting is adopted, the 'human element' can make this a far more irrational, or arational, process than should be the case in theory. Argyris (1953) identified four particular areas where this interaction might lead to conflict. These are:

- The budgeting process, particularly in a time of financial pressure, may be perceived by the staff of an organization as simply a means of control rather than of management and so seek to sabotage its usefulness. The old adage of 'garbage in – garbage out' is particularly appropriate here. Staff must see the positive benefits of budgeting or it will not serve the organization.

- There can be a poor relationship between service delivery staff and the finance section of an organization, which can be seen as simply concerned with figures and not with the 'real' work of the organization.

Effort needs to be made to demonstrate the importance and service actual benefits of such a section. Even in a small organization, where one person may carry out both service and budgeting responsibilities, there can be an unnecessary conflict between these two functions.

- Budgets can often be blamed for problems, rather than alternative explanations sought. Thus overspends can too easily be argued in terms of unrealistic original budgets, rather than possible explanations being sought in the service provision of a VNPO.

- 'Departmentalism' can set in, particularly in large organizations, where the needs of part of an organization became paramount, rather than of the organization, and its goals. For many small VNPO, this is not a problem. However, it can be a real one for many of the large service delivery VNPOs.

CONCLUSIONS

This chapter has outlined the key components of costing and budgeting processes for the managers of VNPOs. These issues will be picked up in more detail in other chapters of this book, particularly in relationship to contractual management and business planning. In closing, it is important to emphasize two points. First, that financial management is a key skill for the service manager of a VNPO, whether in a large or small organization. It is necessary in order to plan the delivery of services and to ensure that the financial resources are there to provide them.

Second, the manager also has to realize the limitations of financial management. Some of these limitations are derived from the information processes and management limitations of their organization. Others relate to the behavioural aspect of organizational life. However rational a financial management system is, it has to recognize and be able to cope with the irrationalities of human behaviour.

REFERENCES

Adams, G. and Perlmutter, F. (1991) Commercial venturing. *Non-profit & Voluntary Sector Quarterly*, **20**, (1), pp. 25–38.

Allen, C. and Beecham, J. (1993) Costing services: ideas and reality, in *Costing Community Care: Theory and Practice* (ed A Netten and J. Beecham) Ashgate, Aldershot, pp. 25–42.

Argyris, C. (1953) Human problems with budgets. *Harvard Business Review*, **31**, (1), pp. 97–110.

Callaghan, J. (1992) *Costing for Contracts*, Directory of Social Change, London.

Chartered Institute of Public Finance and Account (CIPFA) (1991) *Community Care '91: Managing the Money*, CIPFA, London.

Coombs, H. and Jenkins, D. (1992) *Public Sector Financial Management*, Chapman & Hall, London.

Eayrs, C. and Ellis,N. (1990) Charity advertising: for and against people with a mental handicap. *British Journal of Social Psychology*, **29**, pp. 349–66.

Gronbjerg, K. (1993) *Understanding Non-Profit Funding*, Jossey Bass, San Francisco.

Knapp, M. (1984) *Economics of Social Care*, Macmillan, London.

Knapp, M. (1990) *Time is Money. The Costs of Volunteering in Britain Today*, Volunteer Centre, Birmingham.

Leat, D. (1988) *Voluntary Organisations and Accountability*, National Council for Voluntary Organisations, Worcester.

Leat, D. (1989) The significance of fees and charges, in *Sources of Charity Finance* (ed N. Lee) CAF, Tonbridge, pp. 65–72.

National Council for Voluntary Organisations (NCVO) (1994) *Local Authority Funding for Voluntary Organisations*, NCVO, London.

Netten, A. and Beecham, J. (1993) *Costing Community Care: Theory and Practice*, Ashgate, Aldershot. A thoughtful book giving some conceptual background to the practice of costing, and containing some useful case studies.

Nutley, S. and Osborne, S. (1994) *Public Sector Management Handbook*, Longman, London.

Osborne, S. and Waterston, P. (1994) Defining contracts between the state and charitable organisations. *Voluntas* **5**, (3), pp. 291–300.

Osborne, S. and Hems, L. (1995) The economic structure of the charitable sector in the United Kingdom. *Non-profit & Voluntary Sector Quarterly*, **24**, (4), pp. 321–36.

Osborne, S. and Hems, L. (1996) Estimating the income and expenditure of charitable organizations in the UK, in *Non Profit Studies*, **1**, (1).

Passey, A. (1995) Corporate support of the UK voluntary sector 1993/94, in *Dimensions of the Voluntary Sector* (eds S. Saxon-Harrold and J. Kendall) CAF, London, pp. 57–62.

Public Sector Management Research Centre (PSMRC) (1991) *Managing Social and Community Development Programmes in Rural Areas*, Aston University, Birmingham.

Sugden, R. and Williams, A. (1978) *The Principles of Practical Cost Benefit Analysis*, Oxford University Press, Oxford.

GUIDED READING

On fund-raising

Leat, D. (1990) *Charities and Charging. Who Pays?* CAF, Tonbridge. A good study of the impact of charging for services.

Christie, I. (1991) *Profitable partnerships. A Report on Business Investment in the Community*, PSI, London. An interesting research study on the role of business funding for VNPOs.

Gronbjerg, K. (1993) *Understanding Non-Profit Funding*, Jossey Bass, San Francisco. The bible on fund-raising. Essential reading for anyone working in this field. Its only limitation is its American context, which can make some of the examples and legal framework less clear.

Lee, N. (1989) *Sources of Charity Finance*, CAF, Tonbridge. A useful short collection of essays, considering the policy implications of charitable finance, for funders and fundees.

Saxon-Harrold, S. and Kendall, J. (1995) *Dimensions of the Voluntary Sector*, CAF, London. Essential reading for anyone wanting to appreciate the breadth and depth of the funding patterns of voluntary organizations. Well presented with plenty of diagrams to make the statistics accessible.

On general financial management

Coombs, H. and Jenkins, D. (1992) *Public Sector Financial Managment*, Chapman & Hall, London. Despite its public sector focus, this is probably the best guide to financial management for people working in VNPOs. Some of its examples are perhaps too rooted in the public sector, but it is clearly written and comprehensive.

Costs, costing and budgeting

Adirondack, S. and Macfarlane, R. (1990) *Getting Ready for Contracts*, Directory of Social Change, London. A useful introductory guide to some of the costing issues involved in contracting for VNPOs, and in particular of the impact of legal status upon tax liability and costs.

Callaghan, J. (1992) *Costing for Contracts*, Directory of Social Change, London. An excellent practical guide to basic costing for VNPOs, whether they are involved in contracting or not.

Knapp, M. (1984) *Economics of Social Care*, Macmillan, London. Still the best guide to the more sophisticated theory of costing, and particularly to marginal and opportunity costing. Useful to those outside of the social care sector and lucid in its explanations.

Netten, A. and Beecham, J. (1993) *Costing Community Care: Theory and Practice*, Ashgate, Aldershot. A thoughtful book giving some conceptual background to the practice of costing, and containing some useful case studies.

5 Marketing in the voluntary sector

Tony Bovaird and Anne Rubienska

INTRODUCTION

By the end of this chapter you should be able

- to prepare a marketing strategy for a VNPO which is responsible for several types of service and for fund-raising activites;
- to prepare a marketing plan for each of its activites or services, setting out the decisions about the 'marketing mix';
- to identify marketing techniques, particularly market research, which will be helpful to the organization in tackling specific problems; and
- to recognize the main limitations involved in using a marketing approach within VNPOs.

The chapter starts with definitions of marketing, marketing strategy, marketing plans and the different words used to describe the users and beneficiaries of the services of a voluntary organization. It then shows how marketing is related to other managerial activities, especially strategic management, quality management and customer care. The main part of the chapter demonstrates how a VNPO can prepare a marketing strategy at corporate level, marketing plans for each of its main activities or services and for its fund-raising and how it can do appropriate market research to back these up. The chapter concludes with a summary of the lessons emerging, key issues for the future, a list of the references cited and a guided reading section for those who wish to follow up points from this chapter in more depth.

Some initial words of warning are appropriate. The language of marketing, with its frequent emphasis on militaristic terminology (campaigns, targets, strategies, etc.) can be off-putting to those who regard their work as providing a caring service to those in need. Yet marketing at its best is a blend of rigorous analysis and intuitive flair for understanding the client or user. For a service provider whose gifts lie in responding to people in crisis, for example, it can be valuable to study techniques for assessing what people in distress themselves want from the agency. This is what distinguishes the **market-oriented** approach from the **product-oriented** approach.

Nevertheless, the use of marketing techniques will often require an agency to make some very unpalatable decisions about precisely whom they are serving, what they are providing and what benefits they hope to bring about through the service provided. We mention this because we have often found resistance both to the nature and to the tone of marketing language, and also to the inherent assumption that it is desirable to choose one group of people rather than another as beneficiaries of the service. **If you are determined that this will be your stance, then stop reading NOW**! If, however, you wish to explore the usefulness of ideas from an unfamiliar discipline then the techniques of marketing – if modified sensitively – can be of practical value.

WHAT IS MARKETING?

There are many definitions of marketing. In running courses for people who work in the voluntary sector, we have often come across such definitions as 'marketing is about being commercial', or 'marketing is about selling our services more successfully'. While there is a kernel within these definitions which does relate to marketing, they are rather distant from the kinds of definition which marketing people choose. For example, Michael Baker, who once wrote that 'marketing is selling goods that don't come back to people who do', now suggests that 'a marketing orientation starts and ends with consumers and requires one to make what one can sell rather than struggle to sell what one can make' (Baker 1991). This clearly does focus on selling, but not in a mechanistic way – indeed, these definitions subtly combine elements of service design, selling and customer care. For a VNPO, this emphasizes the aspect of marketing which deals with the creation of loyalty toward the organization on behalf of those people whom it hopes to attract to use its services again. (Of course, this does not cover everyone – there are some people whom an organization would not hope to see again; an organization dealing with young offenders is unlikely to define a successful marketing campaign as one which results in its clients coming back each year for a further course of counselling, as a result of repeated offending.)

Another definition which we like is that of Peter Drucker, who suggested that 'the role of marketing is to make selling superfluous' (Drucker 1974), which nicely illustrates the importance of the non-selling side of the marketing function. In the case of an overseas aid agency like Oxfam, this might, for example, entail that people automatically increase their regular subscriptions every time a major famine or flight of refugees occurs, simply because Oxfam is widely identified with programmes of aid in such contexts.

However, the definition of marketing which we think is most useful for VNPOs is:

marketing is identifying the needs of your target audience and satisfying them according to your objectives.

Although this may appear straightforward, it is actually a highly challenging definition. It requires market research with your clients; a definition of the needs of your clients (which may or may not coincide with those needs identified by the clients themselves); an explicit statement of the target audience (and, by implication, of those groups which do not constitute your target audience); a strategy for statisfying these needs; and an explicit trade-off between the needs of your clients and the objectives of your organization (so that marketing contributes to your organization but does not necessarily drive it).

So how does marketing in the voluntary sector differ from approaches in the private or public sectors? This definition makes it clear that marketing in the voluntary sector is **not** simply about meeting the demands of the clients, as it would be in the private sector. A private firm is explicitly concerned with making money. Therefore, it is essential that it understands very clearly what the buyer wants and provides exactly that service. For VNPOs, there are a number of different groups or stakeholders which may need to be served. A decision must be made as to the priority between these groups and the level of satisfaction they are to be granted. Thus, a paternalistic definition of needs is often arrived at, which does not give dominant weight to the needs specified by the clients themselves. In a VNPO it is possible that the definition of client needs can come from a variety of sources – such as the management committee, the professional staff, its major donors or the service users themselves. A key strategic management function is therefore balancing and resolving these different perceptions.

MARKETING STRATEGY AND MARKETING PLANS

We normally distinguish between the processes of setting a marketing strategy and marketing plans. Essentially a **marketing strategy** refers to the overall organizational choices about which target audiences to aim at and which services to concentrate upon, in order to serve these audiences.

For each service or activity which is agreed in the marketing strategy, a **marketing plan** is then usually drawn up, setting out the **marketing tactics** by which the organization will ensure that this service or activity will satisfy the identified needs of the target audience(s). These marketing tactics (referred to as the **marketing mix**) relate primarily to the **Five Ps**, namely **product, promotion, price, place** and **people**.

The definition of marketing strategy which is set out above makes it clear that marketing shares with strategic management a concern for designing services which will satisfy their intended audiences. However, while strategic management focuses on a very full stakeholder analysis, marketing has traditionally concentrated mainly on the external clients of the services. To a certain extent, this has changed in recent years, with more frequent attention by marketing staff to satisfying stakeholders within the organization ('internal marketing'). This more general approach to marketing is called **relationship marketing**, because it focuses not on the marketing of individual services but on the building of satisfactory relationships between all stakeholders.

Again, the attention to customer satisfaction which is the hallmark of marketing is also to be found in **quality management**, particularly when this is formulated as ensuring that 'services meet or exceed customer expectations'. Finally, **customer care** is the process of ensuring that the direct interactions at the point of contact between the customer and the organization are managed so that the customer is dealt with satisfactorily, from the point of view both of the customer and also of the organization.

Preparing a marketing strategy

In this section, we are gong to work through a number of stages which are necessary to build up a marketing strategy for a VNPO. At each stage we will give some examples from marketing strategies prepared by actual VNPOs. The key components will be **sector analysis**, including competitor and collaborator analysis, to help us answer the question 'what business are we in?'; **segmenting the market**, concerning choosing priority groups and service eligibility criteria, to help us answer the question 'who are we most trying to help?'; **activity analysis**, including definition of 'core' and 'peripheral' activites, life cycle analysis, the Boston matrix, and the policy direction matrix and product/market innovation matrices, to help answer the question 'how do we prioritize between the possible ways of helping our target clients?'; and **strategy selection**, concerned with choosing one of the identified strategic options.

What business are we in?

This question is the most direct way of establishing the sector to which a VNPO belongs. Is Oxfam in the business of looking after famine victims, of re-organizing agricultural systems in famine-prone parts of the world, or of raising money for famine victims? The answer to this question will dictate the rest of the marketing strategy, including decisions on relationships with rival organizations and potential collaborators, the kinds of activities funded and the groups of people to whom most help is given. The marketing strategy will be much simpler if just one clear answer can be given. In the case of Oxfam, this is unlikely, since all three questions above may be answered 'yes'. Indeed, most VNPOs will work in at least two sectors – a 'service' sector in which they deliver services to one or more specific client groups, and a 'fundraising' sector in which they compete against many other organizations for funds from a range of sources.

Who are we most trying to establish contact with?

There are many different criteria upon which we might segment the possible client groups who might want our services and the possible funders who might contribute to our fund-raising campaigns. Some of the most frequent categories for segmentation of clients are shown in Figure 5.1 and for segmentation of funders in Figure 5.2.

- DEGREE OF COMMITMENT (Hostile/indifferent/interested/committed)
- DEMOGRAPHIC (age, household structure)
- SOCIO-ECONOMIC (or social class)
- LEVEL OF NEED (usually in terms of need for specific services)
- LEVEL OF DISADVANTAGE (e.g. unemployed, receiving benefit, having a disability)
- GEOGRAPHIC (e.g. inner city, suburban, rural or remote rural)
- LIFE-STYLE/PSYCHOGRAPHIC (e.g. the VALS grouping of 'survivors, sustainers, belongers, . . . socially conscious and integrated')

Figure 5.1 Possible bases for segmentation of clients

Organizational fundraising is most likely to be successful with organizations which have:

- a local base;
- kindred activities to yours;
- a record of supporting your organization or its activities;
- a record of being large givers already;
- personal connections to or contacts with some members of your organization; and
- a specific resource or capability which you badly need.

Individual fundraising can hope to tap some of the following individual giving motives:

- need for self esteem;
- need for recognition from others;
- fear of contracting the illness or experiencing the problem which you tackle;
- 'giving' out of habit;
- 'nuisance' giving;
- required to give because of job or public profile;
- captive giver, due to personal relationships or circumstances;
- people-to-people giving; and
- altruistic giving from 'concern for humanity'.

Figure 5.2 Possible bases for segmentation of funders (Adapted from Kotler and Andreason 1991)

Prioritizing our potential activities

This can be done in a number of different ways. A useful starting point can be life cycle analysis of the various activities which the VNPO is already undertaking (Figure 5.3). There are two reasons why services may reach the maturity phase of the 'product life cycle' – they may either become physically obsolescent (some other product or service can do their job better) or psychologically obsolescent (the clients begin to see them as 'old hat' so that they are less attractive than before). In either case, they need to be replaced by other activities or to be redesigned and relaunched in a way which will make them more appealing to their prospective target groups.

Once a life cycle analysis has been carried out, services can be analysed further by means of a series of 'portfolio' analyses. The basic purpose of these analyses is to help to design a portfolio of services or products which is balanced, which corresponds to the strategic capabilities of the VNPO and which meets the needs of the target groups of clients. First of all, existing services can be fitted into a Boston Matrix (see Figure 5.4), an approach originating in the private sector. A public sector version is shown in Figure 5.5, in which the 'market share' axis is replaced by a 'net social value' criterion. (The definition of 'net social value' must essentially be made by the agency itself, but would usually refer to the achievement of its highest level impact objectives). VNPOs may often want to carry out both

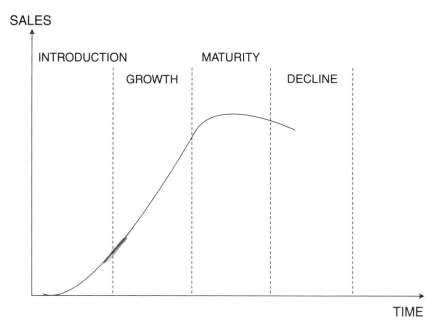

Figure 5.3 The 'product life cycle' or 'service life cycle'

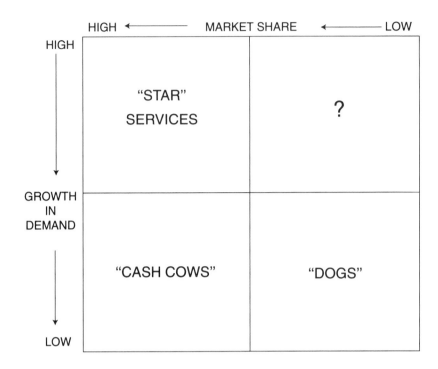

Figure 5.4 Boston Matrix for commercially-orientated services

analyses, since both market share and net social value may be important criteria in deciding which services to provide.

A further refinemet can be added by means of the policy direction matrix (see Figure 5.6). In each of the boxes, there are some tips given as to what should be done to any services which fit into that box. These tips highlight lessons from past practice, but they do not necessarily apply in any particular situation.

Selecting a marketing strategy

In deciding between options for a marketing strategy, there are a number of different steps which usually need to be taken. First of all, options need to be screened to remove those which are **infeasible**. The most common reasons are that the strategy requires more funds than can be raised by the VNPO, or would place the organization in cash flow difficulties. Of course, these constraints on the feasibility of options must never be taken for granted – it is sometimes important to question and challenge them, otherwise highly desirable options will get ruled out unnecessarily.

Second, those options have to be eliminated which would entail a higher **risk level** than is acceptable to key stakeholders, such as funders or interest

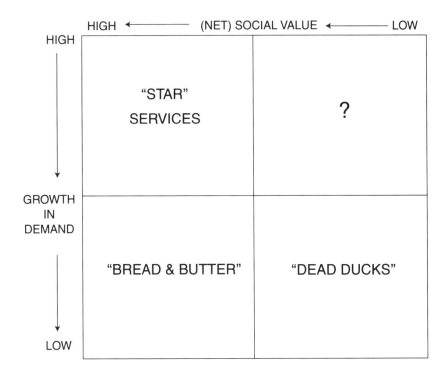

Figure 5.5 Boston Matrix for socially orientated services

groups representing users. In community care, for example, for some client groups it would be unacceptable to propose independent living in the community without the regular supervision of a warden or caretaker in their accommodation. Third, some options may be rejected because of their lack of **cultural fit** in the organization – for example, an option which involved staff of Age Concern in a sales effort to get elderly clients (or their families) to buy health insurance might be regarded as distasteful, or even unethical, by the staff concerned.

Fourth, there is a need to test how well **different objectives meet the objectives** of the VNPO or its key stakeholders. Techniques such as the Goals Achievement Matrix (Figure 5.7) may be helpful in determining the ranking between options. Fifth, the **overall costs and benefits** of each strategic option need to be assessed. Cost–benefit analysis is one technique that can be applied. It entails an assessment, and if possible a quantification, of the different costs and benefits arising anticipated from each strategic option. It is discussed in the chapter on financial management.

While these steps form a useful checklist in helping to sift strategic options, we should not overestimate the role of rational analysis or 'objective' information. Obviously, most strategy selection is influenced very powerfully by the politics of different interest groups. Indeed, it can seem

Prospects for Profitablility

	Unattractive	Average	Attractive
Weak	**Disinvest**	**Phased Withdrawal**	**"Double or Quit"**
Average	**Phased Withdrawal**	**Proceed with Care**	**Try Harder**
Strong	**Cash Generator**	**Growth**	**Leader**

Competitive Position

Figure 5.6 Directional policy matrix

Criteria	To provide enjoyment	To improve skills in the water	To attract tourist visits	TOTAL SCORE
	Weightings			
Alternatives	x5	x3	x1	
Traditional Pool	4	7	2	43
Leisure Pool	8	3	9	58

Figure 5.7 Goals achievement matrix for provision of new swimming pool

that rational evaluation methods are often applied to strategic options in order to rationalize a choice already made, rather than to inform that choice.

Preparing a marketing plan

For each of the activities or 'businesses' which a VNPO intends to provide as a result of its selected marketing strategy, a marketing plan has to be drawn up. As mentioned earlier, this usually entails concentration on the 'four Ps' of product, promotion, price and place. Sometimes a 'fifth P' is added – 'people', referring to the customer care relationship with staff. We will concentrate here upon breaking down the 'four Ps' into six different dimensions of the marketing mix, by dividing both pricing and place into two separate dimensions. These are **product** or **service design**; **promotion**; **pricing**; **other income generation** including fund-raising, sponsorship, sales and merchandising; **place accessibility**, bringing the service and the customer together; and **place 'atmosphere'**, about designing facilities to be customer friendly.

Product or service design

This needs to conform to both the needs of the customer and also to the purposes of the VNPO. Many VNPOs have strong feelings about what is in the interests of their users. This means that often they are only prepared to offer a limited range of services, compared to the full range which these users might want and be prepared to pay for. But in designing each of these services, the organization is likely to want to ensure that the services attract and satisfy their users as far as possible. In Figure 5.8 there is an outline of the factors which need to be thought about in service or product design, to ensure that the organization has the proper product or service design requires appropriate market research.

Promotion

The essence of this in the marketing mix is successful communication. The key questions are what, to whom, how and why? This is shown in Figure 5.9. Clearly promotion may need to send to each target audience a different message through a different medium – a service for drug users may need to promote itself very differently to young people using 'social' drugs compared to hardened heroin addicts. This may not always be successful, especially if the different target audiences are likely to come across the campaigns aimed at other audiences, giving what they may perceive to be a clashing image.

The main promotional methods are public relations, advertising (by press, radio, TV or by posters and hoardings), direct mail, telephone selling and special events (or 'promotions'). It is important to note that it is widely suggested by promotions experts that advertising is quite ineffective ('We know that only 50% of advertising works, but we never know in advance which 50%!'). However, advertising persists since it often is the simplest and fastest way of making contact with your audience. Other promotional methods entail a higher use of staff time, particularly of senior staff. Nevertheless, these other methods may be much more cost-effective if pursued systematically.

Pricing

There are two main kinds of pricing decisions to be taken by VNPOs – pricing of contract bids in negotiation with a purchasing agency (often in competition with other bidders) and pricing of services to customers on a 'take it or leave it' basis. In both cases, a key principle is that differentiation of prices will increase the achievement of your objectives.

This can occur in two ways. First, extra revenue is generated if different prices can be charged to each identifiable market segment, so that those willing to pay more are indeed charged more. Second, the targeting of the

Tangible service features
Ease and comfort of use

Reliability
Low failure rate
Rapid and effective response to failures
Clear and easy-to-use complaints procedures
Redress opportunities

Responsiveness to customer needs
Provision of customer choice
Clear information, made widely available to potential users
Comprehensiveness for all customer tastes
Specific attention to each user's different tastes
Prompt delivery of service

Reassurance
Competent staff and appropriate procedures
Polite, respectful, considerate and friendly contact staff
Privacy in contacts with staff
Trustworthy and honest service provider
Service delivery system (and transport which is free from risk, danger or doubt)

Empathy with customers
Approachability and ease of contact
Keeping customers informed in language they can understand
Listening to customers and their representatives
Making the effort to know customers and their needs

Wider social implications
Equitable between clients and between client groups
Tested and monitored for side-effects of service
Controlled and acceptable environmental impact

Source: Adapted from Zeithaml, Parasuraman and Berry (1990: 21–22) and Healey and
Potter (1987: 16).

Figure 5.8 Features of products and services to be included in design for customer-
oriented quality

service to priority target groups will be more successful if each target group
is charged a price which is appropriate to its means and its desire to have
the service. In negotiating prices with clients who are purchasing agencies,
the skills involved in standard negotiating procedures are critical. In particular, there is a need to have a clear picture of their reasons for using your
service – and specifically the unique benefits which your service offers and
which will therefore be lost if the client purchases less of your service in
reaction to a price increase. Second, it is important to have a clear picture

WHO are you?	*IDENTIFICATION*
WHAT are you trying to say?	*MESSAGE*
WHY do you want to say it?	*OBJECTIVES*
TO WHOM do you want to say it?	*TARGET AUDIENCE*
HOW are you going to get the message to them?	*MEDIA*
WHAT EFFECT have you had?	*FEEDBACK*

Figure 5.9 Key questions in the communication process

of what you believe to be their maximum willingness to pay and also what you regard as your minimum price, based usually on your costs. Again, negotiating procedures are needed to deal with the standard objections by clients that your proposed prices are too high. You need to have a ready answer to the normal objections that 'we haven't got the money' (usually you will argue that the client will make a long-term saving by going for the better service), that 'your competitors are cheap' (to which you will normally respond that the comparison leaves out service quality), or that 'it's not worth it to us' (which you should be able to counter by pointing out the benefits of your service to various aspects of their needs).

When dealing with customers who argue about price, there is a need for staff to feel comfortable with the price levels set by the organization. VNPOs have good grounds for being less self-conscious about their prices than private sector organizations. Nevertheless, many staff need to be convinced that it is respectable or valid to talk about price. Without such an orientation, signals may be given to users that the organization does not believe in the worth of its own services. Of course, staff must never be placed in the situation where they feel they have to put undue pressure on customers to buy or use a service.

In setting prices to those customers to whom you can dictate prices on a 'take it or leave it basis', one of the key issues is how to raise prices in such a way as to minimize resistance or reduction in take-up. This is usually a fraught area, since users will perceive themselves to be made worse off by any price increase, notwithstanding that your organization is clearly giving good value for money and may be charging well below the going 'market price'. Some tactics which may be useful include:

- putting up your prices when everyone else does or when demand is 'sleeping';
- not increasing prices too much at one time;
- not increasing prices too often (usually no more than once a year);
- moving some prices **down** when you move others **up**;

- looking after your key customers by making them valuable offers of discounts, but only if they increase their usage; and
- providing sound and true explanations of why you are raising prices (based on Winkler 1984).

Other income generation approaches

There are a number of other ways of raising revenue which are important to VNPOs, in addition to pricing. Indeed, for some VNPOs these alternative methods may be much more important than pricing. These include ancilliary sales and merchandising, franchising, sponsorship, selling advertising in publications, fund-raising, attracting skills from volunteers and attracting 'free/at cost' goods and services.

Place accessibility

We considered two very different aspects of 'place' in the marketing mix – 'accessibility' refers to the ease or difficulty of bringing the service and the customer together. This can be broken down further into issues of the proper location of services and facilities, the transport of customers and the possibilities of contact with customers through telecommunications. In respect of the **location** of services and facilities, important choices need to be made between centralized and decentralized services; widespread and concentrated customer access points and service delivery points; and fixed and mobile services.

Given that your priority users are often economically disadvantaged and may also be physically frail or have disabilities, the arrangements to be made for the **transport of customers** are extremely important. Indeed, proper transport for priority users may justify a higher level of expenditure by the service than provision of service to lower priority users. This is a nettle few VNPOs have been prepared to grasp, even though public transport, in Britain at least, has increasingly become expensive, less frequent, more unreliable and less safe (in terms of door to door travel). VNPOs should consider the proper balance for their users between use of public transport, mobility allowances, community transport schemes, car-sharing and minibuses.

Finally, there are opportunities to substitute telecommunication contact for face-to-face contact with service users. At the moment, this is largely restricted to telephone provision, especially in respect of emergency services and information and advisory services. However, there are already major opportunities to extend telephone services to include instruction, tuition and problem-solving services. In the future, there are likely also to be more extensive television outlets available to VNPOs, especially through local cable TV operators. The potential of the Internet, perhaps accessed through publicly-available terminals in libraries, medical surgeries and local authority neighbourhood offices, is only just now being explored in demonstration projects, but this may grow fast in the near future.

Place 'atmosphere'

The other dimension of 'place' is the need to design spaces and facilities to be customer friendly. In Figure 5.10, we list the features which Foxall (1983) suggests have a major short-term effect on service user perceptions and reactions. Given that it is essential to start interactions with your users on as favourable a footing as possible, it is vital to plan and manage those elements of Figure 5.10 which lie within your control – and these relate mostly to the physical and social surroundings. The effect of the physical surroundings on the 'atmosphere' of the interaction with users is probably much more important than service professionals realize, engrossed as they are in the intricate details of the core service itself.

Physical surroundings

sound
decor
weather
lighting
temperatures

Social surroundings

presence of other people
their characteristics and roles
nature of interactions

Temporal perspective

time, day, year
intervals between purchase/choice
gap between purchase and consumption

Antecedent states

acute moods
availability of cash/resources
illness

Source: based on Foxall (1983)

Figure 5.10 Features of 'place' affecting user perceptions and reactions

Doing market research

Purposes

There are may possible reasons for carrying out market research. They include, for example, identifying service gaps which the organization might fill, identifying new service segments, spotting what competitors or other providers are offering to users or funders, getting market feedback from users, helping to redesign the product or service, and identification of which promotional methods have been most effective.

Myths about market research

Kotler and Andreason (1991) usefully list a number of myths which have grown up about market research. These myths need to be exploded, as they can lead VNPOs to undertake too little market research, of an inappropriate type. These myths are:

- The 'Big Decision Myth' – that is, 'only big decisions need market research'. NO, NOT NECESSARILY! In practice, many big decisions are relatively easy to make or are not influenced by what the users think. It is often relatively small decisions which are most able to be influenced by feedback from the 'market'.
- The 'Survey Myopia' Myth – that is, 'market research means surveys'. NO, IT DOES NOT! In fact, there are many different ways of doing market research, including focus group discussions to explore the qualitative reasons behind the decisions of service users and other stakeholders.
- The 'Sophisticated Researcher' Myth, that is, 'market research is very complicated and can only be done well by experts'. NO, IT IS NOT! Indeed, service professionals and managers can be especially effective in doing market research, for example, in asking frequently for informal feedback from users – after all, they know what questions to ask and how best to implement any suggestions emerging from such feedback.
- The 'Most Research is Not Read' Myth – that is, 'market research is ignored in practice'. NO, IT IS NOT. When it is well planned, by the people who want to have the results, it is likely to be influential. And indeed, many market research reports have possibly too much influence – their results become part of the fundamental beliefs of the organization, long after they have ceased to be relevant.

CONCLUSIONS ON THE LIMITATIONS OF MARKETING IN THE VOLUNTARY SECTOR

We should end this chapter by emphasizing what marketing cannot do. It cannot provide an answer to the knotty question, 'Who is our main customer?' This has to be resolved by the VNPO itself. Again, it cannot tell an organization which services to offer; although it can throw light on which services its users would prefer, the final choice of which services to offer has to remain with the organization. Finally, marketing cannot demonstrate that 'the user is always right' – only that there may be real difficulties in convincing your user to do things or accept services which do not seem designed to meet their needs.

In addition, there are some other limitations on marketing in VNPOs. **Philosophically**, marketing tends to assume that satisfying the needs of stakeholders is a process which can be improved by the use of rational procedures. In fact, this is a rather debatable proposition, as is evidenced by the way in which some for-profit organizations with carefully thought out marketing strategies sometimes fall flat on their face.

There may be serious **ethical issues** confronting a VNPO in its choice of marketing strategies or of marketing tactics. In choosing a marketing strategy, a VNPO may be tempted to concentrate on target groups or on activities for which it knows funding will be easy, although they do not correspond to the central purposes for which it was founded. Conversely, it may be tempted to divert funding to groups in high need, even though the funds were given with the understanding that they would be primarily for another group, with 'lower' needs. Again, some kinds of promotion campaign may be ruled out because of ethical concerns. Many adoption agencies are opposed to using photographs of real children in their advertisements.

Political issues may also severely hamper a VNPO in its marketing. While charities must avoid political activities, and many VNPOs also wish to maintain a strictly non-political stance, it is often the case that public sector bodies are ultra-sensitive to marketing activities which have political implications. For example, when a charity for the elderly launches a campaign against government cuts in home improvement grants for energy conservation, it runs the risk of being branded 'anti-government' and thereby endangering its funding from local authorities which have the same political colour as central government.

The key **managerial issue** in marketing usually revolves around the choice of who should be responsible for marketing in the VNPO. While there is truth in the common saying that marketing is part of the job of every member of an organization ('marketing is too important to be left to marketing staff'), there is a need for a focus somewhere in the organizational structure. There is a tendency in some small VNOs to fall back on occasional help from a member of the management committee with marketing expertise. This is rarely an adequate substitute for proper regular marketing effort. It is therefore likely that one senior manager will need not only to take on lead responsibility for marketing, but also to undertake training and to spend considerable time in marketing.

Costs remain a fundamental stumbling block to many VNPOs in undertaking their marketing efforts. Typically, staff time spent in marketing is not separately costed and accounted for – therefore marketing techniques which are staff intensive are easier to implement than those which require extra budgets, e.g. advertising campaigns or market research. This bias is inherently irrational but the reluctance to spend money on marketing when it reduces the funds available for the provision of front-line services is understandable. This bias is likely to persist while it remains difficult to evaluate clearly pay-offs from the marketing effort in terms which allow comparisons with marketing expenditure.

REFERENCES

Baker, M. (1991) *The Marketing Book*, Butterworth-Heinemann, Oxford.

Drucker, P. (1974) *Management: Tasks, Responsibilities, Practices*, Heinemann, London.

Foxall, G. (1983) *Consumer Choice*, Macmillan, London.

Healey, M. and Potter, J. (1987) Making performance measurement work for consumers, in *Performance Measurement and the Consumer*, National Consumer Council, London.

Kotler, P. and Andreason, R. (1991) *Strategic Marketing for Non-Profit Organisations*, Prentice Hall, New Jersey.

Winkler, J. (1984) *Pricing for Results: How to Wage and Win the Price War*, Pan, London.

Zeithaml, V., Parasuraman, A. and Berry, L. (1990) *Delivering Service Quality: Balancing Customer Perceptions and Expectations*, Free Press, New York.

GUIDED READING

Casson, D. (1995) *Guide to Company Giving 1995–96*, Directory of Social Change, London. A valuable guide which allows voluntary organizations to target their company fundraising and sponsorship campaigns more accurately.

Clarke, S. (1993) *The Complete Fundraising Handbook*, DSC, London. Just what it says!

Hannagan, T. J. (1992) *Marketing for the Non-Profit Sector*, Macmillan, Basingstoke. A well-written textbook aimed solely at VNPOs.

Kotler, P. and Andreason, R. (1991) *Strategic Marketing for Non-Profit Organisations*, Prentice Hall, New Jersey. The 'bible' of non-profit marketing – comprehensive, rigorous, easy-to-read. The place to look if other books only seem to scratch the surface. The only snags are that it is very USA-oriented and the *very* high price.

Kotler, P. and Roberto, E. (1989) *Social Marketing: Strategies for Changing Public Behaviour*, Free Press, New York. Comprehensive guide for planning and organizing campaigns. In spite of its USA-orientation, valuable because it is so thorough and systematic.

Leat, D. (1990) *Fundraising and Grant Making: A Case Study of ITV Telethon 1988*, CAF, London. Interesting and revealing case study of a broadcast appeal, showing lessons to be learnt not just in raising the money but also in organizing the grant-making process to disburse funds raised.

Walsh, K. (1995) *Public Services and Market Mechanisms*, Macmillan, Basingstoke. A thorough and rigorous critique of government policy in respect of using the market mechanism for providing public services. Sets VNPO marketing in its political context.

Winkler, J. (1984) *Pricing for Results: How to Wage and Win the Price War*, Pan, London. An engagingly outrageous approach to using the price mechanism to your advantage. While entirely private sector in focus, its down-to-earth advice on how prices really work will be valuable to all VNPOs who are concerned that their current pricing policy is out-of-date.

6 'On a clear day . . . '
Strategic management for VNPOs

Mark Lyons

INTRODUCTION

Management is a difficult and complex activity. Managers often experience pressure and look for ways to improve their performance. As a consequence, they are much preyed upon by purveyors of slick solutions and quick fixes for the often insoluble dilemmas managers face day to day. Sometimes, out of this melee of competing remedies, a term and the set of practices which it loosely encompasses achieves a longevity and a standing above the others. This is usually because beneath the array of often contradictory advice there is a core of good sense. Such is the case with strategic management. Strategic management has been a popular remedy for many organizational problems for over a decade. Its predecessor, strategic planning, is twenty years older. Together they have created a huge literature, much of it contradictory and a good deal of it critical of what has gone before. Yet within it there is an insight and a core of practice that is of fundamental importance to management. However, it can be difficult to chart a course through the vast array of writings on the topic. A recent study identified thirty-seven books in print with the title *Strategic Management* (Whittington 1993). There are hundreds more articles in academic and professional journals.

This literature can be grouped or categorized in many different ways. One way is to distinguish between writings that seek to instruct the reader in strategic management and those that seek to describe the process and its consequences. Sometimes the two are linked, usually with instruction following description. This chapter seeks mainly to instruct, though some reference to the descriptive literature will be provided.

The chapter begins with a brief review of writings about strategic management. It recognizes that many who work in voluntary and non-profit organizations (VNPOs) are suspicious of strategic management; this chapter argues that while some of their mistrust is well founded, there are important insights in strategic management that should be practised. It then goes on to outline an approach to strategic planning which is fundamental to strategic management. It concludes by suggesting that a strategically managed organization is one whose managers and staff act in ways that make it a **learning organization**. Four case studies and one example illustrate the points made in the text.

By the end of this chapter you will:

• be familiar with the main features of strategic planning and management;
• be able to recognize the value of strategic planning and strategic management for VNPOs; and
• be able to manage the process of developing a strategic plan for your organization and be better able to manage it strategically as a consequence.

WHAT IS STRATEGIC MANAGEMENT?

One of the most important distinctions in the descriptive literature is between strategy as a consciously designed plan of action and what Mintzberg (1994) calls **emergent strategy**, or a strategy that an observer (or a participant) discovers, after the event, to have been present. This is, in effect, a post-hoc rationalization. Actions which seemed piecemeal and uncoordinated at the time are found later to have had a coherence that constitutes a strategy. This may be an accurate description of how most organizations work, but such an expansion of the term strategy drains it of almost all meaning. Some of the descriptive writings about strategy develop categories of strategies, such as competition and co-operation, or acquisition, divestment, merger and so on. Again, this literature can be helpful to the reflective manager, but is not much of a guide to the practice of strategic management.

Finally, there is descriptive literature that aims to see if strategic management actually matters. It reports the results of research that seeks to discover if organizations that are strategically managed do better than those that are not. The results of these studies are mixed and seem to vary with the number of organizations included in the study. Those which review a relatively small number of organizations, particularly those that use a case study methodology, suggest that strategic management does matter (e.g. Robinson 1982; Stone 1989). Those that draw a larger sample, and by necessity are restricted in the number of variables that they can examine and the criteria of success they can use, tend to find that it does not matter (e.g. Fulmer and Rue 1974; Gup and Whitehead 1989). It is a matter of conjecture whether this dichotomy reflects either faults in strategic management or limitations of the respective research designs.

There are many methods proposed in the instructive literature on strategic management and its close relatives, strategic and corporate planning. At the core of much of this literature, mostly written for managers of for-profit corporations, are (at least) three propositions. These have in turn been criticized, sometimes by those who would argue for an alternative approach to strategic management and sometimes by those who would dismiss it as a waste of time and resources. Many in the voluntary and non-profit sector reject strategic management because they reject one or more of these propositions, or what some proponents argue are the necessary consequences of adhering to them. Such a rejection is too sweeping and prevents appreciation of the core truths of strategic management.

The first proposition is that **it is important for at least the top managers of an organization to have an appreciation of where their organization is located in its wider environment**. This is why the term strategy has been borrowed from the generals. Strategic management requires that managers look at how their organization is located in its wider environment, take a long-term view and develop an holistic organization perspective. This is why it is called strategic as opposed to tactical and why it differs from, but ideally should encompass, the operational plans which various units of an organization might develop. The term 'strategy' also suggests competition ('it's a war out there'). This is the central belief of writers who focus on for-profit firms struggling for competitive advantage in the market place, (e.g. Porter 1980; 1985). However, strategic management can still be a useful practice for organizations that are not fighting for market share. Competitors are only one possible component of the wider environment of an organization.

The second proposition is that, **thanks to science, the world is now relatively predictable and managers can use 'scientific' methods to forecast their future environment and to chart a course that will realize their objectives**. This proposition embodies two views of science. It endorses a possibility of being able to develop laws to describe and predict the outcome of interactions not only in the physical world but in society as well. In addition, it endorses a model of decision-making that has adopted the term 'rational' to describe its processes. To be rational, decision-makers must be clear about their objectives, identify alternative means for obtaining those objectives and, after evaluation, choose the most effective and efficient of these means. The wrong-headedness of these assumptions has been criticized from many quarters (e.g. Lindblom 1968; Fay 1975; Mintzberg 1994), but they persist, perhaps both because they are not so much fundamentally wrong, as just grossly oversold and because they offer relatively easy tools for managers to use.

The third proposition is that **senior managers have perfect control over their organization, so that once decisions have been taken and, once a strategic plan has been adopted, the execution of that plan follows without difficulty**. The distinction between thought and action is endemic to writings about policy as well as strategy and, again, a good deal of criticism of strategic management has been directed against this assumption. Nonetheless, a good deal of writing about strategic management recognizes that implementation is a highly problematic matter and that the key stakeholders of an organization, including their staff, must be involved in the planning process if there is to be any likelihood of that process producing specified changes in the structure and practices of an organization.

The best way to understand strategic management is to recognize that it is a perspective or an orientation to management. To practise strategic management means incorporating as a central component of that practice a recognition that an organization exists in a changing world and therefore must change and adapt if it is to survive, to continue effectively to pursue its mission and to make a difference to that world. In the first instance, strategic management entails building a formal process of strategic planning into the long-term cycle of organizational tasks. It also means trying to foster and encourage a similar orientation in other staff (or at least senior staff, if it is a large organization). Strategic management is an orientation to management which is vital for all managers, including those of VNPOs, to possess and to practice.

However, it must be recognized that while strategic management, if well practised, can assist an organization to adapt and prosper in an uncertain world, it cannot guarantee this. Strategic management can help managers and their organizations handle uncertainty, it cannot eliminate it.

To restate the proposition offered immediately above, strategic management is an approach to management which has the following characteristics:

1 it encompasses the whole organization;
2 it is outward looking; that is, it looks out from the organization to the wider environment in which the organization is located and seeks to understand what is happening there and to develop strategies for action based on that understanding; and
3 it is forward looking; that is, it seeks to develop an appreciation of the likely shape of the external environment in three, five, ten, even twenty, years ahead and to identify what major changes may need to be made to the organization to enable it to continue to pursue its mission effectively into that future.

Strategic management is based on this simple observation: 'All organizations operate in an environment which is changing all the time.' These changes in its environment require an organization to change and the best way to do this is in a pro-active and adaptive way. Organizations cannot control their environment, but they can read it or anticipate it. To adopt an Australian analogy, strategic management is a bit like riding a wave. Surfers are carried in one direction, but by reading the wave and using a variety of techniques, can ensure that they stay on the wave and to a certain degree are able to control where they end up.

STRATEGIC MANAGEMENT AND VNPOs

There is a great deal of suspicion of strategic management in VNPOs, especially amongst smaller organizations and those with a strong commitment to social change and advocacy. At least four types of objections are made against the use of strategic management in the voluntary sector.

Strategic management is a business idea, a business technique that is designed to improve profitability and enshrines a set of values that undermines the essential values of VNPOs (Bush 1992). Yet, as has been argued above, there is a core insight in the practice of strategic management that makes it applicable to all organizations and indeed, arguably makes it even more useful to mission-driven voluntary organizations which have no ready method, such as profitability, for assessing their performance.

Strategic management is an aid for, and indeed might be said to mandate, competition which is a value and an orientation hostile to the voluntary and non-profit sector which is about collaboration and partnership. Yet VNPOs do sometimes compete – for government grants and public donations, and sometimes for clients. But once again, strategic management is primarily a management orientation that recognizes the inevitability of change, not of competition. The environment of a voluntary organization may change because of competition, but it is more likely to be because of a range of other factors such as changes in government policy, shifts in population, scientific or technological developments that create new problems to be addressed or change the character of populations being served or methods for aiding them. Strategic management is as vital for anticipating and managing these issues as that of competition.

Strategic management is a method of control that contradicts the commitment of the voluntary and non-profit sector to participation, and to giving voice and power to the disadvantaged. Again, while the core of much strategic management/planning literature does make that assumption, it is not a necessary character of strategic management and some approaches to strategic management have been developed in order to give opportunity for workers and clients to shape the overall direction of their organization.

Strategic management is too elaborate and too time consuming for small VNPOs that operate in a survival mode, living from one month or one year to the next. Yet strategic management as an orientation is just as important for the managers of small, highly stressed VNPOs as it is for the managers of large, well-endowed bodies. It is probably even more important for the former than the latter. It does require paying some attention to the mission of the organization, to what is happening around it and to how it can reduce its vulnerability. That does mean time out from daily crises, but it is time which should be spent. In a small organization, a basic adaptation of the formal practices of strategic planning or management is not particularly time consuming and can be an essential step if the organization is to survive.

THE PROCESS

At the heart of strategic management is strategic planning. This is best understood as a process in its own right. One of the key outputs of the process is a strategic plan, but the value of the process, if it is well conducted, lies not so much in this formal output but in the enlivening affect it can have on an organization and on its relations with its key stakeholders. It is in the process of developing a plan that its staff can develop new insights, adapt their behaviour or the structure of their work and where stakeholders can develop new commitments to the organization. At the end of the day, there may (or may not!) be a strategic plan, but many valuable changes will have occurred in the process.

This section draws on an approach to strategic planning set out by Bryson (1988). This approach has been widely used in the voluntary and non-profit sector. The strategic planning process can be described, and undertaken, as a series of steps. These will be outlined below. It should be stressed that these need not be slavishly followed, but neither should they be largely or entirely dispensed with. Rather, they should be modified according to the size and the complexity of the organization and its circumstances. The steps are iterative – that is, after proceeding through, say, steps one to four, it may be necessary to revisit steps two and three again in the light of information or ideas that have been generated in step four.

It is important that the strategic planning process moves forward according to a realistic time frame and so it is important to recognize that the process is not a call to perfection. Strategic planning should be seen as a collective learning process. It should be easier, and less time consuming, in an organization which has already developed a strategic plan at some point in the past, than for one of a similar size and set of programmes that has never undertaken such a review before. (See Case Study One at the end of this chapter.)

Step 1 – getting started, and who to involve

Someone with influence in the organization has to propose that it undertake a strategic planning process. That person should be the chief executive of the organization, but sometimes it might be the chair of the board, a government funding body or a senior manager. If it is not the chief executive who suggests it, it is important that he or she should embrace the idea and champion it. If there is not enthusiasm or commitment at the top of the organization and, ideally a full understanding of the process, then there is no point in beginning.

It is at this point that the decision must be made about how the process is to be carried forward. This is because it entails a certain amount of work (indeed, a good deal of work) that is outside the routine allocation of responsibilities amongst the staff of the organization. In a small organization it may be sufficient to agree that all or most staff will participate in the process and share responsibility; in a larger organization it is important to have a small team that carries it forward.

It is at this point, too, that consideration must be given to the question of whom, other than some or all of the paid employees, should be involved in the process, and in what way. Clearly (some) board or management committee members should be involved. The commitment of the board to the process is as important as the commitment of the chief executive. But should some of the volunteers be involved? And what of other key stakeholders from outside the organization, such as users of its services, funders, or staff from other organizations with which it frequently collaborates, or representatives of intermediary or umbrella organizations from the field or fields of service the organization is active in?

Several different structures may be needed to involve different stakeholders in different ways. Clearly, anybody with a capacity to prohibit the organization from changing needs to be involved, and involved in a way that ensures that they feel part of the process and committed to whatever might emerge. In a large organization, in addition to a small strategic planning group which has overall responsibility for the process, it is sensible to establish a wider reference group containing more members of staff but also members of other key stakeholder groups such as volunteers, clients and supporters. These might include government staff or senior representatives from other bodies with authority over the organization, such as a church synod or a religious order.

Some writers on strategic planning for VNPOs suggest a further initial step, that of clarifying their mandate (Bryson 1988). It can be an important preliminary step. Often long-established organizations and those with links to some other organization, such as a church, need to review their constitution and the degree to which they can, or can easily, modify their mission or field of service. In many cases it is sensible to include key mandate holders in the review process, either as part of the wider reference group or via a separate reporting process that recognises their special situation. Of course, if a key stakeholder withholds permission or resources needed for the strategic planning process, there is little point in pursuing the matter further.

It can be sensible sometimes to engage a consultant from outside the organization to assist the strategic planning process. It is important that the consultant recognize that his or her role is to act as a facilitator of the process, responsible for ensuring it happens and possibly even performing a number of key tasks to ensure that it does, but no more than that. It is important that the consultant is not engaged to develop the strategic plan in isolation, meeting with staff and other stakeholders of the organization only to seek information.

Step 2 – develop or review the mission of the organization

This is a succinct statement about what it is the organization exists to do. It should describe whatever problem or issue it tries to address and say what the organization is and what it is doing about that issue. Many VNPOs do not yet have mission statements; others have them, but either they have changed or the issue they were formed to address has changed without them reviewing and adapting their statement of mission. An example of a mission might be:

> People with developmental disabilities are frequently discriminated against, especially in the labour market. This diminishes their capacity to live full and normal lives. Job-Support exists to help people with developmental disabilities living in Habitat City to obtain the employment they want by educating potential employers and employees, by placing its clients in interesting and fulfilling employment and by providing them with appropriate and unobtrusive support when needed.

At this step, the strategic planning group reviews and clarifies the organizational mission. In this process it is sensible to seek input from a wider set of stakeholders. In the end, though, it is the strategic planning group who have to agree on a new or revised mission and the board who have to approve it.

Step 3 – conduct an internal scan

At this step the current activities or programmes of the organization are reviewed. It is important at this step to gather whatever (relatively) objective data there is about what the organization does, what it uses to do it and how well it does it. It might be helpful to use a checklist to ensure the scan covers key areas, including funding, workforce, clients, technology and information.

Some VNPOs monitor their output routinely, but many do not and cannot say how effective their programmes are or how much each discrete set of activities cost. It is also useful at this point to review the contribution of various revenue sources and volunteer input. Ideally, this should be done over a period of five to ten years to discover if there is any trend that can be discerned. How well the organization is known and its reputation should also be assessed at this point. To some organizations, collecting this data will be easy; for others it will be very difficult. If this is the case, it is important not to seek too much detail at this point or else the whole planning process grinds to a halt.

Step 4 – environmental and future scans

This is the most important part of the strategic planning process. It is here that the strategic planning group needs to collect and review as much data and as many ideas about the environment of the organization and likely future developments in that environment, as it can.

The factors that need to be considered can be summed up in the acronym PEST: Politics (including likely policy and regulatory developments), Economy, Society (including demographic changes) and Technology (including the impact of technologies developed outside the immediate field of interest of a VNPO but which could have a likely impact on that field). For a VNPO these could include: trends in government methods of funding a particular set of services (political); a continuing decline in numbers of traditional male jobs with a consequent impact on family poverty (economic); the ageing of the population (social); computerization and miniaturization bringing about an increase in mobility and communication capacity for people with severe disabilities, generating the possibility of new programmes of support (technology). In addition to such 'hard' technologies, this heading also includes 'soft' technologies, such as new therapeutic approaches to working with people with disabilities. Although it is not possible to predict future developments with certainty, good analysis based on a close appreciation of the structures that underlie political, social and economic change and generate incentives for technological development, can help.

Some more sophisticated approaches to environmental scanning seek to give some order to the variety of proposals that can be generated, by developing a limited number of alternative scenarios. This can be particularly useful when trying to foresee ten or more years ahead. It is often claimed by staff of VNPOs that trying to look more than one year ahead, the period covered by the budget cycle, is impossible. This is not true. It is true that the further ahead one looks the more difficult it becomes to forecast with the degree of detail used for an annual budget, but some attempt to understand the likely outcome of the interaction of major structures, themes, interests and technologies is both possible and necessary. Great detail is not possible, but descriptions of likely developments and their implications for the organization and its mission, are and should be attempted.

The process for doing this can rely mainly on the organization's stakeholders (e.g. staff, clients, major funders) or on experts. If stakeholders are used they can be asked to predict the way they see the environment of the organization developing. Those who are expert at reading industry trends also may provide a longer term perspective, but they may paint it with a very broad brush. Ideally the views of both groups will be sought. These views can be sorted and turned into a picture or pictures of the future environment of the organization, or they can be used as a starting point for further analysis by the strategic planning group.

So far this section has stressed the importance of understanding the dynamics of the environment in which the organization is located. In doing this, consideration should be given to the strengths and weaknesses and the plans, as far as they can be determined, of other organizations in the same line of work. Even if your VNPO values collaboration, that may not be true of all other organizations and is certainly not true of for-profit organizations which might be operating or preparing to operate in your field.

Step 5 – SWOT analysis

SWOT stands for Strengths, Weaknesses, Opportunities, and Threats, and is perhaps the best known of the strategic planning/management acronyms. At this point of the strategic planning process the strategic planning group, and perhaps the wider reference group, need to develop an appreciation of the strengths and weaknesses of the organization and the opportunities and threats which confront it in its environment. Essentially the analysis of strengths and weaknesses draws on, but seeks to evaluate, data gathered in step three, while the appreciation of opportunities and threats relies on information and judgements formed in step four.

What distinguishes this step from the two previous steps is the element of strategic **evaluation** that is involved. The two previous steps attempted to gather data in an objective manner and forecast changes in the environment without specific reference to the impact upon the organization. In this step this data is evaluated. This distinction is not always easy to draw. Some characteristics of an organization can be both a strength and a weakness and some aspects of the environment both an opportunity and a threat. It is necessary only to note this ambiguity; it is not necessary to force all assessments into one category or another.

It is often the case that at this step the strategic planning group and the wider reference group become preoccupied with strengths and weaknesses, i.e. with internal processes of the organization with which they are associated. In order to avoid this impasse, it is sensible practice to begin this step with opportunities and threats before moving to looking at strengths and weaknesses. It is also important in this step to attempt to build together the two aspects of the analysis, the internal and the external. Kearns (1992) rightly insists on the importance of bringing together the analysis (he calls it 'mapping the interaction') of strengths and weaknesses and opportunities and threats. The strategic planning team can only determine what should be done in response to perceived opportunities and threats by reviewing these in the light of the strengths and weaknesses of the organization; that is, some aspect of the environment is only an opportunity (or a threat) if there is a corresponding strength (or weakness) in the organization.

It is also important to involve the wider reference group in this step. One way of doing so is to have one (or several, depending on size) meetings where the group brainstorms opportunities and threats and strengths and weaknesses. These can be written on large pieces of paper which can be stuck to a wall and moved around as the meeting reviews earlier judgements about whether a particular factor is a weakness or a strength and how it relates to a particular opportunity or threat. They also can be grouped together to simplify later analysis and to help the group discuss and explore the links between internal and external factors.

Example of a SWOT analysis

The staff and management committee of a childcare centre conduct a SWOT analysis. The centre is licensed to provide care for 40 children aged between two and five years. It was started twenty years before by a group in the local Anglican parish and is still formally responsible to the Parish Council, which provides a small subsidy. Most of its revenue comes from parent fees and government subsidies. Its **strengths** include this link with the parish and its large outdoor space which most parents find attractive. It has also managed to retain its senior staff for several years, unusual in an expanding industry. Its **weaknesses** are seen to include its location on a busy road, which makes parking while dropping off and picking up children difficult and the fact that part of the centre occupies an older church building. Several of its rooms are of an awkward size and one extra staff member is needed than would be the case in a purpose built centre catering for the same number of children. This weakness was given added point by the emergence of the **threat** of competition from two new privately-owned childcare centres within a five kilometre radius of this centre. Both offer slightly lower fees. As well, some members of the parish question the policy of continuing to subsidize the centre. However, the parish connection provides two **opportunities**. None of the three existing centres provide care for under two year olds, a category of care for which there is high demand. Their parish and the adjoining two parishes are seen to provide the nucleus for developing a family day care network; that is, a group for mothers who are looking after their own young children at home who are prepared to take in several other young children for a fee. Second, some parishioners have good connections with businesses moving to a new light industrial estate not far from the centre. This provides the opportunity to negotiate with several companies an agreement whereby the companies pay the centre a retainer to keep open a small number of places for members of their staff who wish to return quickly to work after child birth and for the young children of staff transferred from interstate.

Step 6 – identifying strategic issues

A strategic planning process can generate a long list of issues needing attention. Many of these will be relatively unimportant, especially from a strategic perspective. Before any further action is determined, it is necessary to review these issues in a disciplined way and identify those which are strategic. They include issues which need to be addressed if the organization is to respond to new needs in its client group and issues which, if they are not addressed, will lead to the demise of the organization. Bryson (1994), who rightly insists on the importance of this step, describes strategic issues as 'fundamental policy questions affecting the organization's mandates, mission and values, productivity level or mix, clients, users and payers, costs, financing, management, or organizational design.' They may be issues which need immediate attention or they may be issues identified as emerging from trends in the environment. In such cases, the exact shape or timing of a threat, or an opportunity, might not be clear but it is important to begin paying such matters attention and, if necessary, making adjustments in resource allocation to ensure that attention is given.

Step 7 – strategy development

For each strategic issue, an appropriate action should be developed. The larger reference group of staff and other stakeholders can be involved in this process, which flows on naturally from the SWOT analysis and strategic issue identification. It is often helpful to allow people in the reference group to meet twice in this process, so that there is a chance for reflection and an opportunity to talk with others in the organization who are not part of the group about the analysis and possible proposals. It is important for all stakeholders of the organization to share at least a broad outline of insights generated by the strategic planning process. It is also important that this process be done in a non-threatening environment; that staff are reassured that their interests will be looked after in any organizational change. It is also very important that participants in the process be encouraged to be ambitious for the organization, to develop their 'ideal vision' for the future, and that they 'think outside the lines.'

Possible responses for each strategic issue can also be recorded and together with the relevant issue, these can be moved around into related groups of issues and responses. Frequently, any particular response (a new service programme, a reallocation of resources or staff responsibilities, a new way of relating the organization to significant players in its environment) will turn out to address several issues. In the end, however, the strategic planning group has to sort through the array of ideas and reduce them to a coherent set of actions that can be performed by the organization, given its various resource restraints. This is a difficult task. It entails confronting the ideas and ideals of those involved in the planning process with organizational realities, but doing so in a way that retains a confidence and an excitement about the future. This should be distilled into a succinct description of how the organization will look in five or ten years time. Bryson (1994) calls this the 'organization's vision of success.' It is at this point that the chief executive will be called upon significantly to ajudicate in decisions.

It is important also for the strategic planning group to take account of any disagreements or strongly expressed opposition to a particular response or direction of response. It may be necessary to propose some movement across these 'no-go barriers' erected by staff or other significant stakeholders, but only after a great deal of work has been put into demonstrating that the fears or values that lead to the creation of those barriers will not be breached by such a movement. The chapter on managing change addresses such issues in more detail.

Step 8 - operationalizing the strategic plan

The penultimate, formal step in the strategic planning process is to develop operational plans that implement decisions taken in the preceding steps. To a significant extent, if the process to this point has been successful, it will already have transformed the way staff and other stakeholders view the organization. The strategic planning process will have changed how they work within it and relate to it, and their vision of its future, but the implementation of strategies emerging from the strategic planning process will usually require some reallocation of resources, some repositioning within the organization, some change in procedures, new approaches to other organizations and so on. The timing of these steps and responsibilites for their execution must be clearly identified in advance. This is where the publishing of the strategic plan becomes important. It sets out for staff and other stakeholders the range of changes to be pursued and the reason for them. **It should also include a time-frame for the changes**.

The new strategy may involve a large scale reorganization of the VNPO, such as the shedding of large parts of it or the acquisition of, or merger with, another organization. If strategies encourage significant changes, they must be operationalized in a sensitive manner. Once again, the leadership of the chief executive is crucial and, especially in a large organization, a great deal of time must be spent in establishing and overseeing processes that enable staff to recognize the correctness and the legitimacy of what is being proposed.

Step 9 – further review

The final step entails building into the routine planning cycle a regular review of progress according to the new strategies. It also involves reviewing the appropriateness and correctness of the strategies themselves. It is important that benchmarks to be achieved by adopting new strategies are clearly specified during the planning process and that data is subsequently collected to measure their achievement. This may be, but it need not be, an elaborate data collection exercise. Sometimes the judgement of some key stakeholders, one or two years on, will suffice.

It is also important to review, every one or two years, the original forecasts made in the environmental and futures scan. This is because a forecast may turn out to be wrong, or only partly correct. In so far as an organization has adopted a new strategic orientation because of a pre-viously forecast opportunity or threat, then the analysis that led to that new strategy needs to be reviewed in the light of developments in that environment since then. That is why it is important to retain at least a summary documentation of the strategic planning process and of the analysis that led to certain decisions being taken. If that analysis, two years on, looks faulty, it may be necessary to review the strategies that flow from it.

Of course, a whole lot else may have happened to have taken the organization in a different direction. That is the reality of organizational life and although the strategic planning process outlined above is designed to try and give to the management of an organization some degree of control over its direction, sometimes opportunities that were not predicted emerge and need to be grasped and sometimes disasters happen. None the less, strategic planning can help improve the capacity for an organization to know where it is going and, under most circumstances, to be able to move in that direction (See Case Study 4 below.)

CONCLUSION: A LEARNING ORGANIZATION

The argument so far has been that strategic management is management which is orientated outwards, to the environment of the organization, and forwards, towards its future. The strategic planning process described in some detail above is offered as a formal process that can initiate a strategic orientation to management. It is offered not as a recipe but as a guide; as a series of steps which hold some promise to the management of a VNPO which wishes to orientate itself strategically and to take some control over its destiny. Once undertaken, it should not be necessary to repeat the strategic management process for five or more years.

However, strategic management requires the maintenance of that out-ward and forward orientation. It means not simply maintaining that orien-tation in the chief executive but within the whole organization. The interactions which an organization has with its environment are many and have the potential to keep the organization well-informed about its environment. Such interactions include staff working with clients, profes-sional staff mixing with other professionals at conferences or reading professional literature, and management or professional staff mixing with colleagues in other organizations or with government officials. In a well-run, consumer focused organization, a good deal of data from client interactions will be maintained and reviewed. In a strategically oriented organization, a good deal of other information will be formally assimilated and reviewed. The best way of doing this is by holding regular meetings of relevant staff for pooling and analysing information. This will not be easy. When resources are stretched, the commitment of even a relatively small amount of time for strategic review will be given reluctantly. It is important, too, that such sessions be characterized by hard-nosed analysis and not the articulating of old slogans or the parading of voluntary non-profit sector fears.

What is being suggested here is that each VNPO be thought of as a **learning organization**. This is a currently fashionable term which is in danger of being oversold, but has at its core an important truth. It sometimes is used to refer to organizations as a site for learning; to encourage a constant review of practice in the light of output to ensure a constant improvement in quality. But it can also refer to their capacity to learn from the environment and to adapt quickly and appropriately. In this sense, a learning organization is one that readily assimilates and consciously reviews information from its environment. It is an organization where staff share an outward orientation, who recognize the inevitability of change and who collectively seek to orientate their organization so that it is able to prosper and effectively pursue its mission into the future. This concept is discussed further in the chapter on the management of change.

CASE STUDIES

1 The Help Foundation

This had been established over a decade ago to work with people suffering from a new and debilitating condition. It had grown fast, with a good deal of government asistance. By the early 1990s it employed almost 200 staff and spent almost £3 million annually. A range of factors, including an extremely politicized client community, public hostility to those with the condition and disagreements within the medical research community meant that the Help Foundation occupied an extremely turbulent environment. For its first ten years it had operated on an annual or biannual planning cycle. In 1993, the Help Foundation senior management team decided that a longer perspective was needed and agreed to develop a strategic plan to guide the organization over the next five years. They sought to achieve several goals via a strategic planning process. The intentions were

● to review the Foundation's mission;
● to highlight future scenarios which the Help Foundation might find itself operating in;
● to identify key strategic issues which it needed to address;

- to ensure co-ordination and consolidation of the various areas of activity; and
- to encourage strategic thinking and planning throughout the whole organization.

A discussion paper, proposing a strategic planning process was circulated to the Board and endorsed at a joint planning day between the Board and the management team. At that meeting, an oversight committee was formed from Board members and eight members of a strategic planning team (SPT) were identified. Their role was to oversee the process and to keep moving it forward. The SPT were all members of the management team, apart from one member of the client community. The CEO and deputy CEO were both members. A list of external stakeholders was also developed via a brainstorming process. A six month timeline was determined. When these proposals were put to staff, there was some dissatisfaction, particularly with the composition of the steering group. This unease was mollified by further discussions with certain groups. The SPT met every month for two hours. Each member undertook other tasks. Essentially, the senior staff who were members of the team arranged their other work around their commitment to the strategic planning process.

Following Bryson (1988), the major task was seen to be the identification of organizational mandates, clarifying its missions and values and asessing its external and internal environments. To this end, a questionnaire was 'borrowed' from another organization which had recently undertaken a strategic planning process. It was modified to suit the Help Foundation and was sent to all stakeholdes identified earlier, with a request for either a face to face or a telephone interview. The questionnaire sought their views on the strengths and weaknesses of the Foundation, on likely changes in its environment over the next five years and the way that Help should respond to these.

When these interviews were completed, the data was analysed by three members of the SPT. A report of the findings was placed in the Help Foundation library for perusal by staff, volunteers, and members of the client community. After appropriate modification, the same questionnaire was then given to all staff. Staff responses were collected via small group meetings, using a nominal group technique. Staff were invited to submit written responses as well. Their results were also analysed. Some of the issues emerging from the staff groups were more operational than strategic and were referred to the management team for immediate action. The responses of staff and external stakeholders were found to be very similar, however.

The SPT then faced the challenge of pooling and assimilating the large amount of raw data and reducing it to three possible future scenarios and a workable number of strategic issues. During this process, other valuable insights into the structure and operations of the Help Foundation emerged.

A series of four one-day workshops were held to confirm and clarify 14 strategic issues which had been identified by the SPT of Help. These were arranged for each of its four major areas of work and were open to staff, volunteers and interested members of the client community. Each workshop was facilitated by an independent facilitator who was familiar with the work of the Foundation.

Following these workshops, the SPT spent further long hours building a strategy plan that was both user friendly and action orientated. Two breakthroughs were achieved when it was realized that the 14 strategies could be grouped into five and when someone saw a strategic plan prepared by a government agency, which suggested a sensible way of setting out objectives, desired outcomes and strategies. This offered a useful structure.

The plan was endorsed by a Board/management team planning day and presented to staff at a monthly staff meeting. The plan identified those responsible for different areas of activity and these groups were then required to develop action plans which were approved by the management team and enacted. The deputy CEO was given responsibility for monitoring the continuing implementation of the plan.

Overall, the strategic planning process did not suggest any significant changes to the work or structure of the Help Foundation. Stakeholders and staff both endorsed the existing mission and praised its overall responsiveness. The value of the process was in helping to identify and clarify three ways in which the organizational environment might develop over the next five years, to prepare a strategy to respond to the most likely developments that did not close off the possibility of responding to either of the other two scenarios, should one of them turn out to be the more accurate prediction. The process also served to clarify and consolidate various activites within the organization. As well, it helped sensitize all staff towards future developments. Finally, although the Help Foundation already had structures and processes in place (such as regular staff meetings) that made it something of a learning organization, the strategic planning process added to staff understanding the importance of information retrieval, analysis and dissemination, thus further enhancing the capacity of the Foundation to respond to continuing change.

2 St Brigid's School

This had been a secondary school for girls run by a religious order in a large country town. It had begun about 100 years before to provide boarding school education for the daughters of families living on grazing and farming properties and from small towns across an area of thousands of square miles. Over the past 30 years, as the population in the bush dwindled, numbers enrolled also fell. Parts of the school were closed and other parts converted to retirement living for older members of the religious order. Another change had occured also. As with many religious orders, since the 1960s, the numbers of young women joining fell away. In the 1980s the order had decided to cease teaching at the school and instead to send girls who still attended the school to a new diocesan high school. The school had effectively become a hostel for those girls, although the sisters still helped with homework.

In 1994, the leader of the congregation at St Brigid's agreed that they should review whether the resources that the order had tied up in St Brigid's could not be used more effectively in pursuit of the order's mission to aid the most disadvantaged in society. The last decade had also seen a considerable increase in rural poverty and suicide rates, especially amongst young men living in rural areas, while the aboriginal population continued to experience discrimination and extraordinarily high levels of poverty and mortality.

With the permission of the leader of the religious order, the school mapped out a process for reviewing the work they did and identifying other fields of possibly more effective mission. They organized focus group discussions among present and past pupils; they sent a questionnaire to parents of present and past pupils and prepared to talk to clergy and parishioners of far-flung parishes.

They realized that the success of any reorientation hinged upon the question of resources. They recognized that they needed to retain some of the existing accomodation for older members of the order and that they might need to arrange some way of continuing to provide accommodation for the dwindling numbers of girls who attended the diocesan high, even if for no more than a phasing out period. The key resource they held was the school and its extensive grounds on the edges of a fairly prosperous rural city. **However, there was a catch**. They knew that some of the land belonged to the diocese (a small portion, they thought). But the deeds to the whole portion were held by the bishop. The bishop also had the right to oppose any change in the order's activities within his diocese. Consequently, the school team invited the diocesan administrator to join two parent representatives and themselves on the planning team. However, without explanation, the administrator refused and also refused to make available the title deeds of the land. Faced with this notable lack of support from a key stakeholder, the leader of the order then withdrew her support and instructed the school team to do no more than survey the parents to discover their views on the future for the school.

What had happened was that someone from outside the organization, but someone who was a key stakeholder in it, a person who controlled the mandate of the organization, had stopped the strategic planning process almost as soon as it had begun.

3 Justice Mission

This was a large (£10 million annually) provider of social services in a large metropolitan city. It has a national reputation for innovative programme development and for its social policy analysis and advocacy. Most of the services provided by Justice Mission are devoted to either the long-term unemployed or to older people. Almost 50 years before, Justice Mission had pioneered new forms of providing housing for the aged. The methods they pioneered were endorsed by the government, which provided grants and many thousands of other voluntary organizations followed the path pioneered by Justice Mission. Aged care consumed more than half of the budget of Justice Mission and because of the highly intensive nature of care for the very frail aged, a good deal of that expenditure was committed to services to relatively few people. Approximately 40% of the revenue of Justice Mission came from government grants; the rest from client fees (25%) and from fund-raising and business ventures. Justice Mission was closely tied to one of the major Christian denominations.

Not long after a new chief executive was installed, she and the board determined to review their strategies and possibly to reorient the organization. The main focus of the review was its aged care programme.

When Justice Mission had become involved in aged care, the aged were heavily over-represented amongst the very poorest in the nation. Over the past 40 years, increases in aged pension levels, the expansion of specialized housing and ready access to health care had considerably improved the position of older people. There were still some older people, such as elderly migrants with no family networks, who were badly off, but in general, the most disadvantaged in the society were now sole parents, the long term unemployed and more recent migrants from Asian countries, especially refugees. For Justice Mission, with its strong commitment to aiding and empowering the most disadvantaged in society, the level of its resources going to aged care, particularly in parts of the city which were now quite prosperous, seemed anomalous. Other Christian organizations which specialized in aged care might be encouraged to buy a large part of its aged accommodation, freeing up resources for other programmes which were more clearly an expression of the mission of the organization.

The matter was discussed at several seminars and the views of social policy experts and some stakeholders were sought. It was agreed to subject the matter to further review and a small consultancy team was employed to do this.

Several months later, the consultants came forward with recommendations for the disposal of large parts of aged services and for other major changes in the structure of the organization. Some of these appeared to be no more than an application of currently fashionable theories in the public sector, which is where the consultants had previously done most of their work. Some staff were unhappy with the proposals and some of this unhappiness was reported in the press. The consultants made matters worse by deciding to reply (the chief executive was out of town at the time). Upon returning, the chief executive agreed on certain compromises to mollify some of the staff unrest, but that only frustrated others.

A good deal of unrest and turmoil continued, both among staff and for many of the aged care residents and their families. The major reason for the change was not clearly and frequently articulated. Morale in the organization was damaged and its reputation suffered, though not greatly. It was clear that although staff generally affirmed the mission of the organization, they were not prepared to concur in a large scale reorientation. Perhaps if the process had been extended over a longer time, if more staff had been involved in the process (instead of relying on the consultant) or perhaps if other alternatives had been explored more fully and if a clear vision of the future for Justice Mission had been articulated and 'sold' by the chief executive, a slow adaptation of the strategy to the vision could have been successfully negotiated. As it is, the changes are going forward, but amidst a good deal of unhappiness.

4 Learning Radio

This was one of more then 60 community radio stations which have developed since the 1970s. Incorporated as a non-profit company, it is jointly owned by two metropolitan universities and has a licence to broadcast over the whole city (most community radio stations have a far smaller broadcast range). It is one of the leaders in community radio, but its size is sometimes resented by smaller community broadcasters. It employs about 10 staff who work in management and the technical side, as well as programming support. All the programme develement and broadcasting is done by volunteers. Some of the programming is an alternative version of the familiar: news, current affairs, music; but some is provided for and by specialized groups such as gays and older people. During weekends, the station is leased to various ethnic communities. Although the universities had originally formed the station to provide some sort of formal educational programming, this had not eventuated. The board is still appointed by the two universities but, over time, has come to adopt a far looser description of education or learning. This could be demonstrated by the provision of alternative views and perspectives not likely to get an airing on mainstream radio and by its provision of metropolitan-wide coverage for the variety of community groups that could utilize the radio's resources. Its revenue came from subscriptions, university grants, occasional government grants for innovative programming, sponsorship and from the sale of airtime to special interest groups.

By the early 1990s, it was clear that the extraordinary revolution in communications was going to transform the radio and indeed, the entire communication industry. In the long-term future lay the complete convergence of currently separate forms of communication such as telephone, radio, television, newspapers, videos, computers and so on. More immediately, the government had announced a commitment to introduce a new digital standard for radio transmission which would require entirely new equipment and, for technical reasons, would prohibit any broadcasting that was less than metropolitan-wide. Existing community radio stations could continue to operate, but only people with pre-digital radio receivers would be able to pick them up. It was not clear when this change would take place, but it would be within the next decade. A more immediate threat to Learning Radio was another, somewhat contradictory, government policy of allowing a large increase in community radio licences to enable much smaller groups to broadcast over a limited area. This had within it the possibility that many of the special groups, such as different ethnic communities, which bought time on Learning Radio would run their own radios with a consequent loss of income for Learning Radio.

The station manager was a member of several government committees and was better informed of the ways things were developing than most in the community radio sector. With the agreement of the board and senior staff, she engaged two university staff who agreed to facilitate a learning process for a group of about 20 staff, board and volunteer members. The object was to lead this group through the key steps of the strategic planning process, so that they developed a strategic plan for Learning Radio. The process progressed by a series of four half-day meetings approximately a month apart, with different sub-groups doing work between meetings. The first meeting began with a review and reshaping of its mission. The group then conducted an internal review and uncovered a number of areas of dissatisfaction with aspects of the station's management and disagreement between staff and volunteers about the purpose of the station. These disagreements were partly worked through and resolved and partly suspended so as to move on to a review of the external environment of the station. An extended SWOT analysis produced a long list of strategic issues, but further discussion focused on several long-term issues to do with its possible support in the new but as yet uncertain technological future, with a focus on relations with other community radio stations and community television.

It was agreed that the station should gradually acquire equipment that could be used when radio went digital. It was also agreed to make a bid to utilize unused video production facilities in one of the universities in order to acquire a learning capacity in this medium for Learning Radio. Finally, a number of relatively minor adjustments to the organization were made.

The major issue, however, that of trying to forecast the technological future and to envisage a role for Learning Radio in this future, was found to be too difficult at this point. Instead, it was agreed that the organization should become better able to receive, monitor and interpret information from its environment. A regular monthly meeting with five key staff was scheduled as a place to share information and try and make sense of future trends. In this way, it was hoped, the organization would be able to respond to emerging trends in a timely way.

In the strategic planning process it had been realized that many of the staff possessed information of strategic significance because of the different groups they interacted with, the technical magazines they read and so on but that this was not used to help the organization keep up to date with its rapidly changing environment and enable it to interpret various new developments. It was agreed that it needed to become a more efficient learning organization and that a new process for information retrieval and assimilation needed to be created. Although it was not yet possible to chart a strategy for the future, various alternatives were sketched and kept under constant scrutiny in the light of new information. It was anticipated that as a result of this process, alternative scenarios would develop and at some time in the future, the organization would be in a better position to make the significant adaptation which would be needed. In effect, one of the major outcomes of the strategic planning exercise was to create a **learning organization**, one that was better attuned and would be more responsive to changes in its environment.

REFERENCES

Bryson, J. (1988) *Strategic Planning for Public and Nonprofit Organisations*, Jossey-Bass, San Francisco.

Bryson, J. (1994) Strategic planning and action planning in nonprofit organisations, in *The Jossey-Bass Handbook of Nonprofit Leadership and Management* (eds R. Herman and Associates) Jossey-Bass, San Francisco.

Bush, R. (1992) Survival of the nonprofit sector in a for-profit world. *Nonprofit and Voluntary Sector Quarterly*, **21** (4), pp. 391–410.

Fay, B. (1975) *Social Theory and Political Practice*, George Allen and Unwin, London.

Fulmer, R. and Rue, L. (1974) The practice and profitability of long range planning. *Managerial Planning*, **22** pp. 1–7.

Gup, B. and Whitehead, D. (1989) Strategic planning in banks – does it pay? *Long Range Planning*, **22** (1) pp. 124–30.

Kearns, K. (1992) From comparative advantage to damage control: clarifying strategic issues using SWOT analysis. *Nonprofit Management and Leadership*, **3** (1), pp. 3–22.

Lindblom, C. (1968) *The Policy Planning Process*, Prentice Hall, Englewood Cliffs.

Mintzberg, H. (1994) *The Rise and Fall of Strategic Planning*, Prentice Hall, Hemel Hempstead.

Porter, M. (1980) *Competitive Strategy: Techniques for Analysing Industries and Competition*, Free Press, New York.

Porter, M. (1985) *Competitive Advantage: Creating and Sustaining Superior Performance*, Free Press, New York.

Robinson, R. (1982) The importance of 'outsiders' in small firm strategic planning. *Academy of Management Journal*, **25** (1) pp. 80–93.

Stone, M. (1989) Planning as strategy in nonprofit organisations: an exploratory study. *Nonprofit and Voluntary Sector Quarterly*, **18**, (4), pp. 297–315.
Wittington, R. (1993) *What is Strategy – and Does It Matter?* Routledge, London.

GUIDED READING

Much of the past literature on strategic management is of limited value to managers of VNPOs. It is written for business managers and does not look beyond that group. Some of the general literature is of value, however.

One of the best overviews of the strategic management literature is Whittington. R. (1992) *What is Strategy – and Does It Matter?* Routledge, London. 1992.

One writer who has done more than any other to popularize strategic planning and strategic management is Henry Mintzberg. One of the best of the proliferation of business course texts (voluminous and full of extracts from articles and other books) is edited by Mintzberg and Quinn (1993) *The Strategy Process*, Prentice Hall, Hemel Hempstead. Mintzberg is becoming increasingly critical of many of the claims made for strategic planning and management. His latest book (1994) *The Rise and Fall of Strategic Planning*, Prentice Hall, Hemel Hempstead, is well worth reading and, because it is not focused on the business enterprise, it is quite accessible to voluntary and nonprofit managers.

The most widely used prescriptive, or 'how to' books on strategic management/ planning are North American. Most are written for business organizations, but there are some which are directed at government and the nonprofit sector. The most popular of these is Bryson, J. (1988) *Strategic Planning for Public and Nonprofit Organisations. A Guide to Strengthening and Sustaining Organisational Achievement*, Jossey-Bass, San Francisco. Another useful guide, complete with worksheets, is Barry, B. (1986) *Strategic Planning Workbook for Nonprofit Organisations*, Amherst H. Wylder Foundation, St Paul, Minn.

With the exception of Butler R. and Wilson D. (1990) *Managing Voluntary and Non-profit Organisations: Strategy and Structure*, Routledge, London, descriptive studies of strategic management and voluntary organizations are to be found in journal articles. Middleton Stone, M. and Crittenden, W. recently published an excellent survey – A Guide to Journal Articles on Strategic Management in Nonprofit Organisations, 1977–1992 in *Nonprofit Management and Leadership*, **4** (2) pp. 193–213. It is the best place to start for a more comprehensive review of a growing body of literature.

7 Business planning for voluntary and non-profit organizations

Jill Schofield

INTRODUCTION

By the end of this chapter you

- will be introduced to the various components which make up a business plan;
- will understand the processes involved in business planning; and
- will have thought through the links between the planning components and processes of business planning.

It will be helpful to the reader of this chapter if they are familiar with the concepts involved in strategic and financial management from earlier in this book. Whilst it is possible to have a strategic plan without a business plan, a business plan which has not been informed by a strategic direction will be neither helpful nor robust. Both strategic and business planning involve the puposeful collection and selection of data, the specifying of arrangements and the organization of resources to help make future decisions about actions over a variety of timescales. Strategic plans, however, are more concerned with a longer timescale than business plans and cover broader, often less articulated, issues about the future. Business planning, on the other hand, is very much about bringing the strategic direction to fruition in the 'here and now'. There is no one established blue print for developing a business plan. Scholes and Klemm (1987) emphasize that it is organizational 'circumstances' which will fashion the nature of the plan, whilst Richardson and Richardson (1990) model the organization as a 'complete business planning system' aligned to produce strategic success.

CONTEXTS AND CHARACTERISTICS OF VNPOs WHICH AFFECT BUSINESS PLANNING

There is a general agreement that there is no one right way to compile a useful business plan. However, the pedigree of business planning is one very much situated in the for-profit sector (Lenz and Lyles 1989; Shim and McGlade 1989). To convince us of the relevance of business planning for

VNPOs, it is helpful to specify the particular characteristics and challenges of VNPOs which differentiate them from for-profit organizations and which impact upon business planning. We shall then use these characteristics to assess the usefulness of business planning and to assist in our critique of it as a management process of relevance or otherwise to VNPOs. There are seven characteristics of VNPOs which impact upon business planning.

Organizational characteristics

Both Billis (1993) and Poulton (1988) have provided useful critiques of the organizational variations within the sector. There are, however, two themes upon which a number of writers agree; namely, that VNPOs possess a high degree of ambiguity regarding their role and that their membership comprises people with a diverse range of motivations. What this in turn means for the business planning process is that, by comparison to their for-profit neighbours, many VNPOs demonstrate a lack of **corporate single-mindedness**. In turn, this may result in some organizational tension in deciding upon a strategic direction and this will be reflected in the business planning process.

Ideological characteristics

Kanter and Summers (1987) provide us with a very helpful philosophical 'test' of non-profit vis-à-vis for-profit organizations, namely, that the mission of a VNPO is built around service which is further defined by some societal value of 'doing good' (ibid: 154). Financial values become subservient to these social values and these values themselves only have meaning for as long as they are regarded as being beneficial. This theme of action which has a social value, is reinforced by the definition of VNPOs as organizations which fulfil public tasks which neither for-profit organizations nor the state are willing to perform (Dobkin Hall 1987).

Less easily identifiable values such as grass roots involvement, local responsiveness, community orientation and equity are also important tenants of a voluntary philosophy and have been explored by Salamon and Anheier (1995). It is because these values are difficult to quantify that they are also difficult to include in a business plan. As such, they may need to be conveyed in terms of value-laden statements of organizational mission and as critical success factors by which the results of the plan can be assessed.

The role of patronage and philanthropy

A cursory glance through the established business planning textbooks would never reveal such vocabulary as philanthropy or charity. Such a gap once again is explained by its commercial, for-profit, background. Business planning is very well-established within the public sector in Britain, though that sector is not dominated by philanthropy either. Herein then, lies a key distinguishing characteristic of VNPOs (Joseph 1995; Prince and File 1995) and one which needs to be reflected in their business plans.

A recent study of corporate philanthropy in the UK (Lane and Saxon-Harrold 1993) identified corporate social responsibility and corporate perceptions of self-interest as the main motivations for charitable giving. Depending upon the level of donation, the business plan of a VNPO may well reflect this philanthropic involvement in its policies.

Volunteering

Smith and Lipsky (1993) emphasize the local, or community based, nature of volunteering arguing that, as such, volunteers have personal, often empathetic, knowledge of their clients. It might be suggested that the compilation of a business plan itself can be a move towards professionalization within a VNPO, drawing it ever more into the mainstream of commercial or bureaucratic models of organization. The essence of volunteeering can, though, be reflected in a business plan. Indeed, a volunteer and group of volunteers can be the authors of such plans with or without specialized training.

Financial characteristics

The financial context of VNPOs in relation to business planning is a complex one. There is now the added complexity of VNPOs being more widely used in the provision of services which were previously within the remit of the statutory sector, particularly for human and welfare services. As a consequence of this, VNPOs are increasingly involved in financial contracts for services. These contracts can have targets in terms of service volumes and specifications, all of which require sophisticated and timely financial monitoring and reporting systems.

Smith and Lipsky (1993) have argued that contracting has had, in some cases, a detrimental effect upon the cash flow of VNPOs due to delays in payment from government agencies. Contracting arrangements such as these also raise the issue of the basis for charging. A VNPO needs a financial information system which allows them to do activity based costing or they may find themselves at a price disadvantage because of lack of information. Baine *et al.* (1994a and b) have shown the need for effective contract monitoring systems supported by a business plan.

The financial complexity of VNPOs has a huge impact upon the business planning process because finance is a functional support area to be managed and used to facilitate organizational aims. The business plan also needs to take account of financial **resources** and how they act either as an organizational opportunity or constraint.

Collaboration

With the increased pluralism in welfare provision and the role which VNPOs are playing, they are becoming more involved in inter-agency collaboration. VNPOs need to understand the ramifications of collaboration and reflect this in their business plans. This means some research of the strategic and business documentation of other agencies, which may not always be easily available. One of the advantages of the business plan is that it could well act as a focal point to clarify inter-agency responsibilities and action plans.

Stakeholders

Part of the distinctive history of VNPOs has been the key role played in them by particular individuals willing to step outside the mainstream and take risks. This is particularly the case in neighbourhood VNPOS, where the membership can have a sense of embeddedness in the local community. Given this situation, those responsible for drafting the business plan and for ensuring its relevance need to explore how the views and commitment of stakeholders can be incorporated in to it.

THE COMPONENTS OF A BUSINESS PLAN

It will help us if we view business planning as part of a tripartite planning system which commences with strategic planning, is followed by business planning (sometimes referred to as management planning) and ends with operational planning. Each level involves a further amount of detail, with operational planning being the most detailed. In terms of a working definition, **business planning is about making strategic vision a reality and it does this by identifying the tasks which need to be completed and then allocating these tasks into particular organizational functions**.

Strategic plans tend to be writen in the five to ten year timescale with three-yearly reviews. Business plans tend to be written on an annual basis. Operational plans are often not formally collated into a document but are guided by the business plan and involve the day-to-day running of an organization such as job schedules and all the normal functions needed to keep the organization going.

An important point to note is that business planning goes beyond a collection of functional plans (such as finance or personnel plans). It is much more focused toward achieving strategic action – and in turn the functional departments become just that, a means to an end. To many

VNPOs this may involve a culture change, as these departments may feel that their power base is being eroded.

Figure 7.1 shows the business planing 'route map'. It contains thirteen interrelated stages. The shaded sections of it relate to the activities and decisions which have been made in the organizational strategic plan.

Step 1 – Analysis of internal environment

This analysis is intended to provide a brief review of where the organization is currently, in terms of its key fiscal and human dimensions. It is descriptive, but the mere act of counting and describing all the resources at its disposal helps to clarify its capabilities. It also only needs to be done once and then updated annually for the production of the next business plan.

The resource audit should list all capital assets of the VNPO. It should also provide a broad financial statement of total income and expenditure and the major income and expenditure groupings used in the organizational accounts. The skills audit refers particularly to all the people, employees, volunteers and non-executive members, who make up the organization and identifies, again in broad groups, the major skills which the organization possesses. The analysis of the audit should provide more detail, such as the age of staff, expected retirement patterns and expected lifespan of capital equipment. This exercise will also help in understanding workforce and volunteer flexibility.

The importance of this exercise lies in its ability to describe the **internal environment** of a VNPO and will link to the SWOT analysis which has already been completed during the strategic planning phase. The exercise also allows the organization to perform simple checks upon its efficiency and productivity.

Steps 2–3 – Test of consistency and business aims and objectives for the coming twelve to twenty four months

Having completed Step 1 and incorporated the information here with the external analysis from your strategic plan, the organization can now assess how the business of the organization fits into its stated strategy and how its internal environment can respond to external contingent factors. This is termed **a test of consistency**.

It is at this point in the business plan where key decisions about the future direction and the commitment of resources are made. The aim and objectives of the next twelve to twenty-four months are laid out and refined in terms of what the organization is going to do, who is doing it, and where and how it is going to be done. These appear to be four very simple questions, but answering them in the context of a clear strategy means exercising considerable thought and skill. Some VNPO business plans will

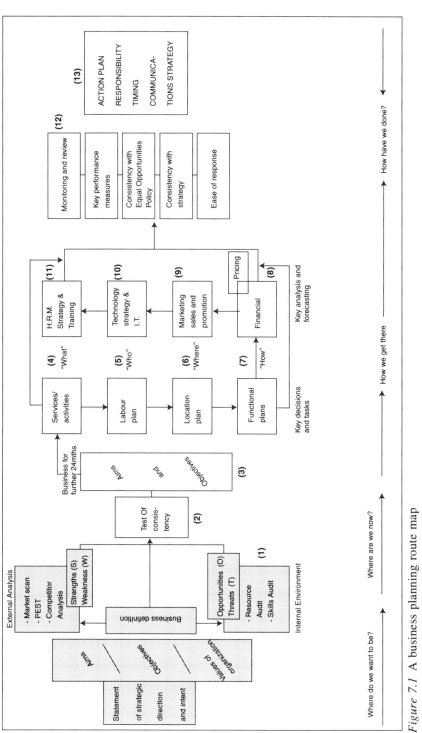

Figure 7.1 A business planning route map

be 'more of the same' and continue patterns from previous years. For others, it can be the beginning of a major strategic shift. Given the patterns of recession in the developed world, it is very unlikely that any organization will not have to address their future financial security and how their business must change to ensure this security.

Steps 4–6 – Activity statement, labour and location plans

The **activity statement** is a description of what the organization is going to do. It is helpful if this can be segmented into areas of activity which share similar characteristics. For small VNPOs this may not be necessary (such as a women's aid project or a small day centre), but for more diverse VNPOs it will be more pertinent – and difficult!

The most important aspect of the activity statement is to be able to define the unit(s) of activity in which the organization intends to be involved in the coming years. This will require an element of forecasting and again, the definition will be easier for some than it is for others. Thus a charity which funds medical research may define its units as a certain number of projects which it can support. A luncheon club may define its units as the number of people served on an annual basis. The unit of activity will vary between VNPOs but it is the **amount and type of activity** to be undertaken which drives all business plans. Activity statements will need to be expressed in draft form to begin with until the remainder of the business planning analysis is completed and, in particular, the financial analysis as this will indicate the feasibility or otherwise of achieving the activity targets.

The labour plan is a future statement about the amount and type of labour needed to support the proposed activity. It is a very important part of the business plan and often one which is overlooked. The labour plan will be informed by the skills audit which was completed in Step 1, but it also needs to specify how shortfalls or excesses in skills and numbers will be addressed. It will address such issues as recruitment, retention, redundancy and planned labour turnover.

The location plan is a statement about the organizational geography. It describes where its physical assets are located, where its key people are located and how mobile or permanent such locations are. The location plan is particularly important if an organization is planning on growing, either in terms of its functions or, in terms of its geographical spread. Basic geographical factors, such as transport networks and proximity to important social or service networks nodes, are important here.

Steps 7–11 – Functional plans: finance; sales and marketing; technology and IT plans, HRM plans

We now turn to the activites required to discharge the planning assumptions made in Steps 4–6, or how to achieve the 'what, who and where' of the integrated business plan. The execution of these activities can be achieved by the **functional division of labour, skills and resources**. These are commonly discharged by the familiar specialist departments found within large organizations of Human Resource Management, Finance, Marketing, and Information and Technological support. Not all VNPOs will have such clear divisions and some may not have any specialist departments. In such circumstances all staff will need to have multi-functional skills.

Finance

Within a number of organizations there exits a tension between what is regarded as the most important or foremost function in the business planning process. This tension is often polarized around whether the business plan should be predominantly marketing led (and so ideologically reflecting an organizational response to the environment and consumer) or financially led (and so reflecting resource control). In for-profit organizations the finance function does tend to dominate activites, because of its clear association with monetary liquidity and profitability. Financial liquidity is equally important to VNPOs for their continued survival, but the profit motivator is less clear, or not a motivator at all. Acceptable levels of surplus not for redistribution are an issue, but the role/use of these surpluses is to continue the work of the organization.

Within the financial plan there are a number of requirements – namely, the need to estimate and forecast expenditure and income and to link these ideally to some measure of activity. Capital expenditure plans will need to be itemized. A cash flow schedule needs to be prepared and an overall statement of the organizational funding, expressed in a balance sheet, needs to be presented. Where relevant, a forecast of surplus/or loss can be presented together with a statement of liquidity and cash flow. These issues are covered in detail in the chapter on financial accounting later in this book.

Sales and marketing

This area is dealt with in detail in the chapter on marketing, and if an organization has a strategic marketing plan then these need to be fully integrated into the business plan. The business plan will need to be well-informed by feedback from users and funders either by *ad hoc* or continuous user satisfaction and consumer surveys. From the point of view of the business planning aspects of marketing, it is difficult to improve upon the classic marketing mix definitions of product, promotion, price and place. These can be used to design the service characteristics to meet the needs of the organization and of the user (product); to have effective communication (promotion); to place a real nominal value on services (price) and to have an effective organization and distribution (place). In turn, the VNPO can design their support marketing functions accordingly.

Technology and information systems

Technology can be viewed as a source of innovation within an organization, or it can be viewed as a functional support to help innovation. Much will depend upon the reason for the existence of the VNPO. The UK Keep Able Foundation exists to make available the very best of cutting edge technology for physically disabled persons. As such, therefore, technology *per se* is part of its strategic aims and objectives. For others, the existence of technological possibilities is a contingent factor for an organization to take account of and respond to. The key issues with regard to information technology are covered in another chapter in this book.

Human resource management

It could be argued that it is only through the human management of technology and the work and commitment of human labour that any of the aims and objectives within the business plan are achieved. Human Resource Management (HRM) encompasses a number of functions. The personnel function involves labour data management, counselling, health and safety, the implementation and monitoring of employment law within the organization, recruitment and administrative duties (such as the interpretation of contracts, terms and conditions). Usually these functions will continue without undue alteration. However, when the consequences of the business aims and objectives result in change to the organization then the HRM function is required to adopt a more strategic and forward thinking role.

In particular, the VNPO may require a review of its skills profile. In part this will have been completed during the resource audit stage, and any excess or lack of skills will now need to be addressed. Skill mismatches will involve solutions which are dependent upon recruitment of permanent or temporary staff and volunteers, or they can be addressed by training and development. The need for training is a very important and often disregarded consequence of the business planning process. It is also likely that there will be further training needs as a result of the planning process. Inevitably these have financial costs which need to be built in to the business plan.

Steps 12–13 – Implementation and evaluation

These final two steps are not ones specific to business planning. They are part of the ongoing management of an organization. The key issues here have been covered elsewhere in this book, and in particular in the chapters on equal opportunities and anti-oppressive practice, project management and performance/quality management. It would be useful to review these chapters in tems of their role and impact upon the business planning process.

PROCESSES, SKILLS AND TECHNIQUES

Forecasting

Business plans can vary considerably in respect of their degree of sophistication and level of analysis which are used. Almost all require some form of **forecasting** – particularly in respect of forecasting future measurable activities, and of finance. Forecasting is all about predicting the future and as a consequence involves a number of pitfalls, not least our inability to predict uncertain events and the need to try and reduce the probability of errors. There are a number of quantitative techniques which can be used in forecasting. These are quite technical and one of the specialist texts (such as Richardson and Richardson 1990) should be consulted.

There are also qualitative approaches to forecasting, namely scenario planning (Shim and McGlade 1989) which requires the generation of a number of descriptive options about the future which try to incorporate some extremes to evaluate future outcomes. Hence a 'worse case' and 'best case' scenario of the future can be envisaged. It is possible to incorporate some of the quantitative techniques mentioned above with the scenario planning approach to give a more informed approach and in turn to perform some sensitivity analysis upon the forecasts. This can be done by altering some of the variables which were used within the future forecasts and considering their impact. This is covered in more detail in the chapter on marketing.

Obviously, all these techniques are dependent upon some availability of reliable data – and in some cases, specialist skills to analyse it. This availability will vary enormously between VNPOs. A long-established housing charity or an international aid organization is more likely to have access to historical data for trend analysis than a newly established community sports and recreation club. Nonetheless, there are other sources of data available, particularly in the form of published data and also specially commissioned survey data. They key is to use what you have available and can handle.

Nationally published census data is a vital first step in business planning forecasting since so much of future activity is dependent upon the various socio-economic patterns of the population. Much detailed information can also be found in governmental social statistical publications. A recent development are **Geographical Information Systems** (GIS) which seek to provide computer-based correlations of socio-demographic variables with spatial variables. These can be either at a national, regional, or very local level such as a census enumeration district.

A final word upon forecasting should also be given to staff experience.

Many field workers have a wealth of experience about how a range of factors operate in reality, though it is unlikely that they have ever written down such experiences. A short amount of time spent gathering some of this experience by talking to field workers can be enormously beneficial to the business planning teams, and particularly for scenario planning.

Modelling

This is about trying to simulate some interrelated aspects of reality. It is a technique which can be used in conjunction with forecasting. Shim and McGlade (1989) provide a useful summary of the techniques. The beauty of modelling for business planning is that it allows for the interrelation of the activity targets, contract targets and financial data and so integrates much of this data in a summary form. Modelling does require access to a computer and sufficient skill to be able to construct some computerized routines. However, the more recent versions of commercial spreadsheet packages, such as Excel or Lotus 123, are more than adequate for the construction of models. Other computer-based techniques which may be of use are critical path analysis, networking and scheduling packages. These are particularly useful and, again, many commercially based **project planning** software packages incorporate these techniques which can be adapted for business planning purposes.

PRACTICALITIES

Business planning consumes resources: skills, money and time. Depending upon the complexity of a VNPO and its experience, some of these resources may be available in-house or may need to be brought in on a consultancy basis. Figure 7.2 summarizes the range of processes involved in business planning. Each has its associated resource requirement. The use of computer-based data storage can greatly assist the data gathering, analysis and assembly stage. Similarly, the availability of desktop publishing allows far greater flexibility in terms of amending the plan after consultation and reflection. The practicalities relating to decision-making, and the allocation of responsibility relate more to good communication and to having the time and space to reflect upon the consequence of decisions.

CONCLUSION AND CRITIQUE

How relevant is business planning to VNPOs? Using the seven differentiating criteria described earlier, it is possible to answer this question. In respect of the organizational, financial, collaborative and stakeholder characteristics of VNPOs there would appear to be direct relevance. This is reflected in the need for VNPOs to direct their efforts towards their strategic aim through their organizational structure, incorporating their wider audiences and partners. Through the rigour of planning and the

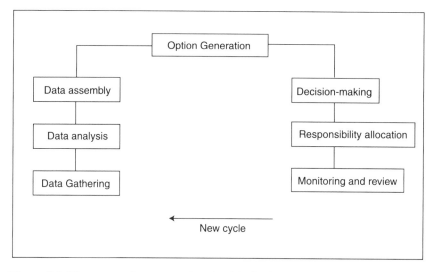

Figure 7.2 The range of processes involved in business planning

technical treatment of data which generates options for decisions, the business planning process can greatly help VNPOs achieve their strategic direction.

It is in terms of the core behavioural characteristics of VNPOs, like their ideology, philanthropic roots and encouragement of volunteering, that business planning may appear to have less relevance. However, this point relates very much to the **tone** of the business plan in terms of how it is expressed and presented. It is possible for the values of a VNPO to suffuse a business plan and make it value-based, rather than being a neutral collection of data and objectives. The decision to do this is your own. As a result of their increasing importance in our lives and their growing complexity, VNPOs are worthy of good management. Business planning is a technique which can assist in this process.

BUSINESS PLANNING CASE STUDY

The Armour Trust is an inner city voluntary organization specializing in providing practical support and counselling to people suffering from substance abuse. It has three full-time paid members of staff, headed up by a general manager and a non-executive board of eight members. It has been in existence for seven years and has a stable turnover of £370,000 per annum and variable additions of up to £50,000 per annum. Funding for the organization comes from local authority social services, two local health authorities, a charitable trust specializing in support for alcoholics and a small amount from voluntary fund-raising.

It was the general manager who initiated the idea of a business plan. The board and volunteers were quite happy 'to do more of the same', building on previous work patterns. Her idea was very unpopular with the other paid staff and even more so when she recruited, on a temporary basis, an ex-management consultant to assist in the business planning process, even though he was very empathetic towards the aims of the Trust having, in the past, suffered from drug abuse. The consultant brought with him an approach similar to the one described in the 'route map' in this chapter and the team of three staff and one volunteer clerical assistant set about their task.

The team had given themselves four months to develop the final draft of the business plan from scratch. It become immediately obvious that whilst most people felt that they knew how much activity went on in the Trust they were unable to quantify it. Nor was it possible for them to agree upon what a 'unit' of activity was; was it how many people who were assisted in their lives through the trained counsellors, or was it the total number of contracts in place with the local authority social services? The team was more successful in completeing its resource audit since it was a small labour, rather than capital, intensive organization. However, when it came to linking their various sets of data together to generate options for their future direction, the Trust realized that it had no idea where its future lay or what shape it wished to adopt for the future.

There were a number of practical difficulties too. The consultant had access to a PC with sufficient capacity to cope with spreadsheets and extensive word processing. However nobody, including the general manager, had anticipated just how long it would take to collate what data they had, and to edit and present the final copy of the plan. The consultant and the Trust parted company as a result of these difficulties, but a commitment to change had been established. In desperation, the general manager reached for the *Ron Johnson 24 Hour Business Plan* (1990) which gave her a page by page pro-forma approach to organizing the plan. The resulting plan may not have been the most sophisticated or comprehensive, but it did meet both the immediate needs and the resource constraints of the Trust.

The Trust learned a number of important lessons during the process. It was quite stressful for the team and involved additional work and considerable frustrations. On the other hand, the actual process issues involved (see Figure 7.2) made the Trust realize that it had more potential than it was exploiting and that their business systems were in need of improvement. At the end, the Trust was more clear about how its activity fitted to its strategic plan, its possible options for survival and growth in the future, and the financial and other organizational implications of each of these possibilities.

REFERENCES

Baine, S., Coleman, N. and Hilditch, S. (1994a) *The PCP Management Health Check*, NCVO, London.

Baine, S., Coleman, N. and Hilditch, S. (1994b) *Management Standards and the Voluntary Sector*, NCVO, London.

Billis, D. (1993) *Organizing Public and Voluntary Agencies*, Routledge, London.

Dobkin Hall, P. (1987) A historical overview of the private non profit sector, in *The Non Profit Sector: A Research Handbook* (ed W. Powell) Yale University Press, New Haven.

Johnson, R. (1990) *The 24 Hour Business Plan* Hutchinson Business Books, London.

Joseph, J. A. (1995) *Remaking America*, Jossey Bass, San Francisco.

Kanter, R. and Summers, D. (1987) Doing well while doing good: dilemmas of performance measurement in non profit organizations and the need for a multiple constituency approach in *The Non Profit Sector: A Research Handbook (ed W. Powell) Yale University Press, New Haven.*

Lane, J. and Saxon-Harrold, S. K. E. (1993) Corporate philanthropy in Britain, in *Researching the Voluntary Sector* (eds S. Saxon-Harrold and J. Kendall) Charities Aid Foundation, Tonbridge.

Lenz, R. T. and Lyles, M. A. (1989) Paralysis by analysis: is your planning system becoming too rational, in *Readings in Strategic Management* (eds D. Asch and C. Dowman) Macmillan, Basingstoke.

Poulton, G. (1988) *Managing Voluntary Organizations* Wiley, Chichester.

Prince, R. and File, K. (1995) *The Seven Faces of Philanthropy*, Jossey Bass, San Francisco.

Richardson, B. and Richardson, R. (1990) *Business Planning: An Approach to Strategic Management*, Pitman, London.

Salamon, L. and Anheier, H. (1995) The emerging sector: the non profit sector in comparative perspective – an overview, in *Researching the Voluntary Sector* (eds S. Saxon-Harrold and J. Kendall) Charities Aid Foundation, Tonbridge.

Scholes, K. and Klemm, M. (1987) *An Introduction to Business Planning* Macmillan, Basingstoke.

Shim, J. and McGlade, R. (1989) The use of corporate planning models: past, present and future, reprinted in *Readings in Strategic Management*, (eds D. Asch and C. Dowman) Macmillan, Basingstoke.

Smith, J. R. and Lipsky, M. (1993) *Non Profits for Hire: The Welfare State in the Age of Contracting*, Harvard University Press, Cambridge, Mass.

GUIDED READING:

For practical advice on getting started in business planning, I recommend: Richardson, B and Richardson, R. (1990) *Business planning: An Approach to Strategic Management*, Pitman, London. This is a practical book, well-grounded in theory.

Baine, S. Coleman, N. and Hilditch, S. (1994) *The PCP Management Health Check*, NCVO, London, is a short and effective checklist to help an organization focus upon business issues. It also has the added benefit of being directly targeted at nonprofit organizations.

Finally, a word of recommendation should also go to Johnson, R. (1990) *The 24 Hour Business Plan* Hutchinson Business Books, London. Whilst entirely based on a commercial model, its pro-forma approach really is a help in a crisis.

8 Project management for VNPOs

David Johnson

INTRODUCTION

In common with most organizations in the public and private sectors, VNPOs are increasingly experiencing forces of change which are both rapid and seemingly never-ending. Many of these changes are driven by new legislation, whilst others relate either to the changing client demands for services, or to the expectations of the funders of VNPOs. The outcome of these dynamic forces of change is that traditional organizational structures and management hierarchies are increasingly unsuited to the task in hand, which is more and more concerned with managing change rather than managing ongoing service-delivery processes.

As a result, more and more organizations are turning to flexible organizational structures and to project-based management approaches, two components of what, in the private sector, is increasingly being referred to as **business process re-engineering**. Thus a recent survey of organizations in Norway (Jesson 1994) found that 70% of private sector organizations and 45% of public sector bodies were using project management concepts and techniques to undertake virtually all of their ongoing operations. Similar statistics apply to advanced industrial countries such as Germany, Japan and the USA. Not surprisingly, then, many leading commentators agree with Turner (1993) that 'project-based management has become the new general management through which organizations respond to change . . . and hence project management is a skill that all managers need in their portfolio.'

The purpose of this chapter is, therefore, to look at the scope for applying project management ideas and methods to VNPOs. By the end of the chapter you should:

- have a good understanding of what is meant by project management;
- appreciate why project management is important to VNPOs, but also be aware of its problems and limitations;
- be able to identify a range of projects within your own organization; and

- be able to consider how the project management approach might best be developed for the purpose of addressing processes of change within your organization.

WHAT IS PROJECT MANAGEMENT?

In the most general sense, the meanings of the terms 'project' and 'project management' are virtually synonymous, that is 'to execute an assignment of work which will create beneficial change' (Anderson *et al.* 1987). A simple definition of **a project** is that it should have a reasonably finite beginning and end, and that it should be designed to deliver achievable and tangible results within that time frame, and normally within a given budget. More specifically, it should include the following key characteristics:

- multiple and composite goals and objectives
- uniqueness
- limitations of time, scope and cost
- the use of mixed resources
- involvement of people across organization structures

In addition, it can also be anticipated that multiple stakeholders (both within and without the parent organization) will have an interest in the way that projects are initiated and managed and this multiplicity of stakeholder interests is particularly evident in the voluntary sector. Moreover, this stakeholder interest is likely to relate to all aspects of the project in question, ranging from the aims of the project to its outcomes, and also with respect to the organizational arrangements and procedures that will be used to manage the project. Such a multiplicity of interests inevitably complicates the already complex endeavours which are typically required to succesfully undertake projects in the voluntary sector. They also emphasize the need for project management to embrace issues of objectives, of organization, of process and of outcomes. Far from being just a 'how to do' technique, therefore, project management requires multi-faceted abilities and skills and must also address the full range of management functions. Thus, in common with general management, project management encompasses planning, organizing, staffing, directing, controlling and evaluating functions. Good project management also requires good support systems, notably of information and communication channels, and clear designation of roles and responsibilities. Above all else, successful project management requires committed staff and strong and effective leadership.

It is clearly not possible in this chapter to discuss all these aspects of the project management task in detail; rather our approach is to fit them within the framework of a rational project planning and management (PPM) model, to identify the key tasks and issues associated with each stage of the model and to point the way for the potential development of best practices at each stage. It should be exphasized that, given the enormous range of VNPOs, and the variable complexities of managing such organizations, the use of a rational model to order the discussion is suggestive rather than prescriptive; the aim is to provide ideas and guidance for how these ideas might be developed in the context of an individual organization, not to lay down rigid formulae. Before turning our attention to the PPM model itself, let us therefore briefly consider what types of projects are relevant to you or your organization.

Project types

We have seen that the general purpose of any project is 'to bring about beneficial change' but what does this mean in terms of the actual changes involved? Some 'projects', for instance, may be very small and involve no more than one task or person – reorganizing your reception desk layout, for example – whilst others may involve virtually all aspects of an organization, and require the involvement of most, if not all, staff (for instance, a relocation to a different set of premises). Similarly, projects will vary considerably in terms of time and scope. As far as scope is concerned, Figure 8.1 sets out a range of typical project types under four main headings. It is immediately apparent that projects may relate to any aspect of an organization, with some projects directed to effecting changes under more than one heading. Whilst the list of headings is far from comprehensive, you should find that Figure 8.1 provides a useful starting point in thinking about the changes your organization has been recently undergoing, and those that may be coming along in the near future.

Electability, or, winning support for projects

In making the above suggestion it is recognized that the widespread adoption of the project management approach within an organization creates its own upheavals, so much so that many organizations in the process of transition away from traditional structures and delivery systems seriously question whether it is all worthwhile. Similarly, it is a not uncommon experience for supporters of project management to find themselves iso-

1. Products and Services	2. Organizational Arrangements	3. Physical Assets and Technical Infrastructure	4. People
Changes in/to: products services customers clients etc.	Changes in/to: structure systems processes roles responsibilities etc.	Changes in/to: site buildings plant and equipment computer systems communications etc.	Changes in/to: teams working arrangements incentives appraisal attitudes etc.

Figure 8.1 Project type

lated and unsupported by senior management in the existing hierarchy, who regard themselves as threatened by major innovations.

Certainly, with any project which threatens the status quo as regards either existing services or personnel, it is going to be more difficult to win support than for projects which reinforce the prevailing organizational arrangements or staff attitudes. Consequently, a key task is to undertake a 'pre-project electability appraisal' so that precious time and effort are not wasted at later stages of the process.

For example, trying to introduce a new computerized system of management information might well be a thankless task if senior staff feel threatened by what the information may reveal about themselves or their department. Even if such fears could be allayed, by consultation processes for example, the project could still be threatened by trying to make the change-over too quickly, or by not allowing sufficient time for system breakdowns. Indeed, the introduction of computers into organizations has probably been responsible for more 'unsuccessful' projects than any other type of project (Turner 1993).

As a quick, and very simple way of distinguishing possible 'winners' from almost certain 'dead ducks', you may find it useful to refer to the **Electability Index** set out in Figure 8.2, which scores a number of key, or critical success factors according to whether or not they are likely to lead to support for your project. The overall score will not tell you whether to try and go ahead with the full development of your project, but the technique does have the virtue of revealing danger areas that may need to be tackled if a feasible project is to be developed (for example, by resolving differences between multiple stakeholders, or rethinking the speed at which an innovative form of service delivery is to be introduced). In evaluation terms, the Electability Index can also perform a

Ownership by top management	Low	1	2	3	4	5	High
Stance of senior staff	Unsupportive	1	2	3	4	5	Supporting
Stakeholders	Many	1	2	3	4	5	Few
Purpose of project	Controversial	1	2	3	4	5	Uncontroversial
Process employed	Innovative	1	2	3	4	5	Familiar
Scale of project	Large	1	2	3	4	5	Small
Significance of project	Major	1	2	3	4	5	Minor
Speed of change created by project	Fast	1	2	3	4	5	Gradual
Unknowns and uncertainties	Many	1	2	3	4	5	Few

Maximum score = 45. In general, the higher the score the more likely it is that your project will win support at later stages of its development. Think carefully about projects with a low total score, or scoring only 1 or 2 against individual criteria.

Figure 8.2 The electability index: critical success factors

useful function in reviewing past project ideas that have been unsuccessful in winning support and pin pointing why.

THE RATIONAL PROJECT PLANNING AND MANAGEMENT (PPM) CYCLE

It is now appropriate to consider the various aspects and tasks of 'project management' in more detail and the simplest way of doing this is to consider what you are doing (or not doing!) in terms of the Rational Project Planning and Management (PPM) Cycle (Figure 8.3). The PPM model derives its strength from its universal applicability since, although different projects vary enormously in terms of their individual purpose and content they all, to a greater or lesser extent, require a reasonably common set of tasks to be undertaken if they are to be successful. These tasks (such as identification and design) can, in turn, conveniently be grouped under the four main stage headings of formulation, appraisal, implementation and evaluation. Whilst the term 'project management' properly encompasses all of these stages and tasks, it is common practice to regard the formulation and appraisal stages as comprising the 'planning phase' of projects, whilst the implementation and evaluation stages are sometimes referred to as the 'management phase'.

Irrespective of the terminology employed, it is clear that all projects have to start somewhere, that is, the need for them has to be identified by

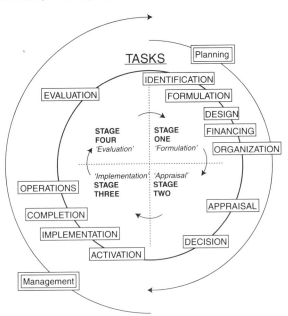

Figure 8.3 Phases, stages and tasks of the Rational Project Planning and Management Cycle

someone or other, and their purpose has to be formulated and articulated in the form of meaningful objectives. Then some more detailed design work needs to be undertaken so that the size, scope, cost and timing of the project in question can be estimated. In this regard, the funding and financing arrangements for VNPO projects are often critical and it is therefore important that this task is singled out for particular attention before proceeding to an overall appraisal of project options. The appropriate organizational arrangements for managing the project also have to be determined before proceeding any further, and it is advisable to establish an appropriate set of monitoring and reporting procedures in order to review progress during and after implementation.

After these intial 'planning phase' tasks have been completed it is essential that some form of formal appraisal is undertaken of the various project options so that an informed decision can be made as to whether or not to commit resources to the implementation of the preferred option. This is stage two of the project cycle and experience suggests that this stage is both the most important and yet the most neglected aspect of project planning. This aspect of good practice is therefore examined in greater detail later in this chapter.

Once a decision to go ahead with the project has been taken the 'planning phase' comes to an end and the 'management phase' begins. Assuming that a sufficient amount of work has been undertaken on the scheduling of the project in the planning phase, this will be primarily concerned with the actual implementation of the project, its control, completion and incorporation into the ongoing activities of the organization. During the management phase various forms of monitoring should be carried out and, in the case of major projects, some form of evaluation and review undertaken after the project has been completed.

Figure 8.3 sets out these various project stages. In practice, of course, many projects do not follow this logical sequence of events, some stages either being omitted altogether or, conversely, undertaken in parallel (for example, a preferred set of organizational arrangements may be identified by a project manager who simultaneously makes up his or her mind regarding the preferred project option). However, irrespective of current forms of practice it is invariably worth comparing such practice against the idealized PPM model if only to confirm that all the various angles have been adequately covered, and the appropriate questions asked. It is also important to recognize that these questions may need to be asked more than once and, indeed, a project may need to pass through the planning phase of the model several times before it is appropriate to operationalize it.

Project appraisal

Project appraisal lies at the heart of project management and is an art which should be learnt and developed by all managers aspiring to lead their organizations into the next decade. It has a number of functions, in enabling better decisions to be made, in providing a framework for rational thinking about the use of limited resources, and in stimulating policy makers and managers to question and justify what they are trying to do.

There are, however, many different kinds of appraisal and it is especially important to recognize the distinction between the use of appraisal techniques for the purposes of project formulation as opposed to the employment of a 'formal appraisal' process to make key project decisions. This distinction is particularly relevant to those VNPOs which bid for public funds for their projects (for example, for monies from the Single Regeneration Budget to assist in the provision of services to inner city residents) as such bids will be subject to a consistent formal project appraisal procedure by government irrespective of the internal appraisal procedures employed. Moreover, in any well-managed organization there should be some functional separation of those who are responsible for intiating and formulating projects, from those who are responsible for making decisions as to whether or not to commit resources to their implementation. It follows that regardless of the particular appraisal techniques employed, the final results of the appraisal process should enable 'information to be gathered and presented in an objective fashion to decision-makers, to assist them to reach an informed and rational choice between alternative courses of action' (HM Treasury 1991).

Fundamental project appraisal questions

This brings us to the question of how project appraisal is acutally undertaken, but before we consider techniques we need to establish some fundamentals. Irrespective of the particular technique employed, project appraisal can usefully be described in general terms, 'as the process of defining objectives, examining options and weighing up their costs and benefits before deciding whether to proceed'. (Johnson 1994).

Thus, if we examine the fundamental reason for undertaking any sort of project ('the creation of beneficial change') we can recognize that, irrespective of our ability to measure and value the particular **benefits** concerned, those benefits are definable by their outputs and outcomes. In short, it is these that provide a project with its rationale or provide the project with its answer to the inevitable question **why?** However, in order to identify, measure and, if possible, value these benefits we need to ask two more fundamental questions, namely **what?** (as in what sort of outcomes, and what volume of outputs) and **for whom?** (as in who gains? and are these the people/clients/customers/target population that we want to gain?). Asking these questions in the early stages of project identification (and, indeed, re-asking them at all stages of project development) is invaluable in terms of focusing projects, the setting of objectives and the identification of relevant output and performance measures. It is these factors which determine the **desirability** of the project under consideration.

Turning now to a consideration of the **costs** of alternative project options, our attention is drawn to the various processes that we are thinking of using and also the way in which we intend to manage these processes – that is, **how** are we going to provide our new service, and **how** are we going to manage the process of setting up a new facility. Then we need to consider the inputs required for the new facility, and how much they are likely to cost.

These questions all relate in various ways to the issue of **feasibility**, which is concerned with how projects work, how difficult they are, how practicable and how costly. In summary, the purpose of the appraisal process is to identify those project options which are desirable and likely to be feasible, likely to be effective, efficient and economical, and likely to show the best return in terms of benefits compared with costs.

However, the particular emphasis of the appraisal process will, quite rightly, vary from project to project. In some cases, for example, everyone in an organization may quickly agree that a certain type of project is both desirable, and likely to be effective in terms of its objectives, but also recognize that there are question marks about its feasibility. In this case, the appraisal process will necessarily concentrate on the feasibility factors relating to **each** project option. Conversely, (and perhaps all too often), projects are pursued because it is thought that they **can** be done (i.e. they are feasible) without sufficient attention being given to the question of whether they **should** be done.

Benefits	Costs
Outputs and Outcomes	Inputs and Processes
Why? What? For Whom?	How?
How Worthwhile?	How Difficult
Desirability	Feasibility
Effectiveness	Economy and Efficiency

Figure 8.4 Feasibility of projects

In practice, of course, desirability and feasibility are only part of the appraisal story for two reasons. The first is that it is often extremely difficult to predict how projects are going to turn out because of the many unknowns and uncertainties that may be present at the project planning phase. Consequently, different project options will carry different levels of **risk**, and these need to be taken explicitly into account. Second, the pressures and realities of the real world mean that VNPOs have to respond to considerations other than just producing 'good' projects. In particular, both probity and accountability need increasingly to be demonstrated by the audit trails that are left on file by the appraisal process, and these accountability requirements can both slow down and, in some cases, introduce undue caution into appraisal judgements. On the other hand, the need to demonstrate action (for instance, following an injection of public sector funding) can lead to pressures in the opposite direction, with short cuts being taken at all stages of the project management cycle. The consequence is that project appraisal for VNPOs, even for highly capable organizations, is a delicate balancing act between the development of good projects, the necessary expenditure and accountability requirements.

Formulating project objectives and evaluating performance

It is one thing to talk about the 'desirability' of projects – it is another to consider how this desirability is to be meaningfully identified and specified in the form of project objectives. The first thing to recognize is that all projects are a means to an end and not ends in themselves, even if project managers sometimes think so! For instance, the construction of a new waiting-room for clients could be seen as completed when it is open, but the real reason for constructing it is the enhanced quality of experience it is capable of giving to future clients. It is these latter beneficial effects which comprise the **outcomes** of the project and, ideally, all project managers should attempt to specify the objectives of projects in ways which relate to project outcomes. In the case of the enlarged waiting room facility, for instance, the project proposal might recommend building a new waiting-room in order to enable the VNPO to see 50% more clients, to enable each client to be seen within 15 minutes of entering the waiting room and to reduce the level of client complaints by 30%.

In terms of our previous discussion, these planned outcomes are the **why**? and **for whom**? of the project, whilst the completed waiting room is its **what**? Whilst, in the above example there will clearly need to be quite specific objectives for the construction of the waiting-room itself (these we can refer to as intermediate objectives) it is the effects of the resultant enhanced service delivery which comprise the final set of objectives. Expressing these final objectives of the project quite specifically in terms of desired project outcomes also means that they score well against the criteria for assessing the meaningfulness of project objectives, namely that they should focus the project, be capable of testing its success and communicate real information rather than vague aspirations.

In order to fully respond to these requirements, project managers ideally need to develop relevant performance indicators and targets, (see the chapter on performance management) and get these agreed by both senior management and the project team itself, before implementing the project in question. In practice, few VNPO projects include performance indicators and targets as part of the project formulation process and hence it is extremely difficult to objectively assess the 'success' of projects after they have been completed.

The role of stakeholders

We have previously referred briefly to stakeholders in our discussion of critical success factors and, in practice, stakeholders are often the most crucial factor governing the success of VNPO projects. In the simplified waiting-room project example given above, it might seem at first glance that there are only three sets of stakeholders, namely the project manager, the constructors of the new waiting-room, and the final service users. However, there are usually many groups of stakeholders who have an interest in the operations of VNPOs, and in the development of new projects, and the waiting-room project would be no exception. These multiple stakeholders can usefully be grouped into six main categories:

- those benefiting from a new facility (users and clients, etc.);
- those involved in the production of new service facilities (suppliers, constructors etc.);
- those involved in the operation of new service facilities (managers, staff etc.);
- those who control or influence resources and funding (Board of Governors, grant awarding bodies etc.);
- those wielding political influence (politicians, media, pressure groups etc.); and
- those who influence the environment within which the VNPO operates (neighbours, local authorities etc.)

In the case of our waiting-room project, it is obvious that several of these stakeholder groupings would be influential in determining the success of the new facility, in addition to the three stakeholder categories mentioned above and whilst it would be unrealistic to suppose that project objectives should be formulated to take account of **all** such stakeholders, it is also naïve to formulate project objectives without at least taking due account of the needs and influence of all **key** stakeholders. In the worst case scenario, key stakeholders might be able to prevent projects going ahead if they are not consulted, but at the very least they may hinder and undermine the effectiveness of otherwise successful projects. It is therefore important, when identifying and formulating project objectives, to identify key stakeholders and win their support before proceeding too far down the line.

Project-based organizational arrangements

Apart from satisfying key stakeholders, the most crucial factor determining whether or not a VNPO will be able to successfully develop project-based service delivery mechanisms is the extent to which the organization can adapt its existing organizational arrangements to incorporate the temporary, cross-boundary arrangements which are needed to plan, implement and manage projects. Thus the typical project will cut across existing professional or organizational divisions and will also require multi-disciplinary teamwork if it is to be successful. It will also need, not only clearly defined roles and responsibilities for a range of people from top management down to support staff, but also properly identified and demarcated procedures and reporting processes so that the progress of the evolving project can be sensibly monitored and assessed by the relevant parties.

In practice, it is often the case that these conditions are not met and project managers may find themselves struggling to communicate adequately with top management, or gaining the co-operation of other departments, even if they are able to manage the work of the project team itself. Moreover, project managers – especially for large or complex projects – need to be equipped with a wide range of interpersonal skills, as well as technical knowledge, if they are to be successful. In order to secure a sense of ownership and commitment to the changes that will be brought about by projects, a participative style of management is required, entailing the ability to communicate, negotiate and team-build and to generally involve staff in the project development process. Whilst many managers have these interpersonal skills already, in others they need to be developed. Hence the instigation of project-based management approaches requires both a culture change on the part of the parent organization, due to the need to be flexible and accept the need for cross-boundary organization arrangements, and the development of project managers having not only the requisite technical abilities but also the inter-personal skills that projects increasingly entail.

LESSONS

In conclusion, what are the essential differences between project management and general, or operational, management and what opportunities and challenges confront a VNPO that is seeking to develop project-based initiatives? As far as the first question is concerned, the main differences between project management and general management stem from the inherent nature of all projects, that they have (or should have) a reasonably finite beginning and end, that they are designed to deliver achievable and tangible results within that time frame and normally within a given budget. Project managers therefore need to be more goal oriented than their general management counterparts since their success or failure depends almost wholly on their ability to deliver effective results within a relatively short time-scale compared with normal operational activities. Projects therefore provide good opportunities for focused efforts, for leadership, and for the development and application of a wide range of management skills and techniques.

This last point is particularly important since, as we have seen, the ability to develop and deliver successful projects requires a wide range of both technical and interpersonal skills. In particular, project-based managment organizations quickly have to learn how to set up teams, how to reconcile temporary organizational arrangements within a corporate structure, how to acquire the necessary skills and techniques for managing projects, how to appraise and evaluate projects, and how to incorporate the lessons of project evaluation for the future development of the organization's service delivery systems.

There is no simple, or single, answer for resolving these questions and it would be unrealistic to expect dramatic changes in managerial practices overnight. Never the less, the early experience of those VNPOs that have been attempting to develop a culture of 'management by projects' shows that significant benefits can be achieved given committed project managers and a willingness to innovate on the part of the organization. These qualities will be increasingly in demand during the next decade as the forces of change, that have become all too evident in the early 90s, continue to exert their influence on VNPOs.

REFERENCES

Anderson, E. *et al.* (1987) *Goal Directed Project Management*, Kogan Page, London.
HM Treasury (1991) *Economic Appraisal in Central Government Departments: A Technical Guide*, HMSO, London.
Jesson, S. (1994) The use of the project approach in Norway, in *Proceedings of the IRNOP Conference on Temporary Organizations and Project Management*, Lycksele, Sweden.
Johnson, D. (1994) *Review of Project Appraisal Systems and Practice*, PSMRC, Aston University, Birmingham.
Turner, J. (1993) *The Handbook of Project Based Management*, McGraw Hill, London.

GUIDED READING

Any of the books below offer a good introduction to the practice of project management:

Boddy, D. and Buchanan, D. (1992) *Take the Lead - Interpersonal Skills for Project Managers*, Prentice Hall, New Jersey.

Burton, C. and Michael, N. (1993) *A Practical Guide to Project Management*, Kogan Page, London.

Cleland, D. and King, W. (1988) *Project Management Handbook*, Van Nostrand Reinhold.

Duff, B. and Haward, J. (1993) *Project Management Manual*, Longman, London.

Harrison, F. (1985) *Advanced Project Management*, Gower, Aldershot.

Thomsett, M. (1992) *The Little Black Book of Project Management*, Kogan Page, London.

9 The management of change

Bill Tassie, Asaf Zohar and Vic Murray

INTRODUCTION

By the end of this chapter you should be able to:

- describe the need for change faced by most VNPOs in the world today;
- to identify the primary approaches to change management that are available to practising executives in this sector; and
- understand their application:

Every VNPO must deal with an environment in which there are stakeholders who have the power to determine whether it lives or dies. For example, it must be able to raise funds and attract those for whom it provides services, as well as the appropriate staff and volunteers; and it must comply with financial and legal regulations administered by various government institutions and maintain the goodwill of a variety of influential groups in the community. The problem is that the agendas of these key stakeholder groups can, and do, change over time and vary between groups. If the VNPO is unable to adapt to their changing expectations and needs, it runs a serious risk of being destroyed.

In the last decade of the 20th century the environment of VNPOs around the world is changing as never before. Consequently, the VNPOs themselves must be adaptable to an as yet unsurpassed degree if they want to survive and flourish into the next millennium. This means that the management skills required to create an organization able to change constantly and effectively become the most important skills a VNPO executive can process.

THE WAVES OF CHANGE AND THEIR MANAGERIAL IMPLICATIONS

Consider the following four trends:

1 In many countries of eastern Europe, Latin America and Asia 'civil society' (the myriad of associations made up of citizens organized to help themselves and others) is only now emerging (or in some cases re-

emerging) from decades during which the state controlled all the areas in which they are now active. These countries are having to virtually create a voluntary sector from scratch, and with it a relationship to government.

2 Most of the countries in the so-called developed or western world have had a voluntary sector for some time, though it has varied considerably from country to country. The characteristic which most distinguishes these variations has been the relationship of the sector to the state. In much of mainland Europe, for example, the sector has been relatively small and heavily funded by the state or sponsored by religious organizations. In Britain and Canada the sector has been larger but also heavily dependent on government for funding. The US has had perhaps the largest voluntary sector, and it has been least dependent on funding from governments – though government support is by no means unimportant even there.

Without doubt, the most significant change in the sector in most of these countries over the past five years has been the changes in the nature of the relationship to government. Some of the ways the relationship is changing is as follows:

- large-scale, across-the-board reductions in government grants and increases in the purchase of contracted services (as in the US);

- changing areas of emphasis – for example, less general support of VNPOs, and more focused support of only certain sub-sectors, coupled with significant cuts in others (as in Britain);

- 'privatizing' quangos (quasi-autonomous non-government organizations), by making them legally independent from government and providing them with substantially smaller 'lump sum' grants, and expecting them to raise far larger amounts of their own income (for example, aspects of the British health care system); and

- 'devolution' – the shifting of control of non-profits from central governments at the national or regional levels to local communities, often through the creation of new community level supervisory organizations. The new community 'overseers' then administer a significantly reduced block grant of money. This is a common phenomenon in the health and social services in many provinces across Canada, where provincial governments used to make decisions about the funding of each individual hospital. This responsibility has now been given to District Health Councils, while at the same time the total amount of money available to be distributed has been reduced.

3 In many countries there is growing disillusionment with what 'professional helpers' are able to do in eliminating the problems they are ostensibly trying to solve. Both government and large mainstream non-profit organizations are being attacked for being self-serving and out of touch with the real needs of the user of their services. The call is

to make those organizations more 'accountable to their communities' (see McKnight 1995).

4 As part of the drift to the political right found in many countries, there is a general belief that organizations not subject to competition and market forces cannot be efficient and effective. This applies to both government and VNPOs. With it goes the call for such organizations to demonstrate that they are accomplishing their goals as inexpensively as possible. This rhetoric is quickly picked up by funders of all types.

In response to these four (and other) trends, VNPOs are having to change. They are having quickly to learn how to do a large number of things differently. Many of the other chapters in this book give examples of the host of changes that are being required by VNPOs. This chapter concentrates on the management of the **change process** for these issues.

SPECIAL CHARACTERISTICS OF VNPOS THAT AFFECT THEIR ABILITY TO CHANGE

One of the reasons that there are so many 'how to do it' books and practising consultants focused on helping executives to manage change is because it is not easy. It may be easy enough for one person to see the need to change but getting others to also see the same need, to agree on what changes to make and to implement them effectively is no mean feat, especially if the changes are large and frequent as the previous section implies they must be for most modern VNPOs.

In addition, VNPOs have a number of unique characteristics which compound the problem of change management. These include:

Commitment to organizational values

Probably the most distinctive characteristic of most VNPOs is that their members are imbued with a strong emotional attachment to 'the cause' (i.e. the mission of the organization). On the surface, it might seem as though this characteristic would **facilitate** change rather than inhibit it ('Anything to help us do our job better,' etc.). Paradoxically, however, the commitment to values can often have the opposite effect because it involves not only a belief in the mission, but also a deep attachment to pre-existing ways of doing things, such as professional treatment modalities, forms of artisitic expression, or policy positions. Values can get to be seen as principles, and nothing is more difficult to change than people who feel their principles are being threatened.

Lack of a market mechanism

For most VNPOs (indeed also for many public sector organizations as well) their sources of income are not directly determined by the willingness of their beneficiaries to purchase the services offered. This means that it is possible to deny one of the most potent motives for change – a steep decline in 'customer satisfaction'. Beneficiaries may be increasingly poorly served but, unless this eventually causes those who control resources to apply pressure for change, it is possible for the leaders of a VNPO to ignore this.

Vague, multiple, difficult to measure objectives

A drastic decline in sales, changing consumer tastes, new, more cost efficient, technologies, can all trigger needed changes in business organizations since they can be measured against relatively clear benchmarks, and connect closely to the bottom line of profit and loss. In many VNPOs, however, it is exceedingly difficult to evaluate outcomes and hence to diagnose what needs to be changed. This is often because of their multiple objectives. Furthermore, these multiple objectives often have no clear priority ranking. In the case of a multi-programme community service agency, for example, which groups should receive what kind of assistance: youth at risk, seniors, or recent immigrants? Moreover, how is one to measure the impact of the help provided? Given these difficulties it is possible for various stakeholders to form their own, diverse, opinions about what needs to be changed and to end up in a 'change gridlock', in which no agreement can be reached, and hence little happens.

Chronic resource scarcity

Especially at the present time, many VNPOs feel extraordinarily pressed for funds. They have had to cut back programmes or staff or to do the same as before with less money. Again, from one perspective, this ought to make the organization more than usually open to change but, again, this isn't necessarily so. The effect of high stress has been shown to bring on a bunker mentality (Osborne 1992) in which denial of the need for change and an inability to think beyond the short-term are prominent features.

Clearly managing change in VNPOs is difficult. Yet, in spite of the fact that there are a number of such conditions facing the VNPO manager and which make it particularly difficult to achieve successful change, change none the less does occur, with many examples of success. The following sections describe and illustrate the essentials of effective change management within VNPOs.

APPROACHES TO MANAGING CHANGE

Drucker (1985) has stated that if the present-day management of VNPOs can be compared to a river voyage most, if not all, are presently attempting to negotiate white water rapids. How can we manage to keep our organisation afloat in these turbulent waters? How can we manage the transition from times of stability and certainty to constant flux and uncertainty? As they ride precariously down the rapids, the advice that VNPOs receive from the academics and consultants that crowd the shore is often confusing and contradictory. In such circumstances it is inevitable that practitioners feel confused, overwhelmed by and ultimately cynical about the enormous amount and variety of choices and advice on how to manage change that they are offered. Who are we to believe? What practices should we follow? Where does the future of effective change management lie?

At the same time, many change management initiatives within many types of organizations have failed or have delivered disappointing results (Beer, Eisenstat and Spector 1990, Hammer and Champy 1993; Kotter 1995). In this section we offer a framework for examining approaches taken to change management, with particular attention to the different conditions and circumstances that may make the selection of one approach over the other more readily apparent. We then address the phenomenon of unsuccessful change initiatives in terms of these approaches, and discuss an emerging approach that may be more appropriae to the situations facing managers in VNPOs. These frameworks and ideas are presented with the intention of charting the ways VNPOs can conceptually and practically determine their own unique starting point for navigating the white waters that lie ahead.

A framework for approaches to change management for VNPO managers

Managers interested in change initiatives can choose from among many prescriptions to fashion an approach for their organizations. One aspect of these prescriptions addresses the **type of change** envisioned. Definitions of the type of change vary. Developmental, transitional and transformational (Ackerman 1986), tuning, adaptation, re-creation and reorientation (Nadler and Tushman 1989), incremental, retro-fit and greenfield (Neal and Trom- ley 1995), or evolution and punctuated equilibrium (Gersick 1991) are all different classifications. Another aspect of these presceiptions addresses the **change process**. Regardless of the type of change, these prescriptions offer 'blueprints' for roles, principles and best practice (e.g. Gabarro and Schlesinger 1983; Jick 1993; Kanter 1983; Price Waterhouse Change Integration Team 1995).

Underlying most typologies and prescriptions in the literature is the notion that successful change is realized through large scale **programma- tic** approach to change management. Large-scale change initiatives, such as business process re-engineering (Hammer and Champy 1993; Watson 1994) and Total Quality Management (Hackman and Wageman 1995) are typically designed and driven by the organization's top management, who subsequently oversee the implementation of the programme. Not as explicit, but perhaps more important, is he deeper assumption that conditions will remain stable after the changes have been planned, a situation similar to that described by Mintzberg (1994) in relation to strategic planning.

This assumption is deeply embedded in the Western cultural assumptions integral to the thinking of many management practitioners and academics, a thinking based on a Newtonian mechanistic paradigm oriented to stability and predicability (Markley 1991; Znaniecki 1980). The argument is that change is transient – a bumpy unstable period where organizations need to ride a brief stretch of rapids in order to resume their placid journey 'just around the next bend' in the river.

An example of a change initiative grounded in these traditional assumptions is the implementation of a new organizational restructuring plan. Faced with mounting criticism from funders that the organization is not sufficiently 'client focused', the Executive Director brings in a team of consultants to address the issue. Detailed analyses are undertaken, resulting in plans and documents that outline a series of new contingencies and structural changes that are directed at addressing the situation. While there may be some disruption and even discontent during the implementation process, organizational members are assured that 'things will stabilize' once the new organizational system is adopted. The immediate threat of funder discontent has been addressed and the ED now feels that, until the next crisis, the VNPO can enter another stable period relatively uninterrupted, routine practice.

There is another view. Its roots lie in the 'new physics' and **chaos theory**. It is oriented to indeterminancy, unclear cause-effect relationships, non-linear relationships between variables and variables whose properties are influenced by the very act of measurement (Barrow 1992; Carnap 1966; D'Espagnat 1985; Glieck 1988). The underlying idea of this alternate approach to the change process is that order, pattern and structure emerge from apparent disorder through a process of self-organization (Wheatley 1992; Stacey 1992). Key aspects of this approach have served as the basis for the development of novel approaches to change management that view **environmental uncertainty** as a key point of departure for generating creative, emergent solutions to organizational problems (Goldstein 1994).

An example of this self-organizing approach to change is the implementation of a new computer system for case management. Starting out as a straightforward automation of case record-keeping, it soon leads to discussion of what constitutes a 'case'. This leads to examining the need to provide support to the family, and the natural network of people in need of services, rather than a 'treat the individual' approach. Soon, the very way the VNPO carries out its activities is subject to revision and ultimately a new mission emerges to refeflect the agency's approach.

Either the programmatic or self-organizing approach can be valid in certain circumstances. The choice of approach will depend on perceptions of the predictability of the external environment of the VNPO, the clarity of the links betwen means and ends, and the relationship between these factors and the approach. Figure 9.1 illustrates these possible relationships.

This figure provides a three-dimensional framework for considering the various approaches to change management. The first dimension relates to the relative predictability of the external environment: to what extent can change in external conditons be clearly understood and predicted? The second aspect is the link between means and ends: to what degree of certainty can one assume that a given process will produce a given outcome? The third dimension is the approach to change management: how programmatic should the approach be, given the perceptions of environmental predictability and means-ends relationships?. The key challenge of successful change management in VNPOs lies in establishing an appropriate degree of 'fit' or congruence between these three critical dimensions. In the following section, we argue that the failure of most change initiatives in VNPOs can be attributed to an inability to match the adopted approach

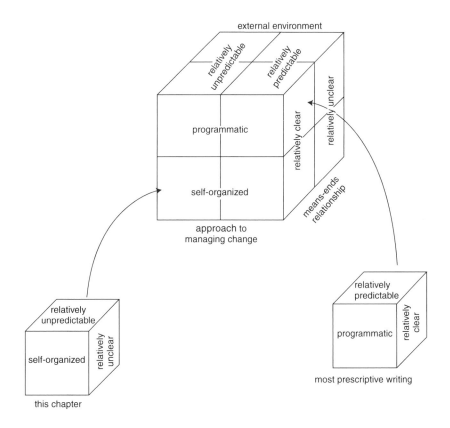

Figure 9.1 Matching the approach with the situation in VNPO management

to change (programmatic or self-organized) with the situation (external environment or means/ends relationships orientated).

Why programmatic change initiatives often fail to produce change

Much of the current writing on change management assumes both environmental predictability and clear means-ends relationships. This is the 'relatively predictable – relatively clear – programmatic' segment of Figure 9.1. These conditions do, in fact, exist for certain situations, such as the devlopment of certain kinds of programme modifications, a move to a new facility, or the implementation of a new technology. For example, an agency serving children might decide to acquire a computerized case management system to reduce the administrative work for its case workers. The functionality of the system can be described in terms of intake, client profiles, resource availability, case history, and the like. Vendor selection, procurement, implementation and staff training can be planned and executed according to plan. Here the future for case management is predictable, the specific activities to be carried out are relatively clear, so the programmatic approach to change is appropriate. The waters are smooth.

This conventional programmatic approach generally involves a split between the role of change strategist (usually top management) and change implementor (usually middle management) – the change is top-down. It also involves a SWOT (strengths, weaknesses, opportunities, threats) analysis, which defines what needs to be changed to lead to a desired future stae, a state that is de-coupled from the past. The strategists are expected to be able to rally organizational stakeholders behind a 'vision', and to convince the stakeholders of the need to change in the line with this vision. Then an implementation plan, with specific goals and clear responsibilities, can be developed. Enabling structures, both practical and symbolic, are put in place as mechanisms for implementing change, and the change process. Through communication and participation, other organizational members are involed in the implementation. Once implemented, the change is institutionalized.

This approach appears to be sound, so long as the critical assumptions described earlier are satisfied. In order to examine the relevance of these assumptions, managers need to ask themselves a number of basic questions. Does the organizational culture encourage a top-down approach? Often with community-based organizations, this top-down approach is an anathema. Can the future state be predicted? Often VNPOs face such uncertainty that a prediction of a specific future state as a basis for action can risk the existence of the organization. Can the future state be decoupled from the past? Often the roots in its traditions are so deep, and devotion to the cause is so strong, that a major change can destroy the essence of a VNPO. Will stakeholders rally around a vision for the organization? Many managers have experienced conflicting stakeholder demands, for example, in boards that are sufficiently fragmented to prohibit consensus on minor issues, let alone major changes to the agency. Can specific goals be developed? As many commentators have noted, it is difficult to articulate clear goals for many VNPOs; articulating both current and new goals may prove to be a daunting task. Should the change be institutionalized? Overcoming 'organizational sclerosis' is one of the key challenges in instituting change, and allowing the change to become institutionalized, while tempting, may make it more difficult to make future changes.

The programmatic approach will work if stakeholders can reach consensus on a desired vision for a specific future state; can agree on the specific goals for a change programme; can determine the links between operations and goal achievement; can develop an implementation plan that foresees future contingencies; and can successfully implement this plan. While this scenario is not impossible, it is certainly atypical for many VNPOs for the present as well as the foreseeable future. Thus it can be expected that in these circumstances, a programmatic approach to change will not produce the desired results – regardless of the degree of managerial effort, sincerity, or dedication to the plan itself.

A self-organizing approach to managing change

The term **self-organization** describes the process of radical transformation and renewal in the structure and functioning of complex systems (Goldstein 1994). Inspired by recent developments in the natural sciences, it describes how complex systems successfully meet the challenges of turbulent conditions through a self-generated, self-guided organizing process (Wheatley 1992). Basically, these natural systems appear to **organize themselves** in fundamental ways in order to adapt to radically changing environments. Research on the dynamics of self-organization by such authors as physicist and Nobel Laureate Illya Prigogine, suggest that complex systems possess an inherent ability to reorganize and renew themselves in fundamental ways. This has led to the development of new ways of understanding of the process of change in **social** systems. Organizational research has witnessed the emergence of novel approaches to the nature of successful leadership, strategy and change management inspired by this perspective (Stacey 1992; Romme 1992).

These novel insights into the nature and process of change in complex natural systems appear to lend support and legitimacy to a well-established, yet often neglected, stream of change management literature in the nonprofit and government sector. Charles Lindblom (1959; 1979) developed a theory of public policy formulation that was based on an incremental, emergent process which he described as 'muddling through'. He used the term **successive limited comparisons** to describe an explicitly incremental method of policy formulation which evolves through a series of relatively small but significant policy choices. From this perspective, successful policies and strategies evolve through the negotiation of multiple competing demands by a ubiquitous, incremental process of successive limited comparisons between frequently mutually exclusive values and preferences. This process offers a more comprehensive regard for multiple values through a continuing process of mutual adjustment. Lindblom further argued that the strategy of proceeding through small yet significant incremental changes avoided serious lasting mistakes in situations where it is impossible to predict outcomes.

In a similar vein, Saul Alinsky, a leading social activist of the 1960s, argued that successful social change results from a synthesis of incremental, evolutionary processes that emerge from a particular sequence of revolutions. These small-scale but significant revolutions can potentially build sufficient critical mass, resulting in what is retrospectively perceived as major social change. In his view, effective organization towards meaningful social change was usually thwarted by the desire for instant and dramatic change – what he termed 'the demand for revelation rather than revolution'. His central message for prospective community organizers was that large scale plans rarely produce change. Instead, he argued that 'tactics . . . come out of the free flow of action and reaction, and requires on the part of the organizer an easy acceptance of apparent disorganization.' (Alinsky 1972).

Together, these works challenge us to revisit our fundamental assumptions about the nature, characteristics, and processes through which change unfolds in social settings. They outline a radically different understanding of the nature of successful change characterized by the spontaneous emergence of novel patterns and configurations; the amplification and incorporation of random events; the self-guided discovery of creative alternatives for functioning; and the emergence of new coherence and co-ordination among the organizational subsystems (Goldstein 1994). Paradoxically, instability and disorder become the source of spontaneous formation of new order or reorganization. The case study below illustrates the relevance of these ideas for the management of change in VNPOs.

CASE STUDY

A voluntary social service organization is facing major challenges. Stakeholders are increasingly critical of its ability to successfully fulfil its mandate. Donor agencies are demanding greater accountability for performance in key areas such as the number of clients being serviced, greater effectiveness in providing clients with measurable, positive outcomes – in short, they are demanding 'more value' for their dollars. The organization is beset with mounting internal problems, and morale has reached an all time low. Staff feel overworked, undervalued, and are still reeling from the last series of cutbacks that saw their caseloads increase while their compensation was reduced. Middle management feel alienated and frustrated by the situation; they are perceived as the bearers of bad news from the board and senior mangement and they are targeted as being autocratic, secretive and generally insensitive to the situation of their staff. Internal political differences plague the organization, as advocates for different client groups all seem to feel that their programmes have suffered more than others. Above all, they feel the organization is drifting into an uncertain and turbulent future with no clear direction.

Faced with these challenges, the Executive Director (ED) decides to launch a major change initiative. In order to address the demands of the board and key funders, she decides that each of the five regional departments needs to redesign its service programmes. She spends long hours masterminding the redesign of programmes and services. At the same time, an increasing workload leads her to the realization that she cannot continue to assume the traditional role as a top-down manager. In a series of sessions with her management team, she outlines the nature and direction of the major restructuring initiative within each department. As her management team begin to formulate detailed strategic plans for their respective departments, important questions arise. Which processes should be redesigned first? What programmes should be used for pilot projects? Who should be involved in detailed decision-making and design?

As the ED and management team wrestle with these concerns, new problems begin to emerge. Employees are becoming increasingly fearful of the changes underway. How will they be affected? Will their programmes and positions be 'restructured' and 'rationalized' out of existence? Staff members secretly question if all the change is really necessary, or is it simply another of a series of plans that will disappear as suddenly as it came? Should they continue to support the change or mount the type of political resistance that has torpedoed initiatives in the past?

As political tensions begin to rise, the ED decides to challenge the 'norm of non-communication' between management and staff. She realizes that staff members are ultimately the ones that have to make change happen; consequently, she directs her focus to increased staff participation in the planning and decision-making process. She decides to demonstrate her commitment to this approach by listening and responding to their needs. She launches a series of facilitated departmental dialogues: staff are invited to openly voice their suspicions, concerns and ideas with their managers and the ED personally. Staff members are assured that no repercussions will result from these sessions, and that all ideas will be given serious consideration.

After a few trying and often painful months, these dialogues begin to 'break the logjam' of conflict between staff and management. Staff members begin to approach the ED and their managers with innovative ideas on service provision. One department is able to reduce its caseload and waiting list by 50% through the introduction of a 'client workstation'. Another department launches a 'cafeteria style' approach to service provision that reduces caseloads by allowing clients to choose their own unique combination of services.

Within a year, the first sign of a new culture of collaboration begins to emerge, based on the success of the initial dialogue sessions and the tangible results of the ED's promise to act on expressed concerns. The organization is now well-positioned to address the concerns of the funders and launch new and innovative programmes in response to clients' needs in the new realities of fiscal restraint. Colleagues from other organizations begin to approach the ED in order to learn her recipes for success in bringing about successful changes.

Our case study begs a simple question: Is this a case of programmatic or incremental change? While this organization was able to achieve large scale results, they were achieved through a process that can best be described as incremental and emergent. **We believe that this is the actual pattern in most successful change initiatives: they are often emergent instead of meticulously planned, self-guiding instead of rigidly designed and controlled**.

This fundamental insight into the self-organizing or self-designing aspect of successful organizational change contrasts sharply with the traditional programmatic approach described earlier. The search for solutions to management problems through planned, programmatic change management reflects a basic misconception of the relationship between transformational outcomes and the incremental processes through which these outcomes typically arise. No rational model, no matter how sophisticated, can properly comprehend the complexity and irrationality of human interaction.

While many non-profit organizations need to achieve breakthroughs that will deliver large-scale changes, it is misleading to translate this desire for major breakthroughs into a search for large-scale programmatic solutions. They understand the objectives or desired **results** of the required change, but not the **process(es)** through which it can be achieved. In the remaining sections, we outline some of the implications of the above case for adopting a self-organizing approach to managing change in VNPOs.

HOW TO MAKE IT HAPPEN

To this point we have shown that the programmatic change approach may not fit the environment in which VNPO managers often find themselves. The present-day setting for change management in VNPOs appears to lie within the 'relatively unpredictable-relatively unclear self-organizing' segment of Figure 9.1. Under these conditions, where should VNPOs direct their efforts for change? The answer is not to develop detailed plans and micro-manage their implementation. Instead, we suggest that VNPOs need to focus on creating a context where successful change initiatives can emerge, guide change agents in selecting a focus for individual change efforts, and create the conditions that will allow such initiatives to flourish. The following section offers a more detailed account of this approach to managing change in VNPOs.

Creating a context for change

As a starting point, the traditional prescription for change calls for identifying outcomes, or the results, expected from the initiaive (e.g. Schaffer 1991). Yet as we have seen, in the voluntary sector outcomes are often difficult to measure, and stakeholders tend to focus on processes (Coulton 1982; Gandy and Tepperman 1990; Rekart 1988). The starting point for successful change initiatives in VNPOs, therefore, should be to **create a context** for successful change to unfold. The fundamental challenge facing VNPOs in turbulent times is to create contexts in which meaningful change can occur (Morgan and Zohar 1995). As in our case study, leaders and managers must focus on 'context making' in a way that embraces the traditional functions of setting a direction for the future, while creating a sense of space and possibility within which meaningful innovation can occur.

A critical aspect of creating a context for change is to establish a shared sense of vision and values that inform the search for major transformation. The ED in our case study quickly realized that she could not possibly control and predict the multiple ways through which her agency could, and could not, enact meaningful change. Instead of trying to generate a detailed 'master plan' for change, she accepted the fact that both at the level of plan formulation and implementation, she needed to rely on organizational members at all levels to find creative ways of driving forth meaningful change. Her approach was to articulate and demonstrate her commitment to an organizational vision and core values, which then gave organizational members a broad yet clearly defined context within which to independently pursue a series of diverse initiatives that fell within that domain.

Establishing a broad sense of vision and values for major transformation allows managers and leaders to redirect their energies away from the creation of detailed large-scale plans, and programmes. Instead, it allows them to focus on co-ordinating, championing and monitoring emergent staff initiatives that find ways of achieving the vision through manageable, 'do-able' initiatives. The role of mangement is to create the enabling conditions, culturally and structurally, that will assure that successful staff initiaives will not fall prey to political or procedural barriers. Basically, their role in the change process is to assure that successful initiatives can develop a critical mass whereby a series of changes, large and small, can accumulate to create truly transforming results. As Lindblom (1979) notes, most bottom-up initiatives fail simply because they do not receive organizational support and commitment from management. Successful organizational change is often driven through small changes and initiatives that generate momentum for further change. The key to unlocking this inherent organizational capacity for 'bottom-up' change is to create a context that will allow small initiatives to thrive and gain critical mass throughout the organization.

Selecting a focus

The initial focus for a change effort should emerge from the actual situation the agency faces. It could begin by the initiation of a dialogue among managers and staff, the development of a change-oriented culture, or the motivation of staff to confront and articulate barriers to change. In our case study, the initial focus was the need to revisit the service programmes of all five agency departments. In other cases, a management development programme may be constrained by a lack of time and money for the needed management training. Perhaps a self-organized, collaborative, inter-agency approach to training would overcome these constraints, pointing to a different way to train managers and pay for this training. An existing change programme may have become bogged down or overwhelmed by day-to-day events. Perhaps there is a need to step back, assess why this has happened and develop a new way to implement the changes.

An agency may comprise a fragmented set of constituencies with board, management and staff representatives which impedes the ability to work together to deal with important issues. Usually there is a need to open a dialogue between constituencies, to reframe isues from a 'win-lose' to a 'win-win' scenario. Agency resistance to change may be rooted in an 'anti-change culture', where change is seen as an unwanted departure from the roots of the organization. Perhaps there is a need to revisit its mission and vision, to reach conclusions on fundamental matters such as the future relevance of the agency as presently constituted. Alternatively, some agency members may be unwilling to confront barriers to change due to concerns with politics, job security or client service. From situations such as these, or any others facing the VNPO, members can select a specific, relevant focus for their change initiative. From this focus, VNPO managers can select specific, measurable objectives for the initiative and go on to conduct group discussions with stakeholder representatives about ways to achieve these objectives.

Developing action plans

Action plans will address the various challenges, opportunities and multiple demands that a VNPO faces. As we saw in our case study, the ED rejected the programmatic change approach in favour of creating a context which would allow a series of multiple action plans to come forth from its departments. In the early stages of the change initiative, staff members identified the need for visible support by the ED and the management team for safe experiments, wherein the success or failure of these experiments would be discussed openly, successes would be celebrated and failures would not be automatically punished.

However, as we described in our discussion of context, organizational members also needed the ED to identify the constraints for these experiments, possibly in relation to the 'old rules and systems'. In particular, if a VNPO is providing services mandated by government legislation, as reflected in regulations/contract governing related agency operations, there will be explicit boundaries beyond which experiments would not be 'safe'.

Action plans can go beyond individual initiatives, such as those related to risk taking. The agency may decide to allow stakeholders to take actions as they see fit – self-organization in the fullest sense of the idea. However, it is important to devote some attention to the 'up' aspect of the bottom-up approach to managing change. This could involve the establishment of a working group to co-ordinate the individual change initiatives, to monitor progress and share lessons learned, to encourage ongoing efforts to explicate contradictions and develop action plans.

It is apparent, therefore, that a self-organizing approach to change management is incremental and emergent, as opposed to the top-down progmmatic approach. There is no clear distinction between change strategists and change implementors. There is no need for a comprehensive diagnostic SWOT analysis that is decoupled from action planning, no need for precisely predicting future states, no need for developing the elusive quantified agency goals at the onset. The self-organizing process is **the enabling structure for change**, embedding a change process inherently involving stakeholder participation in the direction and nature of change. Changes themselves need not be institutionalized; instead, the successful management and implementation of the change process itself becomes that which is institutionalized. For these reasons, it appears that a self-organizing approach is best suited for VNPOs facing relatively unpredictable environments and unclear means-ends relationships.

SUMMARY

We began this chapter by describing the rapid, dynamic changes that are besetting VNPOs today. Perhaps the most remarkable aspect of this account is that it is by no means exhaustive; the 'new realities' facing VNPOs are unprecedented in terms of the fundamental way they threaten the continued viability and success of the sector as a whole. These realities were likened to the 'white water rapids' that present-day VNPOs are required to navigate: unpredictable turbulence, uncertainty and constant flux. Having described the need for change in VNPOs, we outlined a conceptual framework that highlighted the differences between two primary approaches to change management in VNPOs. These were described as the programmatic and self-organizing approaches to change. We presented a framework as a point of departure for asking basic questions about the degree of fit between three critical factors: external environmental conditions; means-ends relationships; and approaches to change management.

Contrasting these two approaches can assist VNPOs in bringing to the forefront of critical attention the different conditions and circumstances that may make the selection of a suitable approach to change management more readily apparent. Throughout our discussion, we have emphasized that the choice of a given approach to change management needs to be determined by the degree of congruence between a particular approach and the environmental context of the situation facing the VNPO. Both programmatic and self-organizing approaches to change will either produce or fail to produce successful change, depending on the degree to which they match existing circumstances and situations. Yet many VNPOs still try to negotiate the 'white water' using only programmatic navigational techniques that were designed for calmer and more predictable waters. We suggest that the self-organizing approach is more appropriate for the harsh and dynamic realities presently facing managers in VNPOs. Hopefully, the frameworks and ideas presented in this chapter can assist managers within VNPOs in charting their own unique course for navigating through the 'white waters' that lie ahead.

REFERENCES

Ackerman, L. (1986) Development, transition or transformation: the question of change in organization. *OD Practitioner* (December) pp. 1–8.

Alinsky, S. (1972) *Rules for Radicals*, Vintage, New York.

Barrow, J. (1992) *Pi in the Sky*, Clarendon Press, Oxford.

Beer, M., Eisenstat, R. and Spector, B. (1990) Why change programs don't produce change? *Harvard Business Review*, (November–December) pp. 158–166.

Carnap R. (1966) *Philosophical Foundations of Physics*, Basic Books, New York.

Coulton, C. (1982) Quality assurance for social service programs: lessons from health care? *Social Work* 27(5) pp. 397–410.

D'Espagnat, B. (1985) *Reality and the Physicist: Knowledge, Duration and the Quantum World*, Cambridge University Press, Cambridge.

Drucker, P. (1985) Entrepreneurial strategies. *California Management Review*, 27(2) pp. 9–25.

Gabbarro, J. and Schlesinger, I. (1983) Some preliminary thoughts on action planning and implementaion. *Managing Behaviour in Organizations.* (ed L. Schlesinger and J. Ware) McGraw Hill, New York, pp. 342–43.

Gandy, J. and Tepperman L. (1990) *False Alarm: The Computerization of Eight Social Welfare Organizations*, Wilfred Laurier Press, Ontario.

Gersick, C. (1991) Change theories: a multi-level exploration of the punctuated equlibrium paradigm. *Academy of Management Review*, 16, pp. 10–36.

Glieck, J. (1988) *Chaos: Making a new Science*, Penguin, New York.

Goldstein, J. (1994) *The Unshackled Organization*, Productivity Press, Portland.

Hackman, J. and Wageman, R. (1995) Total quality management: empirical, conceptual and practical issues. *Administrative Science Quarterly*, 40(2) pp. 309–42.

Hammer, M. and Champy, J. (1993) *Reengineering the Corporation: A Manifesto for Business Revolution*, Harper, New York.

Jick, T. (1993) *Managing Change: Cases and Concepts*, Richard Irwin Inc., Homewood.

Kanter, R. (1983) *The Change Masters*, Simon and Schuster, New York.

Kotter, J. (1995) Why transformation efforts fail. *Harvard Business Review*, (March-April) pp. 59–67.

Lindblom, C. (1959) The science of muddling through. *Public Administration Review*, **19**, pp. 79–88.

Lindblom, C. (1979) Still muddling, not yet through. *Public Administration Review*, **19**, pp. 517–25.

Markley, R. (1991) Representing order natural philosophy, mathematics and theology in the Newtonian revolution,. *Chaos and Order: Complex Dynamics in Literature and Science*, (ed N. Hayles) University of Chicago Press, Chicago, pp. 125–48.

McKnight, J. (1995) *The Careless Society: Community and Its Counterfeits*, Basic Books, New York.

Mintzberg, H. (1994) *The Rise and Fall of Strategic Planning*, Free Press, New York.

Morgan, G. (1994) *Imaginization: The Art of Creative Management*, Sage, Newbury Park.

Morgan, G. and Zohar, A. (1995) *Quantum Change Incrementally!* Working Paper 12-95, Faculty of Administrative Studies, York University, Toronto.

Nadler, D. and Tushman, M. (1989) Organizational frame bending principles for managing reorientations. *The Academy of Management Executive.* **3** (3) pp. 194–204.

Neal, J. and Troomley, C. (1995) From incremental change to retro-fit: creating high performance work systems. *The Academy of Management Executive*, **9** (1) pp. 42–53.

Osborne, S. (1992) Lifting the siege. *Local Government Policy Making*, **18** (5), pp. 17–20.

Price Waterhouse Change Integration Team (1995) *Better Change: Practices for Transforming Your Organization*, Irwin Professional Publishing, Burr Ridge.

Rekart, J. (1988) *Voluntary Sector Social Services in the 1980s*, Social Research Council of British Columbia, Victoria.

Romme, A. (1992) *A Self-Organizing Perspective on Strategy Formation*. Datawyse, Maastricht.

Schaffer, R. (1991) Demand better results – and get them. *Harvard Business Review* (March-April) pp. 142–9.

Stacey, R. (1992) *Managing the Unknowable*, Jossey Bass, San Francisco.

Watson, G. (1994) *Business System Engineering: Managing Breakthrough Changes for Productivity and Profit*, John Wiley, New York.

Wheatley, M. (1992) *Leadership and the New Science: Learning about Organizations from an Orderly Universe*, Berret-Koehler, San Francisco.

Znaniecki, F. (1980) *Cultural Sciences: Their Origin and Development*, Transaction, New Brunswick.

GUIDED READING

Wilson, D. (1992) *A Strategy for Change*, Routledge, London. An excellent summary and overview of change management strategies.

Morgan, G. and Zohar, A. (1995) *Quantum Change Incrementally!* (Working Paper 12–95, Faculty of Administrative Studies, Toronto). A useful guide to change management processes.

10 Managing equal opportunities and anti-oppressive practice

Marian Osborne and Linda Horner

INTRODUCTION

Trying to implement equal opportunities and anti-oppressive practice within any organization is not an easy tasks. Most organizations barely get beyond the equal opportunities statement on their recruitment material ('This organization is an equal opportunity employer . . . etc'), which means very little and causes much cynicism. It is relatively easy to have an equal opportunities veneer, but requires much more commitment especially from the top to go beyond that, and to keep the momentum going. In addition, for voluntary organizations, other considerations, which are to do with their value bases and funding commitments, can pose difficult challenges. The understanding which we have reached about this process has been developed from our own experience and does not necessarily reflect all issues in all VNPOs. What will be common though will be those issues which all such agencies have to address when implementing equal opportunities and understanding anti-oppressive practice. In this chapter, we seek to describe those issues and reach some understanding.

Implementing equal opportunities and anti-oppressive practice is an ongoing process, the direction of which has to be continually reviewed and evaluated. In this chapter, we have sought to highlight issues which are useful to address at the beginning of the implementation process, as well as to share the conclusions we have reached, often based upon the retrospective consideration of mistakes made. By the end of the chapter you should:

- understand the terminology of equal opportunities and anti-oppressive practice;
- understand the differences between anti-oppressive and anti-discriminatory practice;
- be able to understand the models and stages of implementation; and
- be able to analyse the frameworks operating in your organization and plan an implementation strategy.

BACKGROUND

At the end of the 1990's, it feels as though the arguments for the adoption of equal opportunities and anti-oppressive practice for employers should be well rehearsed. Any VNPO wishing to attract statutory funding will be required to give evidence of such a policy, as it is generally part of the grant or contract conditions. A cosmetic exercise is an option for voluntary agencies. However, credibility will be lost and most VNPOs see ethics as an important principle to consider. The main message of this chapter is that if VNPOs try to achieve equal opportunities solely to satisfy the funding criteria of other agencies, it is unlikely to work; nor can it be achieved in isolation from the rest of the work of the organization. If an equal opportunities policy is not firmly rooted within the overall direction of the organization, staff lose direction and begin to question the validity of the approach. Equal opportunities has to be planned within the context of overall service quality – you cannot guarantee a quality service unless it is provided in an anti-oppressive way. Similarly, an organization which does not consider quality issues in its service design cannot provide a service which is truly anti-oppressive in nature. We shall return to these ideas later on in the chapter. To begin with is is important to appreciate that VNPOs face specific issues in relation to equal opportunities. The requirement to provide evidence of an equal opportunities approach for funders has already been raised. Other factors include their value base, structure and size.

The value base

Not all VNPOs have a religious basis for their work, but most of them have a value base. For the newer VNPOs, which have often been set up within an equal opportunities and anti-oppressive context, encompassing that context within its value base is likely to be far easier. However, for those agencies which have been well established with a value base extending back into the last century, the issues around equal opportunities can be problematic. This is especially true for those agencies with a religious base to their constitution. The concept of fair treatment for all service users may well be a core part of the mission statement, but employing staff from a different religious faith can have a major impact upon both the organization and the staff themselves. Fear that its central faith will be compromised by such recruitment is very real for staff who may have joined the organization through a sense of mission. An acid test of how far such VNPOs are willing to move in this area is how far they are willing to extend recruitment of other faiths into the decision-making management hierarchy. Another area of conflict for agencies with a religious foundation is around gay and lesbian discrimination. When these VNPOs include gay and lesbian discrimination within their understanding of anti-discrimination, conflicts can occur yet again within the staff group. Staff with a strong religious conviction can have difficulty in separating out their deeply held religious views on the morality of gay and lesbian actions from the need not to be oppressive to such groups. Some staff can also try to use their religious convictions to support their personal opposition to gay and lesbian rights.

When society as a whole is divided on these issues, the 'morality' of pursuing such an anti-discriminatory stance on gay and lesbian rights may have no validity for these staff. When coupled with the frequent need for fund-raising staff to be in symmetry with their donors, it is not hard to see how VNPOs can be in organizational conflict on this issue. Anti-discrimination is still vulnerable to criticism and challenge from such opinion setters as the press, and VNPOs are wary of exposing themselves to such criticism.

The structure and size of a VNPO

One of the main difficulties in describing the voluntary sector is that it is impossible to generalize. Voluntary agencies are extremely diverse in both complexity and structure. They can vary from being either single issue led and highly focused, or diverse in approach; they can be user or profession-ally led; they can be small and simple in structure, or highly structured and bureaucratic. What impact if any does this have upon the successful implementation of equal opportunities?

We have argued previously that more recently formed VNPOs may not have to face the problems that the more established ones face in trying to adapt. Furthermore, VNPOs which are more simple in structure are more able initially to weave a culture which is anti-oppressive in its nature, than those which are more bureaucratic in nature. We are not arguing that such organizations will be more successful in the long term, because they may face other limitations such as lack of infra-structure and resources. They are also more vulnerable to the vagaries of local authority funding and changes in fund-raising patterns. However, at a more simplistic level they can be more successful in implementing organizational change.

WHAT IS 'EQUAL OPPORTUNITIES'?

We have grown so used to the terminology of **equal opportunities** that we rarely stop to think what it actually means, yet if we posed that question to a group of people, we would probably get a wide-ranging response. The issue becomes even more complicated when we introduce terms such as **anti-discriminatory practice** and **anti-oppressive practice**, by which time at least half of our group will have probably switched off altogether. To try and make some sense of the confusion we shall try to explain all these terms.

There are two theories of equal opportunities which are popularly adhered to and these translate into three commonly used models. The **liberal theory** is based on a belief that if the processes that organizations follow are fair then the end result will be fair. In recruitment, for example, if there is a recruitment policy which everyone follows, which treats every candidate the same, then the best candidate will be appointed. One of the problems with this theory is that it assumes that all of the candidates are starting from the same point and ignores any disadvantage or preferential treatment that candidates may have experienced within society before reaching the interview. The process seeks to ensure that people are not further discriminated against by the recruitment process, but it does not redress the wider societal imbalance in any way. It assumes also that organizations are rational so that rational processes will produce rational results.

The **radical theory** recognizes the imbalances that have been created in services by failing to address discrimination within society as a whole – for example, the under-representation of disabled people who are in employment. In trying to seek to address this imbalance of opportunity, the theory argues that it is the **outcomes** which are important, not just the processes which are used. Therefore, using the example of recruitment again, quotas may be used to ensure the recruitment of poeple from underrepresented groups. There are several problems with this theory which will be explored later, not least the question whether it is realistic to expect organizations to try and redress the imbalance of societal ills.

These two theories translate into three different models of equal opportunities: **equal chance**, **equal access** and **equal share**. The first of these models is grounded in the radical theory. One of the main components of this model is positive discrimination. This means that in relation to recruitment, quotas would be set to establish a balance within the workforce of people from various oppressed groups and preferential treatment would then be given to people from those groups until the quota was reached. Whether you think that this is a good idea or not, it is for the most part illegal in Britain. Positive discriminaion is **only** allowed in relation to recruiting disabled people, up to the 3% expectation stated in legislation.

Even if it were not illegal, you would have to think very carefully about the implications of this model and whether it would achieve the desired outcome. The model has the potential to create a hierarchy between oppressed groups within an organization and reduces people to little more than a label attached to them for organizational purposes. As a short-term strategy, while most oppressed groups are under represented in the workforce, this model may seem attractive. However for staff recruitment, it can set people up to fail if they are recruited on the basis of being the best only within their quota, which may not meet the expectations of the organization or meet the standards of the service required. Furthermore it can have damaging consquences upon the quality of the service to users. This adds to the oppression which people experience every day, both for the member of staff who is expected to provide a service he or she is not able for a variety of reasons to do and for the service user who receives a less than adequate service. We will explore these issues further when we consider the stages of implementation.

The equal chance and equal access models both stem from the liberal theory and have similarities. The **equal chance** model would seek to ensure that all applicants for a job were treated in the same way. It aims to eliminate direct discrimination and argues that if this is achieved, the best candidate for the job will be appointed. Therefore all applicants will be assessed in exactly the same way and subjected to the same criteria of assessment. However, it is somewhat näive, in that it does not recognize indirect discrimination, through the barriers to application, which might exist. As argued before, this rational model denies the complexity of life in VNPOs. For example, the way an advert is worded or the content of additional information in a recruitment pack may actively dissuade candidates from applying in the first place. The **equal access** model takes indirect discrimination as its starting point and seeks to remove the barriers within the process which limit employment opportunites in the first place. In this model managers would be careful, for example, to ensure that there was physical access to the workplace, opportunities for visually impaired staff to travel and deal with information and that the information given about a post would be encouraging to oppressed groups. As a consequence, if access occurs and the fair procedures to remove direct discrimination are in place, proponents of this model argue that the best candidate for the job will be appointed. In order to achieve this it is likely that **positive action** will be encouraged, which is action to ensure that people are aware of the opportunities that are available, but does not given them preferential treatment. **This is different from positive discrimination, which does give preferential treatment, for example, through a recruit quota system**.

Neither of these models takes into account the discrimination or oppression that people experience outside the recruitment process and their critics argue that the status quo will be maintained unless this is acknowledged. It is a matter for debate whether it is näive to think that organizations can significantly influence wider societal forces. Beyond this general issue, it is our experience that there are problems with each of these models, but they do offer a useful framework within which to think through an equal opportunities action plan. In order to illustrate the problems we see with the models, we have used the idea of dividing up a cake at a party. The focus so far has been upon recruitment and selectrion procedures. We will illustrate this approach now in relation to the possible services provided by a VNPO, and the cake eaters are of course the service users themselves. The size of the cake is finite and depends upon the ingredients (resources) available, but with an infinitive number of cake eaters. The slices can therefore vary in size. Applying the three models from above, the distribution of the cake could be approached in three ways.

Equal chance of dividing the cake

In this scenario, all the invitations have been sent out and a procedure has been agreed about how large a slice of cake each person will get. Every cake eater will be assessed within this procedure irrespective of how relevant it is to them. The cake will continue, therefore, to be cut in the way that the cake provider (the one holding the knife!) has decided. Some cake eaters will get bigger slices, and some none at all. There may be cake eaters who would have been at the party but they lacked transport to get there, they were afraid to come, they turned up late because they lived far away or they never received an invitation. The cake provider would feel that as long as the invitations went out, that was the extent of their responsibility. If eaters did not come that was their own responsibility. The cake distributor simply holds the knife and cuts under the procedure that he or she has already decided.

Equal access way of dividing the cake

Here the invitations have been sent to everyone and the cake distributor has laid on transport to the party – he or she has made it their responsibility to ensure that everyone will be there. The cake distributor divides the cake based on advice from the cake eaters and from people who say that they know the needs of the cake eaters. Consequently, although (nearly) every-one can attend the party, some cake eaters will have larger cake slices, at the expense of their fellow cake eaters. Whoever is the most fluent in their argument, or has the best advocate, will get the largest slices of cake. The idea of greatest need would not apply.

Equal share way of dividing the cake

Here the cake distributor has decided before the party both to place all the cake eaters into groups and to allocate how much of the cake should be given to each of these groups. These groups would represent different types of needs and would be based upon his or her interpretation of who deserves how much cake. The invitations have been sent out to all the groups and the cake is distributed equally between the groups, irrespective of their size. However, should more eaters from one group turn up and less from another group, the cake would still be distributed to the groups on the basis of the original decision of the cake distributor. Some cake eaters could have more cake than they can eat, whilst some might have crumbs to share out.

The key point in all the models is that the decision about how to cut up the cake is decided by the cake distributor – who never gives up the knife! Power is never shared and the cake eaters are not able to make their own decisions. Those most in need do not necessarily get what they require, and all the models have the potential to put different disadvantaged groups in competition with each other.

For VNPOs, this is an important issue. Power sharing (**empowerment**) may be a core value of your VNPO, but its implementation is problematic. We assume that we cannot give away the knife, because we have to be accountable for the allocation and prioritization of resources and such an action would be counter to this responsibility. The three models of equal opportunities above do not offer any solutions to this issue of empowerment, nor is there an alternative model of equal opportunities which offers any resolution. This is their fatal flaw. The conceptual thinking around equal opportunities, by itself, can only take you so far. In our view it is necessasry to combine this thinking with that about service quality. Normann (1991) is useful here. He highlights both the importance for service quality of the relationship between the service provider and the service recipient (**the moment of truth**) and its link to resource management and optimization and the point that the service recipient is not a passive receptacle for these services. The recipient has an active role in service production, whether this role is a positive one or a negative one. It is at the 'moment of truth' that the quality of a service is created with the service user being a participant in the service delivery process. Empowerment has to be understood within this interactive context. The empowerment of service users therefore requires their positive involvement. It needs to be understood as an **essential** component of both an anti-oppressive and a good quality service and not as an add-on.

ANTI-DISCRIMINATION AND ANTI-OPPRESSIVE PRACTICE

Having explored how organizations can approach equal opportunities and how the issue of quality management adds the important dimension of user empowerment to this discussion, we now want to look in more detail at the concepts of anti-oppressive and anti-discriminatory practice, in order to reveal further what such a quality service could look like in practice. Whilst **equal opportunities** tends to be used in relation to the recruitment and retention of staff, **anti-oppressive** and **anti-discriminatory practice** refer to the services that a VNPO might provide. Although the terms may be used interchangeably, there is a significant difference.

Anti-discriminatory practice is embedded in legislation such as the *Race Relations Act 1976* and the *Sex Discrimination Act 1975*, which make it illegal to discriminate in certain situations on the grounds of a person's race or gender. Discrimination is therefore recognized and defined in law for race and gender, but not at this time for sexuality. Anti-discriminatory practice recognizes that discrimination in society takes place and that law is needed to mediate this. It attempts to negate the negative effect of discrimination. Anti-oppressive practice is based on a view of fundamental power imbalances in society, which lead some people to be oppressed by others because of who they are. This view includes all discrimination and not just that which is addressed by law. It attempts not just to look at the effects of discrimination, but also to empower people in order to redress the balance. In an attempt to clarify this let us look at two situations which illustrate the differences. An attempt at anti-discriminatory practice would be to provide services to black children which would include interpreter services if English was not their first language, or to provide culturally sensitive toys, books or food. Anti-oppressive practice would include all that, and seek to empower these children to be stronger in coping with discrimination, such as through group work to build up a sense of personal worth (see for example Banks 1992; 1995; 1996). Underlying this would be a belief that these children would and should be better able to handle discrimination in other areas of their lives and not just that which the service affects.

PUTTING EQUAL OPPORTUNITIES AND ANTI-OPPRESSIVE PRACTICE INTO ACTION

It is now time to consider the practical implementation of the above ideas. Most VNPOs go through several stages of implementation, which are driven by the level of understanding held by their staff at any one time. At times it can feel that the final stage will never be reached, because it is so dependent upon current societal thinking. It is like opening a door with a key, only to find another door, requiring another key. It feels as if it is never ending. Because of this, it is easy to lose direction and therefore it is essential to have a clear implementation plan to guide you.

Stages of implementation

There are three key stages to negotiate. As they move between these stages, VNPOs often tackle each problem as it occurs in a reactive manner. This review is intended to forewarn, and hopefully fore-arm you. Moreover, reality is invariably more messy than any model of it can be, so these stages may overlap or be iterative. Staff, in an attempt to achieve change within their own sphere of influence, can try to move the organization on before it is ready to move. A backlash to the ideals of equal opportunities and anti-oppressive practice can take place also if the key stakeholders have not been won over at the start of the process. *In our view, it is essential to take a strategic approach throughout, which places equal opportunities and anti-oppressive practice at the centre of organizational and service management, rather than being a marginal or specialist issue.* Such a strategic approach will not eliminate the difficulties of implementation but it will provide a framework for their resolution. Without this, they may be seen as separate from the task of managing services, rather than as a core part of the delivery of good quality services. Finally, leadership is essential to ensure that commitment to organizational change is maintained. VNPOs can make the error of trying to implement equal opportunities through their training section, thus abdicating their managerial responsibility.

First stage

This is when a VNPO recognizes that there is an issue to tackle. This may be due to pressure from various levels. It can come from the top downwards, because senior management recognizes that there are advantages to achieving equal opportunities and anti-oppressive practice, for funding or for publicity purposes perhaps, or to become congruent with the organizational mission. Pressure can come also from the bottom upwards, with new staff bringing in new ideas from other organizations, wishing to enhance professional practices or to re-interpret the organizational mission. Organizational response to these pressures can vary. However, most VNPOs begin with a recruitment and selection strategy, having identified a disproportionate low number of staff from disadvantaged groups. This may be accompanied by a recognition that the attitudes of existing staff may need to be tackled, usually through training and staff supervision.

Second stage

In this stage the focus is upon anti-discriminatory practice. Disadvantaged groups will begin slowly to be a feature of the organization, usually at the lowest level and individual training will begin. It is felt to be easier to concentrate upon one oppression at a time, and race is a common starting point. This stage is often characterized by a high turnover of black staff who, because there is little organizational support on either an individual or group basis, become quickly disillusioned with the rhetoric of the organization. They may also feel that they were inappropriately selected in the first place and were set up to fail. Eventually it becomes apparent to management that more is required than simply recruiting oppressed groups (usually black staff), into the organization, in the hope that this will be enough to bring about organizational change. Moreover, because only one group is being tackled, a **hierarchy of oppression** can be established. Finally, because the VNPO is investing money in training to achieve organizational change, training costs can be high and cause disquiet to uncommitted stakeholders.

This stage is crucial. It is easy for the process to 'derail' at this stage. Expectations from both staff (including staff from oppressed groups) and management can be high. If these are not quickly met, disillusionment can set in equally quickly. Staff may resist challenges to their personal beliefs (and prejudices), which are hard to change in any case, whilst organizational and indirect forms of discrimination frequently are not addressed. Poor performance issues both in managers and staff from oppressed groups can appear. However, it is difficult for the organization to tackle them because there may be few (if any) standards to go by and few sources of support available.

Third Stage

At this stage, organizations begin to tackle other forms of oppression as they realize that a hierarchy of oppression is divisive. Thus anti-oppressive practice begins to develop. VNPOs realize that training at an individual level alone is insufficient, whilst training for managers starts to tackle the management of the poor performance issues which featured in the previous stage. Support for staff from oppressed groups is also recognized now as a legitimate issue and support mechanisms such as support groups are encouraged. Now feeling less defensive, the VNPO may also consider seeking outside advice and help in further developing its practice.

APPROACHES TO IMPLEMENTATION

Based upon our experience, we wish finally to offer two approaches to the management of this implementation process.

Model one: using the training route

This model uses training the individual as a way to achieve equal oppor-tunities within the organization. The VNPO decides to invest in training programmes so that there will be a positive attitudinal change in staff, enhanced skills and therefore improvements in service delivery. Further-more, it is hoped that this will lead to an increase in the proportion of disadvantaged staff within the workforce, by improving staff recruitment and retention. As the VNPO moves through the stages described previously and faces new challenges, the danger in this model is that managers will use training as **the solution** to problems, rather than as **one resource** among many. Training will be left to provide the standards on which the VNPO bases and evaluates its performance, without any strategic direction from the agency as a whole. At its worst, it can lead to equal opportunities and anti-oppressive practice being marginalized as solely a training issue. In our experience, several consequences can flow from this method of implementation.

1 Senior and middle managers may not 'own' the changes which evolve and there is a danger of organizational drift. Staff will sense this con-fusion and any action plan can lose its credibility.
2 Resentment can build up within the organization, because the standards on which professional practice is based are derived from training rather

than from operational sources; staff may not own such changes and will seek ways to undermine their implementation.

3 Although some managers who are committed to equal opportunities will make changes at their level, implementation will be patchy and dependent upon personal commitment.

4 There may be a danger of a backlash against the plans from both managers and staff, who will perceive it as a personal rather than organizational issue; this will result in negative outcomes for staff who are members of disadvantaged groups because they are the visible components of this process.

5 All of the above. This model may allow staff to turn inwards, through their dissatisfaction, and blame both the organization and the policy; this in turn will lead to loss of organizational direction and lead to staff losing sight of what the purpose was – to provide a quality service to all service users.

Model two: using the strategic management route

This model achieves equal opportunities and anti-oppressive practice through the formulation of organizational direction and the harnessing of resources. It is led from the top and informed by the service user. It is based firmly within the concept of the organization as a service delivery system, as outlined by Normann (1991), where a positive organizational culture enhances and reinforces both a positive relationship with the service user and positive organizational performance. We would not wish to advocate a top down approach in isolation. User participation is an essential characteristic of any such approach in isolation. Of course this is not a new insight. Both Ackoff (1976) and Martin (1986) have made this point strongly before. However, it is one which is, ironically, often forgotten in the context of equal opportunities. The advantages of such an approach are fourfold.

1 It ensures a consistent organizational approach which is supported by its aims and objectives (though this may be problematic where the mission of the organization itself is not consistent with an anti-discriminatory approach, as described earlier in the chapter).

2 The organization sets its own standards to be used throughout practice. These should draw upon both its own and best practice elsewhere, and will need to be reviewed and evaluated regularly to ensure that they still meet the needs both of the organization and its users. Training in this model **supports and underpins these standards**, it does not set them.

3 The process of performance management is easier to implement, because it is part of the overall strategic management of the organization rather than an add-on.

4 If some staff are unwilling to support the direction of change, sanctions will be clearer to implement because of the overall strategic direction.

CONCLUSIONS

Equal opportunities and anti-oppressive practice are not separate goals for VNPOs. They are inextricably bound together and are also an inherent part of delivering a quality service. This chapter has argued for a strategic approach to these goals, which situates them within the context of the strategic direction of the VNPO as a whole. At the core of this approach is the concept of the centrality of the user in service quality and hence of equal opportunities and anti-oppressive practice as an essential component of good quality practice and services. In conclusion we would emphasize five guidelines for managers entering into this important and challenging field.

First, achieving equal opportunities and anti-oppressive practice is an ongoing process, which needs to be reviewed and evaluated regularly. It is also a time consuming and lengthy process. Never lose heart!

Second, equal opportunities and anti-oppressive practice must be planned within the context of overall service quality and not as a separate issue. You cannot guarantee a quality service unless it is provided in an anti-oppressive manner, nor can you ensure anti-oppressive services unless you consider quality issues.

Third, the empowerment of service users is a core component of a good quality service, and is integral to anti-oppressive practice. They are two sides of the same issue, and not separate ones.

Fourth, a strategic approach will provide an overall framework for organizational change and for the resolution of the intra-organizational conflict which is often part of this process. Training is an aid, not a substitute, for this approach.

Finally, leadership is essential to the achievement of meaningful change. Equal opportunities and anti-oppressive practice need clear organizational ownership at the highest level for their successful achievement.

The authors write in a personal capacity. Their views do not necessarily represent those of Barnardo's.

REFERENCES

Ackoff, R. (1976) Does quality of life have to be quantified? *Operational Research Journal*, **27**, pp. 289–303.

Banks, N. (1992) Techniques for direct identity work with black children. *Adoption and Fostering*, **16** (3) pp. 19–25.

Banks, N. (1995) Children of black mixed parentage and their placement needs. *Adoption and Fostering*, **19** (2) pp. 19–25.

Banks, N. (1996) Young single white mothers with black children in therapy. *Clinical Child Psychology and Psychiatry*, **1** (1) pp. 19–28.

Martin, E. (1986) Consumer evaluation of human services. *Social Policy and Administration* **20** (3) pp. 185–203.

Normann, R. (1991) *Service Management*, Wiley, Chichester.

GUIDED READING

Cockburn, C. (1991) *In the Way of Women. Men's Resistance to Sex Equality in Organisations*, Macmillan, London. Highlights the issues that individuals and organizations face in implementing equal opportunities policies.

Jewson, N. and Mason D. (1982) The theory and practice of equal opportunities policies: liberal and radical approaches, in *Racism and Antiracism: Inequalities Opportunities and Policies* (eds P. Braham and R. Raltansi) Sage, Beverly Hills. pp. 218–34. A good introduction to the different theories of equal opportunities discussed in this chapter.

Straw, J. (1989) *Equal Opportunities. The Way Ahead*, IPM, London. A good introductory text – probably a good place to start for the 'beginner'!

11 What is 'IT'? Information technology management in voluntary and non-profit organizations

Mike Luck and Paul Golder

INTRODUCTION

By the end of this chapter you should:

- appreciate the opportunities and challenges posed by IT for managers of VNPOs, and be aware of the current role of IT in the community and voluntary sector;
- have a clearer idea of the meaning of the main terms used in discussing IT;
- understand the different roles of information in an organization, the range of activities on which IT could impact and be able to develop an IT strategy;
- be aware of the importance of developing and maintaining the IT skills of your collaborators;
- be able to carry out a review of your current information systems and be able to develop an information system strategy; and
- have an understanding of the possible alternatives and pitfalls present in the procurement of IT and the other components of an Information System.

THE OPPORTUNITIES AND CHALLENGES OF IT FOR VNPO MANAGERS

We consider that the increasingly competitive environment for VNPOs presents a variety of challenges for managers which require the speedy and accurate searching, collecting, processing and disseminating of information. Information Technology (IT) can assist considerably with these processes if properly introduced and maintained. However, if a VNPO has a poor manual information system, badly organized files, confused categories, out-of-date card indexes, cupboards filled with boxes that no one understands, then introducing IT is unlikely to improve matters – and may make things worse. One of our key messages is that there has to be proper development of the **whole information system** (IS) of the organization: telephones, filing cabinets, cupboards and notice boards, together with proper development of its people including the management committee members, workers and volunteers. IT will only bring benefit to the VNPO if its introduction is part of an IS strategy.

For example, a key information need is for the staff of VNPOs to communicate regularly and clearly to management committee members and volunteers and to community organizations through means such as minutes and reports, newsletters and press releases. Rightly or wrongly, volunteers, supporters and clients all expect a high quality of presentation and communication and a high level of efficiency in managing details like names and addresses and the recording of financial transactions. They associate failure in these areas as indicative of poor organization and ineffectiveness, rather than of the homely image of tea and biscuits that may have been the acceptable face of a voluntary organization in the past. For these reasons we find it difficult to imagine how a VNPO can manage effectively without a well-designed, efficient and responsive information system and a supportive IT infrastructure.

Another example is the need for VNPOs to prepare and submit, and often resubmit, proposals to funders. This requires assembling detailed financial information and forecasts and, increasingly, quantitative information on outputs and outcomes. This information will form the basis for contracts and these will have to be monitored and evaluated. Many organizations have found computer spreadsheets (see below) extremely useful for these non-routine financial tasks.

IT IN THE COMMUNITY AND VOLUNTARY SECTOR

An excellent short review of the issues facing the community and voluntary sector when considering the introduction of IT is provided in the report *Press Enter*, produced by the Community Development Foundation (CDF) in 1992. They identified 20 surveys of IT use in the voluntary sector conducted since the mid-1980s and six of these were carried out in 1991, the year before publication of the report. They found that the successful adoption of IT is mainly associated with the larger, better resourced, organizations. Although there is also evidence of cases where IT has not produced expected benefits, or it has taken much longer to achieve than expected, they were surprised that the majority of non-users of IT showed indifference or considered IT to be an irrelevance without having made any significant study or research. There is the danger that these organizations will find themselves increasingly handicapped without IT in the growing competitive environment of the voluntary sector. CDF recommended that VNPOs make use of networks such as the Community Computing Network (CCN), and other sources of advice such as the Information Services Group at the National Association of Councils for Voluntary Service (addresses at end of the chapter).

CLARIFYING TERMS

One of the key problems for potential and less-experienced users of IT is the jargon. There are, of course, good reasons for having specialized terms for accurate definition and communication, but this can lead to deliberate obfuscation by experts who want to sell their expertise. In this section we shall define some of the key terms which we shall be using in this chapter. Two good basic texts which can be used to extend the reader's knowledge are Martin and Powell (1992) and Sachdeva (1990).

Information Technology (IT) has been defined in many ways but the definition we prefer is **the acquisition, processing, storage and dissemination of information by a microelectronics-based combination of computing and telecommunication**. IT has arisen from the convergence of data processing techniques and telecommunications (Turnbull 1986). Many people consider that IT refers only to computers, mainly personal or desk-top computers, but important changes are currently taking place in the ability of telecommunications to communicate between computers in different places and in giving access to databases held by other organizations in other places, even in other countries.

Hardware refers to the computer with its microprocessor 'chip' which processes the information. Devices for in-putting information include the keyboard, the mouse and the lightpen; devices for outputting information include the visual display unit (VDU) and the printer. It also refers to the devices which enable the computer to communicate with other computers over networks (such as **modems** for use with telephone lines).

The Processor refers to the main unit of a computer system which does the actual computing. Processors are continually evolving and are referred to by code numbers like 286, 486 or names like Pentium. In general, the power of a computer system (i.e. the speed of computation and the size of problems which it is practicable to tackle) increases with each new generation of proccessor.

Software refers to sequences of instructions which are used to instruct and control the hardware in carrying out the information processing. Nowadays much software is bought in prepared programs referred to as 'packages', but it is possible to write or purchase special software for particular applications such as stock recording or payroll. The three software packages which are most likely to be relevant for VNPOs starting out with IT are word-processors, spreadsheets and databases (see below).

The Operating System refers to the special piece of software which runs on a computer and does the main management functions, such as sending data to printers, accessing data in memory and on disc, displaying information on the VDU and responding to the keyboard. Various operating systems are available with different facilities. DOS (Disc Operating System) is used conventionally to refer to a number of programs which offer a text rather than a graphical user interface. Operating systems such as Microsoft Windows 95 support an interface which uses a mouse (a hand-held device which is dragged across a horizontal surface and causes an arrow to move across the screen) to point and click to control the computer. They typically have better integration of images and text in the program interface as well as in the documents produced.

Network refers to the various systems for connecting computers together. These may be Local Area Networks (LANs) which enable people in the same office or department to share printers and applications and to exchange data. These may also be Wide Area Networks (WANs) or networks carried over the telephone system which link different sites together and give users access to remote sources of information.

Word-processing is a way of electronically developing text in documents which allows easy storage, editing and revision, changes of typeface and size of font. Thus standard letters can be stored, retrieved and modified for particular purposes without having to retype the whole letter. In producing a report it is easy to move a paragraph within the document without having to retype the whole. More advanced word-processors, with facilities for incorporating diagrams and pictures as well as producing multi-column layouts are called **desk top publishing (DTP)** packages.

A Spreadsheet is a form of electronic grid where a number or a formula can be entered into each 'cell' in the grid (a formula can relate numbers and formulas in other cells). Any numerical work which requires addition, subtraction, multiplication and division can be made more powerful and flexible. In particular, the strength of the spreadsheet for the manager is that it makes it easy to ask 'what-if' questions, such as what will be the effect on variable costs if the number of our clients increases by 10% next year; or if wages are increased by 5%; or what if a particular grant is not renewed.

A Database is a means of storing records in a way which makes sorting and selection easy. Records can be added, inserted, amended and deleted; new categories of information (fields) can be added to all records. Records can be given markers so that it is easy to select subsets for particular purposes. A database is particularly useful for keeping mailing lists, so that labels and customized letters can be printed.

INFORMATION NEEDS OF THE ORGANIZATION

We have now defined some of the key aspects of IT relevant for VNPOs which are considering using IT or are wanting to review the current stae of their IT for upgrading. In this section we look at the basic information needs of the organization in order to indicate where IT may be appropriate.

These individual needs will then be looked at together in order to decide whether they make a viable strategy which can be evaluated for procurement.

An organization functions at different levels and its information system needs to support different types of information. At the **operational level**, many VNPOs will use their IT to support their day-to-day activities, like producing invoices, sending out receipts and mailing supporters. It is such applications which are often seen as the most cost-effective use of computer technology. In such cases it is usually easy to see the saving in staff time or the increase in productivity achieved by using a computer instead of manual systems.

At the **supervisory level**, an early application is also to set up systems for monitoring operational activity. Simple spreadsheet applications for keeping track of costs and for monitoring returns from a fund-raising appeal, are examples of this level of activity.

Finally, the **strategic level** is often overlooked but here the use of the information system to support strategic planning can be essential. Drafting a mission statement, developing plans for the next few years and assembling the information necessary to support a contract tender or a grant application are strategic uses of an information system.

Typical initial projects for a VNPO investing in IT should address some key aspect of its activity. The management of a list of members, the production of reports and the submission of tenders are all areas which interface with the outside world and have the potential to benefit from the application of IT. VNPOs have to maintain mailing lists of members, funders, agencies, community groups, volunteers and clients. Such lists may be kept on file cards in a manual system. The lists need to be updated for new entries and purged for out-of-date records; the lists may need to be re-ordered on specific characteristics such as name, address, role or task; names and addresses need to be inserted into letters and printed on labels for envelopes. All these tasks can be easily handled by a computer database.

Similarly, a time consuming and largely repetitive task is the preparation and circulation of the minutes of management committees and sub-committees, reports of meetings with funders and internal reports for evaluation purposes. The drafting and revision of such documents is made much easier with a word-processor and their readability can be improved with the more flexible layout. Some of these documents can be prepared in a standard form and then modified quickly on the computer.

Finally, much time in VNPOs is involved in the preparation and submission of tenders for contracts and in providing reports for funders. This involves the assembly and manipulation of financial and other numerical performance data. The increasingly precise and detailed requirements of each potential funder usually differ and mean that changes have to be made to the format for each submission. However, once the basic data has been put on to a spreadsheet it is relatively easy to make these changes, then to transfer it into the word-processed proposal for submission and to store it for future use.

The development of an Information Systems Strategy is more than simply profiling a few initial projects, however. It involves managers in examining the activities of the organization at its different levels and identifying where the use of the IT would have the most impact. An effective system will usually deliver operational benefits, like the initial projects suggested above, but should also collect and summarize the data generated by the operational systems, as input to the supervisory level and to the strategic level management activities. Whereas most information for the supervision of operations will be generated within the organization, for strategic planning data from outside (often qualitative, uncertain and unstructured) will need to be integrated with the internal data to produce the planning information.

For example, a VNPO may rely on appeals to supporters for a major part of its income. The operational systems would be concerned with maintaining up-to-date mailing lists of supporters and records of the income form appeals. The supervisory system would be keeping track of letters returned undelivered and receipts for the appeal and from successive reminders so that the efficiency of the appeal campaign can be assessed. The strategic system would compare returns with the previous years and information from others sources to assess whether this means of raising funds was continuing to be effective and not severely affected by external events, such as the National Lottery and high profile campaigns by other organizations, with a view to developing longer term strategies for income generation.

DEVELOPING AN IT STRATEGY

In considering the use of IT within any organization the management team should plan for the acquisition and use of tools to support their work. Thus a typical component of an IT strategy is the choice of word-processing software. Over the next few years the organization will be making use of word-processing and although it is not necessary to decide in advance every letter or document that will be produced it is important to ask what types of activity the organization will engage in and how word-processing capacity will facilitate or impede these.

An IT strategy must cover at least the following five topics.

Hardware

The choice of hardware is a relatively straight-forward choice between an IBM PC family of machines or an Apple Macintosh. Larger VNPOs may be considering mini computer systems, probably with a UNIX operating system (however, such a system will require some in-house management and the IT strategy will thus be developed in consultation with the in-house IT experts).

Software

The choice of software is more complex. There is a large range of software available but in developing the IT strategy the main issues will concern the choice of operating system, the selection of a word-processing package and a spreadsheet. The power of the hardware available will limit the functionality of the software that can be used. It is unlikely that you will get much use of Windows software without a recent machine with a large amount of memory (at least 8 Mb for Windows 95). Whilst DOS word processing packages will run effectively on an old second-hand machine, if you want to produce DTP material you will almost certainly need a more recent machine. The two main suppliers of IT application, Microsoft and Lotus, each have suites of programs (Microsoft Office; Lotus Smart Suite) which will support word-processing, spreadsheets, business graphics and some database management. Such packages are often offered at a special price and are guaranteed to work together easily transferring data and diagrams.

Communications

Although you may not be currently using networked computer systems your strategy needs to consider if you are likely to move to networking over the strategy period. Quite often the first motivation for networking is printer sharing. You will, therefore, need to ensure that any new hardware or software you acquire is compatible with your planned network. Installing a network is a major step up in technical complexity and should be approached very carefully. Managerial consequences follow, since an individual with networking skills and authority will be required to supervise the network. This is a similar level of commitment to the installation of distributed mini-computer systems and requires an appropriate level of planning and commitment.

Organization

The IT strategy will need to include planning at the organizational level. Who is to supervise the strategy? How is it to be resourced? Who is to be responsible for training, security and the maintenance of standards. For example, it is possible to have a well-thought through IT infrastructure but nevertheless find that a database of contacts carefully entered into the computer by a volunteer is not immediately usable for a proposed mail campaign because it is not set up in the way required by the word-processing package.

Skills

Without proper training a collection of hardware and software could impede rather than support the VNPOs activity. Thus the IT strategy needs to take account of the skills available to existing staff and the way such skills can be increased. An individual may have considerable investment in a particular product, and may be able to do wonderful things quickly with it due to their own investment in learning how to use it. But this investment is not easily transferable and often is difficult to update because any transfer to a new product, no matter how advantageous it may be in the future, will produce a short-term fall in productivity and self-confidence. You cannot afford to allow the strategy to be determined by a particular set of skills possessed by one individual, but any successful strategy can easily become hostage in its own set of skills. The role of training is essential and needs to be identified and staff need to be encouraged to share skills. Learning support, such as the purchase of books and videos, should be seen also as necessary support for the majority of staff whose main activities lie elsewhere than in learning about IT.

REVIEW OF THE CURRENT INFORMATION SYSTEM

Before any sensible decision can be made about IT by a VNPO it is essential that the whole information system of the organization is reviewed. The most important resource in the organization's information system is **people**. This may seem like a truism, but time and again we have found organizations, private and statutory as well as VNPOs, where the people, management committee members, paid workers and volunteers, do not consider that the information system is important and do not invest enough time and money in training and maintaining their information skills. This may be because many of those who are drawn to work in VNPOs are committed to serving people in face-to-face work, so they feel that sitting down and dealing with words and numbers on a paper or a computer screen is not 'real work'. Even when organizations have invested considerable resources in IT, the hardware and the software can be under-utlized because people have not been adequately trained or allowed sufficient time for upgrading their skills. In Case Study One we show some of the simple things that need to be done in a small VNPO to review its IS and its IT.

In all organizations, and VNPOs are no exception, the information system reflects power relationships between people. When IT is introduced the power relationships may change. Unless properly handled, the internal politics may result in IT being resisted, or developed in way that does not exploit its full potential. At the worst IT may just entrench existing bureaucratic practices. Some of these issues in a large VNPO are shown in Case Study Two.

It is important to develop a culture which welcomes the development of IT and new ideas for its use, but at the same time fosters a sense of discipline. Confusion and inefficiency can occur if different people modify the system in uncoordinated ways. Small VNPOs are particularly suscep- tible to the 'Jacko' effect. Jacko was a new volunteer who knew a lot about computers and offered to help. The problem was that he made a number of changes to the software but he did not seek approval nor explain the changes to the regular users. They found they could not use the modified system, and Jacko had to be tracked down to explain what he had done.

Manual Information

Whether or not a VNPO has IT there is still going to be some manual information processing and storage. The so-called 'paperless office' is a long way ahead. It is, in fact, a paradox that in most cases IT actually produces more paper than before! It is best to start analysing the total IS by examining information in the organization without specifying at this stage whether or not manual or IT systems should be used. At the basic level this covers the following functions:

- day-to-day external communications (telephone and 'front-desk' activ- ities) including a way of recording messages and passing on those which need action to the appropriate person;
- day-to-day internal communication and control, such as work plans, notice boards, calendars for meetings and staff leave;
- management and decision-making requiring information preparation, communication and recording through preparing agendas and providing and sending minutes of managment committee meetings, newsletters and annual reports;
- providing a service to clients, lobbying and providing advice, requiring communications with clients and customers and the maintenance of relevant files;
- financial control, including paying wages, paying bills, sending in- voices, monitoring expenditure and auditing; and
- strategy and planning, requiring searching for information on new de- velopments and trends, preparing budgets and submitting proposals to funders.

To carry out the above functions a manual information system needs devices for displaying information such as notice boards and for storing information such as filing cabinets. The filing cabinet needs to be organised into sections and then into individual files in a way which is understood and adhered to by those who have the right of access to the files, some of which may be confidential.

Computer information

In principle any or all of the above information may be acquired, processed, stored and displayed with IT: notice boards can be put on individual PCs so that users see these first thing in the morning when they switch on, or which they call up through an external network such as E-mail; reports and financial information can be recorded in computer files; card indexes can be transferred to a database, and client records could be held electronically. It is a matter of strategy and tactics as to whether a VNPO acquires IT and the sequence in which it transfers information from manual systems and develops new applications.

DEVELOPING AN INFORMATION SYSTEM STRATEGY

An information system consists of two essential components: the data essential to the success of the organization and the software that accesses the data. The basic needs of data management are so routine and common to so many users that relatively cheap software is available for database management and the core of any IS is likely to be a database management system. However, there may be specialist applications of the data which cannot be handled by a general purpose database management system and it may be necessary to consider a variety of other sources for the applications that you need. As well as the data and the application systems, we do need to consider the security of our data and most VNPOs will also need to be aware of the provisions of the *Data Protection Act* governing the storage and use of information about individuals (see below). Seven issues need to be considered in such a strategy.

Database Management System (DBMS)

This is a vital part of the IS and needs to be chosen with care. Depending on the computer hardware you are using, a user friendly database management or file management system is likely to be appropriate for personal computers, whilst a multi-user relational database management system is likely to be used if a mini-computer system is available. All these systems will enable basic operations to be carried out relatively easily but if you need to go further and develop specific applications then you will need programming skills.

Applications software

Many applications are so common that good commerical software is available to implement them. Thus payroll, invoicing and accounting programmes exist which are well developed and tested and respect current best practice and legal requirements. No matter how expensive such software packages may appear it would cost you more time and money to attempt to develop your own. The main advice in selecting such systems is to choose well-established suppliers with a large customer base and check out that data can be relatively easily exported from the application to other parts of your IS. Don't accept vague assurances but demand to see where it is documented in the manual – and see if you can understand what it says!

Complete systems

Some supppliers offer 'vertical' systems for particular applications such as garages or hotels. These systems, although well-tuned to the 'typical' organization, tend to be more expensive and you may find yourself tied into a closed system. In such cases it is very important that there is an active users group (ask for details) to represent the users interests.

Customized systems

An intermediate solution is a 'customized' system. In accounting, for example, a standard package is so flexible and has so many options that it can be configured to suit most individual customers needs. As always there is a catch and the system will inevitably be more complex and harder to support. You are likely to have to be able to cope with doing development at a near 'programmer' level to achieve some of the configuring.

Self-development

Of course you could be tempted to write the system yourself using one of the newer languages (often referred to as 4GLs) or traditional languages like Pascal. Don't! Unless you have a lot of time and resources you cannot afford to take this approach. Even if someone offers to do it for free (student projects for example), the consequent problems of maintenance make it an unsatisfactory choice. It can be difficult for even the author of such software to identify the causes of errors or to make what might appear simple changes (such as to convert from £s to ECUs); for someone who was not the original author it may be impossible.

Backup and security

Remember your data is valuable and you have a legal duty to protect any data you hold about individuals. Ensure that you have an adequate security system to protect against unauthorized access, discourage or ban the playing of games and importing of 'freeware' and check for viruses (programs inserted mischievously or illegally which can destroy data and programs). Make backup copies of your data regularly, store them away from the machine and preferably in a different location. If you have information that is vital for your operations, develop an emergency plan in the event that the computer fails, such as arranging to borrow or hire a system if necessary and check that all the data and applications software that are urgently required can be transferred so that you can remain up and running.

The Data Protection Act

As holders of personal information you are liable to the provisions of this Act and should make yourself aware of your responsibilities (the address of the Data Protection Registrar is given at end of chapter). In general, if you hold more than simply the names and addresses of individuals (data subjects) you should be prepared to show them the information you hold and ensure that it does not get transferred illegally to third parties. In a world where the buying and selling of mailing lists is rife you need a policy and ensure that your data subjects can exercise their rights in respect of any data you hold.

IT PROCUREMENT

There are a variety of ways in which a VNPO can 'procure' IT. Broadly, these divide into providing the equipment and service 'in-house' or using a service company (called out-sourcing), or some combination of the two. The choice relates not only to the best technical solution but also to how the VNPO is able to finance its IT. For example, some smaller VNPOs may find it possible to obtain individual grants which can be used to purchase hardware and software, but will have difficulty including revenue costs for IT in their contract/grant negotiations with funders.

Using a service company can provide faster start-up because the agency already has the IT expertise but they may not know enough about the VNPO in order to provide an appropriate system. Moreover, the VNPO is not developing its own expertise for the future, unless this is part of the contract. However, if the VNPO's future is uncertain because of funding difficulties, and the turnover of staff and volunteers is rapid, the agency solution may be the most practical. This can also take care of maintenance which should be included in the contract. Also the upgrading and replacement of the IT system should be reviewed regularly as the VNPO develops its information needs, and as new equipment or software becomes available.

The in-house solution, either leasing or purchasing, means that the VNPO is developing its own skills and is the system likely to be adapted closely to its real needs, rather than what an outsider thinks it needs. The danger is that the staff and the volunteers will not be able to maintain their commitment to training and development in the face of all the other pressures on the organization, such as funding crises and client and community demands.

Because of the wide range of tasks, the variety of organizational structures and the multiplicity of funding and contractual systems, it is impossible to produce a generalized IT strategy applicable to a large range of VNPOs. It is also inappropriate to make suggestions for those organizations with their own professional IT function, but for smaller organizations it is possible to make the following practical suggestions.

Avoid hype

Every month there is newer, faster, glitzier hardware and associated operating systems available. You cannot afford to ride the crest of the wave; you are not in the business of pioneering IT and debugging manufacturers' products for them. However, each new range means that the last wave or the previous one are becoming 'old hat'. As a consequence, these are often being offered at attractive prices and there is plenty of experience in installing and maintaining them and documentation on how to use them. In September 1996 terms this means don't worry about buying a Pentium processor running Windows 95, unless there is a clear task in the organization which needs this level of support. There are plenty of cheaper machines around running Windows 3.1 which will almost certainly meet your needs.

Avoid bargains

They do not exist! There are no real bargains, unless you have the IT expertise to identify the 'catch' and be sure that it will not impede your mission. Anything being offered with pressure ('last days of sale') should be avoided. Cheap or free software may be illegal, may not have adequate documentation, will probably not interface with other applications and may need a German Keyboard; who knows – you probably will not.

Buy mainstream software

Do not be tempted by enthusiasts who extol the virtues of a particular package. Stick to mainstream applications from major suppliers. They are more likely to be around next year, training material will be available and add-ons and enhancements will be readily available. Avoid the latest version, especially any marked version 2.0 or 3.0. Let others debug the new packages, while you go for version 2.1 or 3.1.

Cascade

Staff tend to become attached to a particular machine and are reluctant to share it (perhaps for good security reasons) yet are quite good at justifying why they need a more powerful one. Equipment gets obsolete, not because it wears out (a problem only with certain mechanical parts such as keyboards, mice and disk drives) but because there is a natural escalation of applications. One is always trying to get more out of the system and what was acceptable last year may be a constraint this. In particular, upgrades of software can impose extra processing requirements and demands on memory and disk space. Given the policy of avoiding hype it is still best to buy the most powerful machine available in the range selected as you will soon need this extra power. Pass machines around so that the newest is used for the most demanding application, not the most important member of staff and other machines are reallocated as appropriate. The last one need not fall off the end, it will be useful as a back up if one of the others fails or enable you to take advantage of that new volunteer. A side benefit of the change around is that everyone concerned will have to tidy up their disks, make back-up copies of files for safety and delete obsolete files.

Because of the rate of obsolescence it may be inadvisable to purchase many machines at once even if the funds are available. They will all tend to need replacement at the same time and the funds may not then be available. They will all be of similar functionality and in practice there will be a range of users and applications. New equipment takes time and energy to introduce into an organization and it makes sense to spread the load. Hardware is becoming better and cheaper so a planned programme of purchase can make financial sense – however, grant makers are not always that flexible!

CASE STUDY ONE: A SMALL LOCAL VNPO

This is a case study of a small VNPO, based upon a real example. It shows how two part-time workers and two volunteers reviewed the IS and that they needed to start with the manual files before they tackled the IT.

The VNPO was founded in 1993. Its primary objective was **to provide a forum in Blankshire for work with men who wanted to stop their violent and abusive behaviour with their female partners**. At the time of the case study the VNPO was running group counselling and a telephone helpline for men who wished to change their patterns of domestic abuse. It rented two rooms, one as an office and the other for the groups and meetings and it employed two part-time development workers whilst volunteers led the group counselling, staffed the telephone helpline and assisted in the office. Its IS comprised a Solidisk PC, with Windows 3.1, Microsoft Works for Windows and Timeworks Publisher 3 DTP. There was an HP Deskjet 500 printer.

The two workers had been aware for some time that they were not making best use of the IT facilities and that 'something needed to be done'. The management committee approved a review but stressed that the review should not take up much time because of the urgent need for the workers to search for funding.

That March, Linda and Chris (the development workers) met together with Mike (volunteer office worker) and Steve (trainee administration

worker). They sat in a semi-circle around the flip chart stand and decided
how to proceed. The steps listed below are a version of what actualy
happened, slightly tidied up for reasons of space.

1 Each person clarified their IT knowledge and skills and their expectations for the review. This helped to deal with potential embarrasment
   from different levels of knowledge and skills; to make clear that this was
   a participative effort; and to clarify the time available today and for
   follow-up.
2 The mission statement was reviewed and updated. This was necessary in
   order to clarify that there were potential future activities for which IT
   could be relevant. Any decisions about IT therefore needed to be taken
   in the light of these potential developments as well as the current
   activities.
3 The current and possible future programmes of work were listed on a flip
   chart.
4 Communications with external bodies were discussed and the different
   types of communications were noted. For a wide range of possible
   funders these included seeking new sources of funding, developing
   specific applications, collecting relevant information to support applications, giving presentations and maintaining informal links with intermediate agencies.
5 Internal communications were explored also. The various 'internal
   actors' included development workers, management committee members, group leaders, helpline volunteers, the men being counselled and
   their partners. The formal and informal communications linkages
   between each pair of actors were identified and listed.
6 Current information and resources were listed. These included the workers and all their formal and informal knowledge and linkages; the
   manual files in the filing cabinet; the Library; handling the incoming
   mail; recording incoming and outgoing telephone messages; and the
   computer hardware and software.

By the end of the morning session an action plan was drawn up. Before
going any further it was agreed that Linda and Chris needed to tidy up and
purge the manual files in the filing cabinet. This would serve several
purposes: Linda was sure that there was a lot of unnecessary material
which could be thrown out; it would get Linda and Chris to establish a
common system; and it would form a clear basis of classification of types
of information which would be necessary when the IT information was
examined in detail. After lunch Linda and Chris put in two hours together
sorting out the filing cabinet. This produced a practical outcome from the
day which was good for the morale of the group.

Two months later, the same group met to continue the IT review. As
before, the steps are listed below in a somewhat tidied up format.

1 Progress since the previous meeting was reviewed. Linda and Chris had not been able to do any more work on the information systems analysis. The pressure of routine work and funding applications had taken up all their time. However, Steve had been able to familiarize himself wih the computer and Microsoft Works using the tutorial provided with the package.

2 The flip charts from the previous meeting were reviewed and some minor changes and additions were made. Tasks were prioritized then in terms of (a) their urgency for the survival of the VNPO and (b) as less urgent steps in developing the information system. The three most important tasks identified were deleting old files on the computer; putting the budgets of the current and previous year on a computer spreadsheet for use in funding applications, and going through the card index of names and addresses, deleting out-of-date cards and transferring the remainder to the computer database.

3 The group sat down in front of the computer and started to review the files and decide which should be deleted. This was a slow process because each file had to be opened and discussed and the procedure for deleting a file in Microsoft Works is quite slow in order to avoid deletion by mistake. After about one hour only a quarter of the files had been reviewed.

4 Finally, Mike put the budgets on a spreadsheet in a way that was convenient for Chris to use in forthcoming funding applications.

It was felt that this had been a useful day, but that there remained much to do and it was not clear when there would be the time to continue the review.

Discussion

Reviewing this case study of a small VNPO we can see how easy it is for information, both manual and computer, to become confused and inefficient. The day-to-day pressures of survival on the small number of key persons in the organization makes consistent maintenance of information difficult. In this case, there was really one central person, the first paid worker, Linda, who held all the strands together. When the information review was undertaken it was necessary to carry it out in small increments, each of which had a clearly defined outcome, because it was never sure if and when the next stage of the review would be carried out.

We also saw that there were clearly defined benefits at the strategic level for the organization of using IT both for word-processing documents and minutes of meetings in order to circulate information quickly to participants and for using spreadsheets to keep financial information in a form which could be quickly adapted for the constant stream of funding proposals.

CASE STUDY TWO: A LARGE NATIONAL VNPO

In contrast with case study one, this is a study of a large national organization. It is also based upon a real-life example, of a long-established national charity with a stong public profile. It had a history of involvement with IT and had its own specialist staff. The case concentrates on the main organizational and internal 'political' issues

In 1987 the VNPO had recognized that IT was becoming an increasingly important operational tool, but that its growth in the organization had been *ad hoc*. The main initiatives in the previous twenty years had been within the Finance section. In 1989 a decision was taken to focus on client records as the next step in the development of a national IT strategy. The criteria that the IT system would have to meet were developed and included the more efficient management of large amounts of information, ease of access to user records; the creation of a database providing a national picture of its work; its contribution to organizational decentralization; and the national compatibility of hardware and software. It was considered that a system could be developed which would meet these criteria and a pilot implementation was planned for early 1991, in two different projects in Yorkshire and London. The main decisions made about the IT system were:

- to appoint a **non-technical** IT Development Officer to oversee and manage the development,
- that the hardware should be micro-computer based; and
- that the software should be Paradox 3.5.

Following the installation at the two pilot sites, a two-week initial training period was carried out with all staff on-site. A user guide had been developed which was designed to be as friendly and jargon free as possible containing all basic information regarding starting up the system inputting data and leaving the system. Following a three-month operational period, staff were asked for feedback on the implementation. The results showed that:

- 85% of staff felt that training had been too little and 76% requested further training,
- 57% felt that the installation had run smoothly,
- 76% felt able to input and access information, and
- 71% felt that it was too early to say whether their work had improved with the new system.

The experience of the pilot studies highlighted some important questions and issues for further discussion. Five issues were of particular import for the organization.

Computerization of client records

The manual system had consisted of a card index and case files. It was essential to have clear objectives for such a process, at both a local and national level. Local user needs were for quick access to information, for the identification of possible areas of practice development and for the avoidance of areas of duplication. National user needs were for the speedy definition of new areas of work, for the creation of a more accurate and accessible database for providing a national picture of its work and for promoting more effective responses to changes in the external environment.

Roles of technical and non-technical staff

It was important that there was a proper balance between the technical aspects of systems design and the user needs. If one or the other was too dominant the result was likely to be sub-optimal. A high level steering committee was used to provide 'championing' and 'ownership' by senior management.

Training

As noted above, many staff felt that training had not been adequate. Further investigation suggested that the main components of a successful training programme would have provided:

- information system concepts;
- a quick start to using the system;
- 'refresher' aids;
- help in overcoming difficulties in more advanced use; and
- an explanation of the assumptions behind the system.

Despite considerable effort being expended on developing the user manual, disappointingly little use had been made of it.

Client access to records

This issue had not been considered in the development of the IS, although subsequently it had become recognized as a key factor. Issues of confidentiality and practical arrangements for access would have to be considered in the future.

Equal opportunities

Again, this had not been considerd in depth in the initial design of the system. However, without careful attention to this issue and positive action around it, the introduction of IT in any organization can further disadvantage some groups, whilst increasing the power of others.

Discussion

This review of a large VNPO showed that the effects of IT were similar in any large organization, public or private. In particular, it should be highlighted that information development cannot take place without altering the balance of power in the organization. People develop vested interests which they may see as being strengthened or weakened by IT and hence support or resist its development (Osborne 1995). These issues are considered further in the chapter in this book on the management of change.

IT must be included in all strategic development and organizational change. It is not really feasible for a large organization today to ignore IT in any of the aspects of its development. The potential for LANS and WANS is growing every day, and these should be seen to be the current focus for IT development by large VNPOs.

CONCLUSIONS

From the wide range of implications of IT for both small and large VNPOs we have selected here a small number of key conclusions which seem to us to be inescapable for any VNPO.

1 Information must be considered an essential resource for VNPOs in the increasingly competitive environment of the voluntary sector.
2 IT must be considered creatively as an **integral** part of strategic development and organizational change, not solely as a way of improving routine administrative tasks or as a later 'add-on'.
3 For all except the largest VNPOs, it will be necessary to obtain advice from sources such as other VNPOs, academics and commercial consultants. But whoever provides the advice, it is essential to build up internal knowledge so as to be able to assess this and any subsequent advice critically.
4 Managers and paid workers in VNPOs need to establish a **learning orientation** within the organisation as a whole, with respect to IT and to be active themselves in acquiring knowledge and skills.

REFERENCES

Community Development Foundation (1992) *Press Enter, Information Technology in the Community and Voluntary Sector.* Report of the IT and Communities Working Party, Community Development Foundation, London.
Martin, C. and Powell, P. (1992) *Information Systems, A Management Perspective*, McGraw-Hill, London.
Osborne, S. (1995) *Don't You Just Love Being In Control? The Management of*

Innovation and Change in a Local Voluntary Agency. Paper to the 1995 NCVO Conference on *Researching the Voluntary Sector*, London.

Sachdeva, R. (1990) *Management Handbook of Computer Usage*, Blackwell, Oxford.

Turnbull, G. (1986) *Information Tecnology and Social Work*, University of East Anglia, Colchester.

GUIDED READING

From the above references, *Press Enter* gives a good over-view of the opportunities and challenges of introducing IT to VNPOs, and *Information Systems* is a good introductory text on introducing IT into an organization, as well as an explanation of its components.

Three further articles from the journal *Administration in Social Work* also cover important issues:

Caputo, R. 'Managing Information Systems: an ethical framework and information needs matrix' (15, 4) pp. 53–64.

Murphy, J. and Pardeck, J. 'Computerization and the dehumanization of social services' (16, 2) pp. 61–72.

Schaech, D. 'Using technology to change the human services delivery system' (17, 2) pp. 31–52.

USEFUL ADDRESSES

Community Computing Network, Bill Thompson, 65 Litchfield Road, Cambridge CB1 3SP.

National Association of Councils for Voluntary Service (Information Services Group), Arundel Court, 177 Arundel Street, Sheffield S1 2NU.

Office of Data Protection, Whycliffe House, Water Lane, Wilmslow, SK9 5AF. (Tel: 01625 535 777).

12 Contract management for voluntary organizations

Richard Kay

INTRODUCTION

By the end of this chapter you should:

- understand the significance of the growth of contracting for the identity, role and relationships of VNPOs;
- have acquired knowledge of the legal position of the range of funding arrangements VNPOs can have with statutory organizations.
- be able to make sense of, and manage, the ambiguous, multiple and conflicting meanings of contracting and the contractual relationship VNPOs are confronted with. Managing contractual relationships has to be contextualized, there is no 'one best way'.

THE CONTRACT CULTURE

Until the 1980s, VNPOs in the United Kingdom were perceived to be primarily playing a subsidiary role to the governmental sector in the provision of welfare services. As Wolfendon (1978) argues, government was seen as responsible for the planning and provision of mainstream services, with VNPOs seen as playing three subsidiary roles:

1 complimentary – providing services that were qualitatively different in kind to governmental services;
2 supplementary – extending the statutory sector provision by providing similar services to it; by extending the range of such services, their 'users' might have increased choice; and
3 substitution – filling service gaps where the statutory sector, for whatever reason, had failed to provide a service.

VNPOs were seen also as having a legitimate role in advocating/promoting the provision of better quality or new services by the statutory sector.

Many VNPOs received grants from local government; and sometimes also through central government funding initiatives such as the Urban Programme, and from 'quangos' such as the Manpower Services Commission.

By 1987/88 local government funding of VNPOs was over half a billion pounds (Gutch 1992).

However, during the late 1980s, there was an increasing move to replace grants with 'contracts'. These would be formalized agreements between the VNPO and the funding statutory organization, which identified the responsibilities and obligations of the parties. These would therefore, in theory, increase the accountability to government of VNPOs. This change was in the context of an increasing emphasis by government on changing the role of local government from a monopoly provider of services to an 'enabler' and purchaser of services from 'the independent sector' – the VNPOs and private for-profit organizations. This began to be called '*the contract culture*'.

A number of different reasons have been given for the growth of contracting (NCVO 1989; AMA 1990). These include:

- statutory organizations being seen as bureaucratic, large, inflexible and providers of poor quality services; VNPOs were identified as flexible, innovatory, and responsive to community needs.
- the desire of the government to change and reduce the role of local government; local government should become an 'enabler' of the provision of services and VNPOs should take on the provision of 'mainstream services'.
- the wish to create **a mixed economy of care**, which would provide 'consumers' with greater choice.
- a drive for 'value for money'; the provision of services should be more efficient, effective and economic. This would be enhanced by 'the disciplines of the market' – the creation of internal and external markets for statutory organizations. Contracting was a core component of this 'arms length' market model.
- the constraints and cuts in local government expenditure, a result of a reduction in public expenditure by government and 'capping' of local government spending, influenced local government to perceive contracting with VNPOs as a means of 'levering in' financial resources not otherwise available.
- VNPOs were identified as having important expertise and skills which would enhance the service to the users of public services.
- Contracts would formalize the relationship between VNPOs and statutory organizations clarifying the parties' obligations and responsibilities and increasing the accountability of VNPOs. The relationship with VNPOs could therefore in theory be effectively managed, and their performance monitored and evaluated. This approach was consonant with the growth of managerialism in the statutory sector (James 1994).
- The independent sector (VNPOs and private for-profit organizations) would provide better quality services since the profit motive and the VNPOs' ethic of voluntarism were more effective motivators than a notion of 'public service'.

- Proponents of community development identified the funding of local community groups as a means of 'empowering' local communities.

A very wide range of beliefs, values and assumptions can therefore be said to have influenced the development of the use of contracts. Moreover, the growth of contracting was taking place at a time of significant changes in the role of VNPOs and the statutory sector. Managing contractual relationship has therefore to be understood not just as a mechanistic, technical process of formal contract creation but also as managing a complex process where multiple, ambiguous and conflicting meanings of contract and the contractual relationship compete and influence practice (Osborne 1993). Managing the contractual relationship will therefore require all the understanding and skills of managing change, complexity, ambiguity and conflict.

WHAT IS A CONTRACT? COPING WITH AMBIGUITY

In English law, for a legally binding contract to exist there must be:

1 an unconditional offer and acceptance by the parties to the agreement, who have the capacity in law to enter into legally binding agreements and who have entered into such agreement voluntarily (not under duress);
2 an exchange of consideration between the parties – for example, in exchange for funding the VNPO agrees to provide a particular service; and
3 the intention of all the parties to create a legally binding relationship.

This last criteria is complex, for in law even if the parties did not explicitly agree they were entering into a legally binding agreement, the courts can hold there was an 'implied intention' on the basis of what a 'reasonable person' would have intended in such circumstances. The fact that the document was called a contract would be an important consideration, as would be the VNPO's understanding of the statutory organization obligations under the agreement. If it believed the statutory organization could not unilaterally refuse to carry out its obligations under the agreement, such as to refuse to pay over the funding or to reduce it (unless there was a clause allowing this) then the courts are likely to view this as a contract. **This is despite the agreement sometimes being called something else, such as a service level agreement.**

In fact, there are a range of financial relationships in law:

Grants

These are generally in law considered to be one-sided and therefore not contracts. This is because there is usually no exchange of consideration since the VNPO has no reciprocal obligations in exchange for the grant. The grant is a gift or donation. Grants given to a VNPO to further their purpose/objectives would be such a gift. However, increasingly grants include a description of the service to be provided and other 'exchange' obligations. These are called 'grant aid agreements' or 'grant aid contracts'; as the latter term implies, they may be contracts in law.

Service level agreements (SLAs)

This term is commonly used in the UK to describe agreements between VNPOs and local government departments. These agreements specify, in varying detail, the service to be provided by the VNPO and their other obligations in 'exchange' for the funding. The SLA will also usually specify the obligations and responsibility of the statutory organization. The degree of involvement of the VNPO in negotiating the SLA will vary. However, even if the terms of the SLA are entirely or predominantly drawn up by the statutory organization, as long as the VNPO accepts the terms voluntarily (as defined in law), the SLA could still be a contract in law, since there has been offer and acceptance, and exchange of consideration. The term **Service Level Agreement** is used in the UK in the *NHS and Community Care Act 1990*. Yet in the debate in Parliament, the government spoke of contracts. More ambiguity? However, in English Law, the courts can take this statement into account, to show parliamentary intention that SLAs were intended to be legally binding contracts (as decided by the House of Lords in *Pepper v. Hart 1993 AC 593*).

Service agreements

This term is sometimes used interchangeably with Service Level Agreements and sometimes to differentiate a type of agreement from SLAs. However, the differentiation has varied. Thus in one publication Service Agreements are said to be more detailed in setting out the parties obligations and responsibilities (Adirondack and Macfarlane 1993). However, in another study (Meadows 1992) the term is used by local government to differentiate the agreements from SLAs, since the latter term is used in a special way in the *NHS and Community Care Act 1990*. Further ambiguity is created by the use of the term by the UK Department of Education to describe 'Service Agreements' as agreements between parties who are not legally separate bodies so cannot contract in law (such as agreements between the departments inside an organization). Thus Service Agreement may or may not be legally binding. This will depend whether they meet the legal criteria for a contract in law.

Spot purchases, or placement fees

Consonant with the growth of the 'purchaser-provider' model of relationship, the term 'Spot Purchase' is now being used more often than placement fees. However, their legal status may be the same or differ depending on the context. It is an agreement to pay for a specified service for an individual such as a place in a residential home. If the agreement meets the legal criteria, each individual spot purchase may be a contract in law. It is unlikely that there would be a contract for a VNPO to agree to take further placements in the future, nor is the initial offer an unconditional offer since a place may not be free at the time of referral.

Core funding

This is a grant to enable the VNPO to meet its core objectives. This is similar to the one sided grant/gift outlined earlier. Core funding, though, is increasingly being given in consideration of the provision of a particular service and so may be a contract in law. Reflecting this change one government department has replaced the term core funding by 'Programme Funding'.

Performance based contracts

These are likely to be contracts in law. Their distinguishing feature is that payment to the VNPO is based on results, such as service users finding employment or gaining qualifications. They are high risk contracts, particularly when the VNPO is dependent on others, such as the statutory organization making referrals to it.

Cost reimbursement contracts

These are very common in the US. Payment is in arrears on a cost-reimbursement basis, that is, for costs actually incurred. These can therefore be very bureaucratic requiring considerable administration by the VNPO. These are likely to be contracts in law.

Capital contracts

The VNPO is provided with capital for expenditure on buildings or other items defined as capital. Whether they are contracts in law will depend primarily on whether there is consideration for the capital payment.

The importance of a legally binding contract is that it can be enforced in the courts. If one of the parties does not fulfil its side of 'the bargain', the other party can sue for damages for breach of contract, and obtain damages for any loss incurred by their breach (such as the cost of obtaining the service elsewhere). As most contracts between VNPOs and statutory organizations are contracts to provide services to people, the legal remedy of 'specific performances' (the court requiring the party to perform its obligations under the contract) will not be available; the remedy will be damages only.

Users and contracts

One of the concerns expressed by various writers (Gutch 1992; Richardson 1993) about the growth of contracting is that the influence of the users of the service will get squeezed out. This is primarily because the client to the contract, it is argued, is no longer the service user, but the purchasing statutory organization. It has been proposed by NCVO (1989) that to avoid this difficulty, there should be a 'double contract'. Thus, not only should there be a contract between the VNPO and statutory organization but also between the VNPO and 'user' and the statutory organization and 'user'. Examples are given of the VNPO having an obligation in the contract with the statutory organization to obtain consumer/user feedback on the quality of service; or of the statutory organization having an obligation to act as a 'watchdog' to monitor the service quality. Whilst this proposal has value in highlighting one of the dangers of contracting in English Law, unless that individual user was a **party to the contract**, and the legal contract criteria were met, that user could not enforce that contract since there was no 'privity of contract'. The contract could only be 'a moral contract' with the user.

There are thus many different terms used to describe the relationship between VNPOs and statutory organizations. In legal terms it does not matter what term is used to describe the relationship except in so far as the use of the term 'contract' would influence the meaning the courts gave to the relationship. In law it is not the **form** of the relationship but its **substance** that matters. It is therefore very important that VNPOs do not enter into any formal agreement unless they understand all the terms and obligations and are sure they will be able to meet them. It is also important to have access to legal advice – the statutory organization certainly will! Because of the ambiguity outlined above, VNPOs must understand whether the relationship that they have entered into is defined in law as a legally binding agreement.

MANAGING THE AMBIGUOUS AND CONFLICTING MEANINGS OF THE CONTRACTUAL RELATIONSHIP

The ambiguity of whether the form of an agreement is a contract in law, is matched by the ambiguity of the meaning of the contractual relationship between the VNPO and statutory organization. In 1989 the Association of Metropolitan Authorities (AMA) in the UK, set up a working party 'to make a preliminary assessment of the issues which are raised by the trend towards contracting' (AMA 1990).

Their report highlighted the clear intention of local government to move towards greater use of 'social care contracts'. They saw these as taking any one of three particular forms:

- the 'firming up' (formalization) of existing grant arrangements;
- the development of new services on a contractual basis; or
- the 'contracting out' of existing, directly provided services to VNPOs and other organizations.

They argued that the move towards the increased use of contracts and service level agreements could easily be accompanied by statutory organizations becoming 'managerial and controlling' in their relationship with VNPOs. They stated that in their view such an approach was unlikely to be helpful in the long run. Instead they proposed 'a refined form of partnership' in which mutual expectations and responsibilities are negotiated and made explicit, 'thereby avoiding a rigid Purchaser-Provider split' (AMA 1990). Competitive tendering should only be used in the short-term for certain services where there is an established private sector market. 'Tendering will almost certainly lead to an increased emphasis on cost rather than service quality' (AMA 1990). They proposed that VNPOs should be involved at each stage of the contracting process. This should include:

- consultation on Community Care Plans;
- involvement in preparing draft service specifications;
- participation in setting performance targets and indicators; and
- participation in monitoring and review.

The ambiguity between contracts, service level agreements and partnerships is emphasized in a recent survey by the NCVO in England (Bolton, Leggett and Thorne 1994). This revealed that local government did not view contracting as an important means by which to support VNPOs, in comparison with grants and service level agreements. Of those who responded, 50% said they did not contract with VNPOs. However, many did have service level agreements, so were these service level agreements contracts in law and what meaning did the VNPOs give to the form and nature of their relationship with the statutory organizations?

Gutch (1992) predicted that the contract culture was likely to change the nature of the VNPO sector – making it more like the private sector; increasing the size of large VNPOs; increasing the influence of 'professionals' in VNPOs and lessening the influence of management committee members, service users and volunteers; and most importantly threatening the independence of VNPOs. By contrast, Richardson (1993) has given a more positive meaning to contracting. He has pointed out that in the US, whilst calls for improving the contracting system were frequent, there were few voices calling for its abandonment. Early studies of contracting in the United Kingdom show that whilst the process of contracting can be difficult, it has ultimately been seen as beneficial by the participants (Hedley and Rochester 1991; Bolton, Leggett and Thorne 1994).

This chapter has already outlined one major ambiguity in the relationship between VNPOs and statutory organizations – are they legally binding relationships? The second major issue for VNPOs is to understand the other multiple meanings that can be given to the contractual relationship. Managing the contractual relationship needs also to be understood as managing the multiple meanings of the contractual relationship. Whilst there are such multiple meanings, in practice it is argued that two 'models' of the contractual relationship are particularly influencing the way statutory organizations in the UK are conceptualizing and influencing their relationship with VNPOs. These are termed here the **market model** and the **managerialist model**. Ironically both these models are the ones the AMA working party was striving to avoid.

The market model

Here, the statutory organization, the 'purchaser' of a service, seeks a VNPO to provide a service, the details of which were set out in a 'specification'. The specified service is identified by the statutory organization as a means to meet its strategic objectives and priorities. Bids for the contract are sought from VNPOs through a tendering process. This may be an 'open' process where any VNPO can bid for the contract; or a 'selected list' process where only VNPOs on a list of potentially suitable VNPOs, drawn up by the statutory organization, can bid; or only selected VNPOs are invited to bid for that particular contract. The statutory organization will select the VNPO 'provider' from bids received by tender. The selection criteria may be price and/or quality or some other criteria such as reliability, reputation, or their ability to lever in additional financial resources. The criteria may or may not be known to the bidders.

The managerialist model

Here the statutory organization will require also the contracted services to be a means to meet its strategic objectives and priorities. The VNPO could be reacting to an approach by the statutory organization to provide specified services, or the VNPO itself may have been pro-active in its approach. The amount of negotiation between the parties about the service to be provided may vary considerably. However, the statutory organization will identify the VNPO as a means to its ends, and not towards shared objectives which both parties have been involved in defining. Generally in the UK, the formalized relationship is set out in a service level agreement or service agreement. Despite these terms, it is likely that the agreements would be held to be legally binding.

Whilst these two dominant models are presently used by statutory organizations to create their relationships with VNPOs two other models can also be found. The first of these is termed here **the collaborative model**. In this model, neither the VNPO nor the statutory organization imposes on the other its definition of the problem or issue to be addressed, the services/ strategies drawn up to resolve these, nor the evaluation criteria for judging their 'effectiveness'. Whilst each party will have a 'self-interest' for entering the relationship, both are 'stakeholders' in a mutual endeavour. The VNPO and the statutory organization bring their individual perspectives to work to create mutually created and shared definitions of the social problem/issue, services/strategies and evaluation criteria. Both parties work together to define their roles and responsibilities and both take responsibility for the achievement of the outcomes of the collaboration. The values of this collaborative relationship are mutuality, trust, sharing, reciprocity, learning from each other; yet also a respect for the priorities, contributions and values of each other, valuing their difference. Dynamic tensions are inherent in such collaborative relationships. The relationships may be formalized in a 'contract' or service level agreement, both of which are likely to be legally binding. This can be problematic. In a recent case, attempts by a VNPO and statutory organization to outline in a contract their shared responsibilities was ruled out by the lawyer of the statutory organization, since no party could be held individually responsible in law for those responsibilities. Those involved in the negotiations felt this legal perspective was undermining the 'mutuality' of the relationship.

The final model is **the community development model**. This model is less evident today, but is still valued by many VNPOs. In this model, a grant is given to the VNPO by the statutory organization as it is a 'community organization' – the VNPO having been identified as being 'of the community' or having a role in 'empowering' the local community.

Two case studies will show how these different models held by different organizations and groups in a 'contractual relationship' created ambiguity and conflict.

Case study one

In 1991, a national children's charity, received a request from the manager of a small VNPO in a UK county town, to take over a local service of the VNPO, funded by central government for a time-limited period of time. The VNPO was to provide a service for young offenders. The objectives of the service were laid down by central government and the service to be provided had also to be sanctioned by central government. This relationship is consistent with the managerialist model. During the two year funding period there had been few referrals to the project. The Social Services Department was not happy with the activities of the VNPO, as the manager was active in promoting work with local community groups and young black people (outside the specified services laid down by government). He spoke of the role of the VNPO being 'community development'.

It was evident that there was little need for the service provided by the VNPO, as originally defined, since most of the young offenders were attending the local Social Services facilities. However, the National VNPO senior management and the local Social Services senior management identified the need for a service to keep young people out of local authority residential care. A task group of their senior managers worked together to design a new service to meet these mutually defined objectives. The relationship had a clear sense of being a 'collaborative' one. The relationship was later formalized with a legally binding contract clarifying the obligations and responsibilities.

Despite the continuance of young people going in to the residential homes, few referrals were made to the project. It became quickly apparent that the local authority social workers saw no need for the project – they felt they could provide the service. The 'collaborative' model was thus not shared across all the organizational levels. The meaning of this new service to the social workers was that it was a challenge to their 'professionalism' – to many of them the VNPO workers were not 'qualified professionals'. The Social Services Department then began to question the VNPO's service in relation to young people referred to the VNPO, particularly young women and young black people. 'You are not contracted to criticize us but to provide a service we require' was their response – the managerialist model.

The director of the VNPO asked to meet with the director of the Social Services Department to discuss the difficulties. During the discussions, the director of the Social Services Department expressed her commitment to a model of 'partnership' with VNPOs, which involved the statutory organization working collaboratively with the VNPO, both parties learning from each other – the collaborative model. However, she then went on to say that this would be different when the Social Services Department restructured in to a 'purchaser-provider' structure. It would then purchase specified services (specified by her department) from VNPOs. VNPOs would not be expected to 'challenge' the decisions of her Department. The new relationship was clearly being seen as significantly different from the model previously outlined by her. She was promoting a **market** model of relationships with VNPOs.

Case study two

The second case study highlights a different meaning of contracting but consonant with the ideologies outlined earlier.

A VNPO had worked for many years in a London Borough, providing services for young people at risk and young offenders. Many of these services had been innovatory. These services were seen by the VNPO as 'complementing' the local government provision in the Borough. Mainly due to financial pressure on the local government, the VNPO was assked to provide all the services for young offenders in the Borough. Some local authority staff would be seconded to the VNPO to provide extra staff. The VNPO had therefore taken on a new role, 'substituting' for local government services. The service level agreement was drafted and a meeting held with the Social Services Department senior manager. He informed the VNPO that the VNPO would be expected to 'add value' to the relationship by bringing in additional financial resources. 'Contracting' meant adding financial value. The VNPO negotiated a different meaning of 'added value' by pointing to the additional skills and experience the VNPO was bringing to the contractual relationship.

These cases show the importance of VNPOs understanding the different models and meaning of contractual relations held by the statutory organizations they work with (and within their own organization). Without this understanding, confusion, ambiguity and conflict is likely. The VNPO may decide, despite its own desire for a collaborative model, that it is prepared to accept a contractual relationship based on a market model. At least this will be understood. It may be that the VNPO, as in the second case above, negotiates a new shared meaning of the contractual relationship. It may be that the VNPO accepts the 'managerialist' framework of the contractual relationship and develops 'collaborative' working relationships with statutory organization workers on providing services for individuals. As in the first case, different meanings of contracting can be held at different levels of the organization. A key skill then of VNPO managers is to understand the different meanings of contractual relations held by others and either work with these differences, or work with others to negotiate new shared meanings of the contractual relationship.

MANAGING VNPOs IN THE ERA OF CONTRACTS

VNPOs need to reflect upon a number of key issues or questions. The management of contractual relationships is above all about managing change in a complex and changing political social and economic environment. The key managerial challenges are:

1 Is there a shared understanding in the VNPO of its mission/purpose, objectives, values and priorities, and of its strengths and limitations?
2 Should the VNPO enter into contracting? What impact will this have on the above mission/purpose, objectives, values and priorities?
3 Should the VNPO tender for contracts? What model of contractual relationships does the VNPO value? Is it prepared to work with a statutory organization with a different meaning of contracting?
4 Would the VNPO take on a 'substitution' role, providing mainstream services? Does this conflict with the existing values? Is there a shared view across the VNPO?
5 What impact would contracting have on its advocacy role (if any)?

6 What would be the impact on the VNPO of not contracting with statutory organizations? Is the VNPO prepared for this?

7 If the VNPO took over 'contracted-out' services, has it considered the implications of legislation requiring the conditions of service of 'contracted out' staffs to be maintained (TUPE)? What impact would this have on its existing staff and their terms/conditions of employment?

8 What impact would taking on 'contracted out' services have on the culture of the VNPO?

9 Are the consultation and decision-making processes within the VNPO clear? The contracting process may require quick decisions. Is it clear who has the authority and responsibility to make such decisions?

10 Are there means of effective informal and formal communication within the VNPO in order to ensure the VNPO can learn and share information about its environment?

11 Contracting is likely to lead towards increased formalization within the VNPO and between the VNPO and the statutory organization, and the need for increased administration. Is the VNPO prepared for this? Will this conflict with the values and philosophy of the VNPO?

12 Will contracting decrease the role of the VNPO management committee? What steps will be taken to ensure the management committee have the necessary knowledge, information and skills to carry out their responsibilities for the VNPO, including having responsibility for the mission/purpose strategic direction and policies of the VNPO?

13 Are the management committee aware of their potential financial liabilities under contracting law? Is the VNPO a company limited by guarantee or some other legal entity so giving some protection to the trustees? Has the VNPO insurance cover to give some protection against their possible financial losses?

14 With a move to contracting, has the management committee the appropriate composition, that is the skills, user involvement, community representation?

15 What steps is the VNPO taking to ensure the staff and volunteers have the necessary skills, information and knowledge, including negotiating skills?

16 What impact will possible changes have on the influence of, and services for, existing users? Will this effect its philosophy and values?

17 What impact will contracting have on its anti-discriminatory services and practices?

18 Does the VNPO have appropriate financial systems and resources to cope with contracting?

19 Does the VNPO have the necessary skills and knowledge to cost a contract bid?

20 Has the VNPO considered the costs (financial, human and time) of entering into contracting, including the cost of unsuccessful tendering?

21 Does the VNPO have the appropriate evaluation systems, in order to evaluate the quality and effectiveness of its services?

22 What are the positions, strategies and policies on contracting of local government/statutory organizations with which the VNPO might contract? Does the VNPO understand the explicit or implicit model of contractual relationship held by them? What do their operational staff think about contracting?

23 What is the minimum length of contract that the VNPO would be prepared to enter into?

24 Does the VNPO have links with key personnel in the statutory organizations with which it might contract in order to gain information and, where appropriate, to influence the contracting process? Does the VNPO understand their decision-making processes?

25 What will be the impact on the VNPO's relationships with other VNPOs, if it enters a contractual relationship with government? What is the position of these other VNPOs on contracting?

26 How will the VNPO manage the change created by the move to contracting – its multiple, ambiguous and conflicting meanings and the changing roles of the statutory and VNPO sectors?

Many of these issues are addressed in other chapters of this book.

VNPOs CUSTOMERS AND QUALITY IN SERVICE CONTRACTS

Quality has been defined variously as 'meeting the expectations of customers' (Feigenbaum 1983), as 'conformance to requirements' (Crosby 1985) and as 'fitness for use' (Juran 1989). The latter two definitions raise the question 'whose requirement' and who decides 'fitness'? The usual response is that it should be the customer (Martin 1993). In the contractual work of VNPOs a key question is 'who are its customers? Koons (1991) describes customers as the **beneficiaries** of work. For a contracted VNPO, the external customers would therefore be both the statutory organization purchasing the service, and its end-users. Their quality dimensions may be very different, though. How does the VNPO reconcile this difference?

Martin (1993) proposes that the quality dimensions and standards of the statutory organization are seen as the minimum or 'floor' quality standards that must be met. Thus the statutory organization may require 'performance' (the service meeting its objectives), anti-discriminatory practice in users accessing the service, a healthy and safe environment, and appropriate staffing levels. The users may require not only this level of performance, but also empathy, reliability and responsiveness. Users may also require particular types of programme, which the funder does not. Your negotiating skills will be important in such cases. The steps in this process are therefore to identify your 'customers', to determine their quality preferences and then to develop appropriate quality measures. These issues are covered in more detail in the chapter on performance and quality management.

SUMMARY OF KEY SKILLS, ABILITIES AND UNDERSTANDINGS FOR MANAGING CONTRACTUAL RELATIONSHIPS

The chapter has highlighted two major areas of ambiguity in 'contracting'. These are whether a formalized funding arrangement is a contract in law and the ambiguity of the meaning of contracting and the contractual relationships. Whilst the legal position of contracts has been outlined and the attention of the reader has been drawn to what are argued to be the present dominant models of contracting, it will be the VNPO which will need ultimately to make sense of, and manage, the meanings of contractual relationships held by others. The key skills, knowledge and abilities for managing contractual relationships can therefore be summarized as:

- understanding the legal definitions and implications of 'contracts' and other forms of agreement;
- the ability to 'read' and understand the multiple and different meanings of contracting and the contractual relationship held by others;
- being able to manage the tendering process, including how to prepare bids which emphasize the quality and value for money of the service and/or meet other tender criteria;
- knowing how to cost services ensuring all direct and indirect costs (i.e. management and development costs) are included;
- having knowledge of how the statutory organizations work and having relationships with key personnel;
- understanding the potential competition from other VNPOs, for-profit organizations and statutory organization in-house bids;
- knowing how to manage quality and service performance; and
- being able to manage change.

REFERENCES

Adirondack, S. and Macfarlane, R. (1993) *Getting Ready for Contracts: A Guide for Voluntary Organisations*, Directory of Social Change, London.

Association of Metropolitan Authorities (AMA) (1990) *Contracts for Social Care. The Local Authority Perspective*, AMA, London.

Bolton, M., Leggett, D. and Thorne, M. (1994) *Shifting the Balance* NCVO Publications, London.

Crosby, P. (1985) *Quality Without Tears – The Art of Hassle-free Management*, Plume, New York.

Feigenbaum, A. (1983) *Total Quality Control*, McGraw Hill, London.

Gutch, R. (1992) *Contracting Lessons from the US*, NCVO Publications, London.

Hedley, R. and Rochester, C. (1991) *Contracts at the Cross-road*, LSE, London.

James, A. (1994) *Managing to Care*, Longman, Harlow.

Juran, J. (1989) *Juran on Leadership for Quality: An Executive Handbook*, Free Press, New York.

Koons, P. (1991) 'Getting comfortable with TQM'. *The Bureaucrat*, **20**, pp. 35–8.

Lawrie, A. (1991) *Quality of Service*, Directory of Social Change, London.

Martin, L. (1993) *Total Quality Management in Human Service Organisations*, Sage, Newbury Park.

Meadows, A. (1992) *Reaching Agreement*, NCVO Publications, London.

National Council for Voluntary Organizations (NCVO) (1989) *Contracting In or Out?* NCVO Publications, London.

Osborne, S. (1993) The governance of public-private relationships. PSMRC Working Paper, Aston University, Birmingham.

Richardson, J. (1993) *Reinventing Contracts. Transatlantic Perspectives on the Future of Contracting*, London.

Sarkis, A. and Webster, R. (1995) *Working in Partnership. The Probation Service and Voluntary Sector*, Russell House, Lyme Regis.

Wolfendon Committee (1978) *The Future of Voluntary Organisations*, Croom Helm, London.

GUIDED READING

Association of Metropolitan Authorities (1991) *Quality and Contracts in the Personal Social Services*, AMA, London. A good guide to the view of local authorities on contracting with VNPOs.

Callaghan, J. (1991) *Costing for Contracts*, NCVO Publications, London. An excellent introduction to this complex area.

Kramer, R. (1990) *Voluntary Organisations in the Welfare State: On the Threshold of the '90s*, LSE , London. A thoughtful review of some of the policy issues which contracting raises for VNPOs.

Osborne, S. and Waterston, P. (1995) Defining contracts between the state and charitable organizations in national accounts, in *Voluntas*, **5**, (3), pp. 291–300. An exploration of the multiple meanings, and their implications, of the term 'contract'.

Rathgeb Smith, S. and Lipsky, M. (1994) *Nonprofits for Hire*, Harvard University Press, Boston. Definitive study of the impact of contracting on VNPOs in the US.

13 Managing inter-organizational relationships

Chris Huxham and Siv Vangen

INTRODUCTION

By the end of this chapter you should be able to:

- understand some of the key reasons why working with people in other organizations is complex and often difficult; and
- identify some of the key things to think about and some of the key skills needed by VNPOs in order to work effectively in such situations.

INTER-ORGANIZATIONAL RELATIONSHIPS FOR VNPOs

Unemployment, homelessness, poverty, crime, care of the elderly, the young, the disabled or ill, youth violence, ethnic conflict, drug abuse, protecting the environment . . . These are but a few of the major societal issues facing those of us living in contemporary society. Tackling such problems is obviously not a simple matter. One factor which contributes to the complexity is that these issues tend to span a wide range of aspects of society; some even span national boundaries. An inherent feature of such situations is therefore that no single agency can ever have responsibility for tackling them. For example, tackling youth violence is likely to need to involve local community groups, youth organizations, the police, social services, health organizations, the education sector, probation and prison services and so on.

If you work in a VNPO or are involved with a community group which has a concern for issues of this type, you are almost certain to find yourself working with people in other organizations and groups. You will assuredly find yourself at least communicating with people in public agencies or government bodies because they will always have some role in addressing societal issues and because they tend to have financial resources available. You will often find yourself interacting with other voluntary sector organizations because they have skills or resources which complement your own. You may even find yourselves engaged in initiatives with business organizations. Indeed, if you are to be really effective in achieving your aims, your connections with other organizations probably need to go beyond a simple reaction to circumstances. It is likely to be advantageous to be actively developing collaborative arrangements with other organizations for mutual benefit.

Many VNPOs also find themselves working with other organizations for more mundane, though never the less valuable reasons. Governments in the west have been increasingly transferring the funding of the delivery of various forms of public service away from 'main-stream' government agencies, such as local government or health authorities, to independent voluntary or community organizations. For example, after school care, children's homes and community development initiatives are now often the province of VNPOs where previously they may have been organized directly by local authorities.

While for some VNPOs such service delivery is directly consistent with their aims, others take it on as a way of generating a steady income stream which may provide some stability in the furtherance of other aims. Either way, taking on such work involves a commitment to working with the funding agency, and often with other delivery organizations, to ensure that the aims of the particular service are met.

Given all these reasons why you are likely to find yourself working with people in other organizations, knowing how to do this effectively is going to be important. Working across organizational boundaries is one of the most difficult activities that managers in any type of organization have to accomplish. Many collaborative arrangements which begin with the best of intentions and goodwill never the less turn out to be frustrating affairs and it is not uncommon for them to dwindle away into non-existence. When this happens, not only are the benefits lost, but also a great deal of resource and effort are wasted and goodwill can be lost in the process. With this chapter we aim to give you some insights into some of the good practices and some of the problems that are experienced by people involved in work across organizations, to which you may wish to relate your own experiences. The insights will also provide a basis for examination of some of the key skills required to manage inter-organizational relationships effectively.

DEVELOPING THEMES IN THE MANAGEMENT OF INTER-ORGANIZATIONAL RELATIONSHIPS

Over the past few years we have worked with many people involved in inter-organizational initiatives in one shape or form. First, we have run a number of 'awareness raising' events aimed at allowing participants to share their experiences of inter-organizational work, providing a framework to describe some of the issues in managing inter-organizational relationships to which they can relate their experiences, and developing with them some ideas about how to manage these situations successfully.

Most of these events have been interactive workshops in which the participants work with each other and with us in order to build up the 'story'.

The kinds of people who have attended these events have had varied experiences of inter-organizational working. For example, one workshop was attended by mixed groups of staff from local government and health departments, from independent but publicly funded community organizations, from national and international charities and from purely volunteer or community groups (who often referred to themselves as community activists).

Second, we have worked with the core groups of specific inter-organizational initiatives; that is, with the people who come together on a regular basis to manage the initiative. For example, we have been involved with a colleague over an eighteen-month period in working with a group of representatives from seven organizations concerned with raising the profile of child poverty in Strathclyde Region in Scotland. Our involvement with this group has been in the form of strategic thinking workshops aimed at helping them to review and revise their collaborative purpose and processes. In the course of our involvement, the group has moved from being relatively unproductive (in their own eyes) to being active, but it has also changed its form substantially following the offer of substantial funding for a development worker from a large charity. So much effect has this had, that less than half of the original core group members are still members and the role of the group has become, at least for the present, primarily one of a steering group for the development worker's project.

Finally, we have also talked extensively with four community development collaborative groups, from different areas of Strathclyde, in order to create with them pictures of their collaborative practice. One of these groups consisted of the paid officers of local authorities and independent agencies whilst another consisted entirely of volunteers from community groups. The other two groups comprised a combination of employees and volunteers. The broad aims of the four groups were, respectively, to create and implement an anti-poverty strategy on behalf of the area regeneration initiative of the Regional Council, to assist residents in the area in claiming government benefits, to campaign about local poverty issues and to provide a forum for local people both to discuss local issues and to represent them on the area regeneration group (itself formed from a collaboration of local, regional and national governments).

In all of these kinds of involvement a first stage has generally been to collect individual views and experiences of inter-organizational work. In some cases, we have done this through personal interviews. In other cases, we have organized a group exercise in which people wrote on cards their thoughts about previous experiences of inter-organizational working (one thought per card). These were then grouped together into clusters of related thoughts, fixed to flip chart paper and displayed on a wall. In either case, the thoughts were in response only to very general questions such as, 'what makes inter-organizational collaboration work?', or 'what makes inter-organizational collaboration go wrong?' In either case, there was an opportunity for the initial thoughts to be developed through further review and discussion. Different events have then proceeded in different ways depending on their purpose.

Through retaining a copy of what people have said on each occasion, we have been able to build up a picture of the issues that seem to be of central concern to those involved. Some themes are raised repeatedly by every group, while other issues emerge from the specific considerations of particular groups. These themes are valuable indications of the issues that cause anxiety or reward in inter-organizational work. They are, however, in a sense quite superficial 'first thoughts' sparked by very general questions. In order to understand more about the deeper nature of the issues we have therefore also been working intensively with a small number of people actively engaged in inter-organizational work, in order to probe into the complexities which lie below the surface.

In this chapter we will discuss six themes that were raised commonly by the groups. The focus of the chapter is in particular on voluntary and informal relationships rather than on contractual arrangements, though much of what is said can be extended to those situations too. We shall use the term **collaboration** to describe such relationships, though other terms, such as **partnership** or **alliance**, would do just as well.

KEY THEMES IN COLLABORATIVE WORK

Managing aims

The one issue that has been raised by virtually every person we have worked with is concerned with the aims, objectives or goals of a collaboration. Typically people argued for the importance of having a clear and agreed set of aims. This, it was argued, allows members to be clear about why the collaboration exists and why they are a part of it. It also minimizes misunderstanding of the tasks to be undertaken and reduces false expectations. More importantly, perhaps, it is thought to provide the basis for who is going to do what towards meeting these aims.

While these are all important considerations, agreeing on aims is not as simple as it may sound. It is highly unlikely that you will find another organization to work with that has aims exactly similar to your own. Even if such an organization did exist, you are unlikely to need to collaborate with it unless pooling of financial resources is the driving force. Indeed, you may even feel in competition with an organization so similar to your own!

You are much more likely to want to collaborate with organizations with **complementary** expertise, and these will have different aims to your own. Organizations of this type are also much more likely to want to draw you

into collaborative arrangements with them. This means that different organizations will be in the collaboration for different reasons. They will often
be wanting to achieve different ends through it – and you may have to
accept that some agencies will have less reason to be committed to it than
others.

We have developed a taxonomy to describe some of the kinds of goals
that are present in collaborative situations (Vangen *et al.* 1994). It would
not be appropriate to describe it in detail here, but it will be useful to
extract one or two key points from it. Our taxonomy characterizes goals as
being on three levels. At the top level there are the **meta-goals**. These are
the reasons for the collaboration – a statement of what it is aiming to
achieve. As we said earlier, on the face of it an explicit statement of meta-
goals is essential to making progress. In practice, however, too explicit a
definition of meta-goals can produce difficulties in itself; the more tightly
you try to define meta-goals, the more difficulty you will have in trying to
get the other organizations with their different aims to agree to them. The
manager of one community partnership recently argued '. . . we have to
write a statement of aims to justify our existence. My job is to find a way of
writing it so generally that none of the parties involved can disagree with
it.'

A second level of goals, the **macro-goals**, are those that each of the
participating organizations is likely to want to achieve for itself through the
collaboration, but which are not related to the overt purpose of the collaboration. For example, one of the organizations might wish to use the
collaboration as a way of raising its profile with a funding body, thus
increasing the chances of securing its own future existence.

The third level of goals, **the micro-goals**, are those which individual
members of participating organizations may wish to achieve through the
collaboration. These tend to relate to career aspirations or job security. For
example, the individual might see the collaborative initiative as increasing
the chances of renewed funding for their own post.

What makes these organizational and individual goals so difficult to deal
with is that they often form part of hidden agendas which are not brought
out into the open. They therefore often cause confusion and tension.
However, it is important to remember that these organizational- and
individual-specific goals often provide the incentive for organizations to
participate in the collaboration, so it is essential for you to be aware of the
existence of such goals for other participants (and for yourself!) even
though they may not have been publicly discussed – and even though
you may not know exactly what they are.

To get the greatest value out of collaboration you need to find a way of
setting it up so that each organization and each individual involved benefits
from it and so that society or 'the greater good' also benefits through you
having collectively achieved something that none of the organizations
could have done acting on their own. We call this combination of meeting

individual aims, organizational aims and wider societal aims, achieving **collaborative advantage** (Huxham and Macdonald 1992).

In order to achieve collaborative advantage you have to decide on the extent to which you want to bring all of these goals out into open discussion. On the one hand it is helpful to have the goals explicitly stated so that everyone knows what everyone else is aiming to achieve and to give a collective sense of direction. On the other hand, opening up discussion can emphasize all kinds of incompatibilities between the different goals. Even if you are able to reach agreement, despite the incompatibilities, this can often require seemingly endless discussion and negotiation. The important thing is to get 'enough' agreement about broad aims and about detailed actions to allow the joint initiative to progress. Being able to judge when you have 'enough' is an important skill that you need to develop.

Participants in our session also noted a number of points about the nature of the negotiation about goals and the goals themselves which made it more likely that the collaboration could make effective progress. In terms of the process of negotiation itself, they suggested that it was important to incorporate different organizational goals in the agenda of the collaboration. This was to ensure not only active participation by all, but also that each party must be aware of the need to compromise on its goals for the collaboration for the sake of defining meta-goals that are realistic for the collaboration as a whole. Finding a way to discourage some agencies from pushing their own goals inappropriately is a part of this process. The participants also suggested that given the diverse nature of the organizations involved in a collaboration, its goals are more likely to be achievable if they are expressed in a task oriented and tangible form rather than in more grandiose terms. Finally, they also suggested that having both too wide and having too narrow a remit can be disabling. In the first case, because it dilutes efforts and weakens the sense of direction, and in the second case because it is unlikely to satisfy all partners.

Compromise

The point has just been made, that being willing to compromise on different agendas is essential to making progress in collaborations. In addition, people involved in collaboration often mentioned a need to compromise on different work practices, different organizational cultures and different individual styles of working.

The need to compromise arises because organizations are different from each other. As well as the differing aims, they have different cultural norms and values. For example, in one group with which we worked compromises were required because one ethnic group involved held strong religious beliefs which were different from their partners. Style of management, decision-making procedures and the speed at which things can be achieved are also likely to differ greatly especially, for example, between a large bureaucratic organization and a small community group. This can mean that tasks you feel ought to be trivial or routine matters to carry out can take a great deal of time and compromise to sort out to the satisfaction of all concerned. For instance, in the child poverty group referred to earlier, the organizations all had very different procedures for evaluating projects and different criteria against which to evaluate them. A great deal of effort and compromise were required in order to decide on an evaluation process for the collaborative project that would not be too time-consuming to carry out and yet would satisfy all concerned.

Many difficulties also arise because collaborations tend to involve people with different professional expertise working together. If you work for a child-care charity you are likely to have different values, goals and styles of working from the people who work for the police, the health service, the local authorities and the schools with whom you are likely to need to interact. In order to make progress it is important that you can all 'move out of your own professionalism' and 'meet the others half-way' from time to time. Breaking down the stereotyped perceptions of each other is also something that needs to be worked at.

Communication

Related to the issue of compromise is that of communication. The plea for good communication is very common among those who have experienced collaboration, probably because of the frustration that poor communication induces. Our participants made a distinction between three different communication channels: communication between the people in the core group, communication between the core group and the organizations concerned, and communication between the collaboration and the wider community.

In terms of establishing good communication between the members of the core group, one issue which seemed to be a concern to many is that of language. The everyday language of one profession can be quite different from another. What seems like ordinary English to one person may appear to be highly specialized (and unfathomable) jargon to another. Volunteers in community groups often express frustration and even anger about the use of jargon by those they regard as professionals; in their perception the term 'professionals' often includes those who work for large charities or even small, funded, autonomous community organizations as well as the more obvious public agencies. The problems of language and jargon are even more pronounced if some groups are more articulate than others, and can be exacerbated if parties come from ethnic groups with different national languages.

There are some obvious lessons for good collaborative practice to be drawn from this. First, it is going to be important to examine your own use of language. Imagine yourself in the shoes of the people with whom you are trying to work and ask yourself what might **not** be obvious to you.

Second, you are going to need to find a way to communicate that is not aggressive, but which maintains your own dignity, particularly when asking others to explain what they mean. It is worth remembering that you are probably not the only one who cannot understand.

Ensuring that you can understand the language of everyone is obviously a prerequisite to good communication. However, even if there is no serious problem with jargon or language, you may find yourselves talking at cross-purposes because your different outlooks lead you to interpret things differently. **Listening** is as important a skill in this respect as **talking**. Our participants stressed the need to pay careful attention to checking that you understand meaning as well as language. Tolerance is essential.

As well as being concerned about communication between core group members, in order to realize the full potential of the collaboration you will also need to ensure good communication between the core group and the partner organizations. Keeping up this communication is likely to be highly time-consuming but essential, in terms of spotting early signs of disagreements and in terms of gaining trust, commitment, support and the required resources from each organization.

Finally, for collaboratives set up to tackle societal problems at a community level, our participants argued that communication between the collaboration and the wider community as a whole is vital, in keeping the group up to date and in maintaining good relations with the community. For instance, for the successful combating of problems such as ethnic conflict or drug abuse, gaining the goodwill of the community at large could be crucial.

Democracy and equality

We argued above that different organizations will have different values. However, there is one particular set of values that is common among most or even all VNPOs which can distinguish them – at least in terms of the **strength** of feeling about these values – from public and private sector organizations. This is an ardent concern for democracy and equality in the process of collaboration. There are at least three aspects to the way democracy is viewed.

The first aspect of democracy is concerned with who should be involved in the collaboration. Some people express a concern to ensure that the group is not too exclusive. More commonly, people go further and argue that everyone with a stake in the issue should be involved. However, while this sounds like a good democratic practice, our participants have also argued against it as a practical way forward suggesting, for example, that organizations which cannot commit sufficient time to the collaboration should be actively discouraged from participating. They also recognize that having too many organizations involved exacerbates the communication problems and the difficulty of reaching agreement about aims and actions, and may thus reduce the chance of achieving anything of value. Balancing the size of the group to reduce exclusiveness but at the same time to ensure that it is relevant for all members is important.

In practice, few collaborations seem to be convened in any sort of thoughtful way; instead membership tends to be created out of existing contacts and evolves in a rather unplanned way as new issues suggest new partners or new contacts become drawn in. Never the less, we think that it is valuable to consider explicitly who should be part of your collaboration. In particular, you need to identify those organizations (or even key individuals) who could give significant help toward achieving your collaborative ends, those who will be affected positively by your collaborative work and those who might wish to sabotage your endeavours. In a truly democratic world all of these 'stakeholders' should be involved in the collaboration. In the practical world some aspect(s) of democracy usually has to be sacrificed to pragmatism. Not everyone can be involved so you have to decide who should be.

One way of thinking about these stakeholders is in two categories. **Internal stakeholders** are those that are a part of the collaboration. **External stakeholders** are those that remain outside (Finn 1996). When you have decided who you would like or need to be internal you have to persuade them to join. You should be aware that they will be certain to want to renegotiate with you the aims of the collaboration. Each extra internal stakeholder also adds another dimension to the difficulties caused by differences in working practices, culture and language. These are things you would be advised to bear in mind and make a judgement about before you invite more organizations to take part. Increasing the group numbers tends to increase the difficulties of collaboration geometrically, rather than arithmetically.

External stakeholders should not be forgotten, either. These are people/organizations that will also have a significant interest in the outcome of a collaboration, but do not or cannot necessarily be involved in it. They need to be managed in some way. If they are organizations that you are concerned about for democratic reasons, you may want to consult them from time to time. If they are potential saboteurs, you may need to take evasive action!

The second aspect of democracy is concerned with the processes of the collaboration itself. There is a legitimate concern to ensure that what the collaboration ends up deciding to do emerges from 'proper democratic discussion'. Having effective communication is obviously important to this, but it also means that regular attendance at meetings of the collaboration is important. Ensuring that no one is allowed to 'take over' is clearly an issue here, but this may conflict with a need for strong leadership to help the group progress. Achieving shared control is not always easy and the price to pay for pure democratic processes might well be that no one takes responsibility for the collaboration. This is a problem that co-operatives and collectives in particular have to address (Landry 1985; Stryjan 1989).

There is also a concern with equality and credit. Recognizing the value of each contribution and ensuring that everyone gets credit for joint action is essential in this view. An important consequence is that you may sacrifice some of the credit which ought to be due to your own organization or to you in the interests of democracy. While this may not seem to matter in the abstract, 'so long as the ends are achieved', when it comes to the crunch you are likely to regard it as more significant for two reasons. First, being visibly seen to be achieving will be crucial to your organization receiving funding for the future. Second, receiving credit where it is due may be vital to maintaining high staff morale. Further, it could reflect upon organizational perceptions of your performance as a manager, by your colleagues and/or governing body.

The third aspect of democracy is concerned with accountability and representativeness. Clearly, individuals who represent their organizations in the collaboration are constrained in what they can agree to, by their accountability to their organization and sometimes to even wider constituents. For example, if you have an elected councillor in your collaborative group they will feel themselves answerable to their electorate as well as to the council. Similarly, representatives from charities may feel accountability to donors as well as to colleagues. Collaborations therefore have to satisfy each of these constituencies. This severely reduces the autonomy of the collaboration to act as it sees fit. This important point is explored further by Leat (1988).

The other side of this coin is to be clear about the way in which participants in a collaboration are actually representatives. For example, community representatives may express views which are beyond the sphere of the particular community group that they represent on the collaboration. Given that such representatives are not accountable to anyone for these views, it can be often difficult for other collaborators to judge just how representative of community views they actually are.

Power and trust

Closely related to the issue of democracy is that of power. For instance, people who work for large international charities sometimes say they feel like small players on the global scene, when compared to the various government bodies with which they have to work. On the other hand, these same organizations can seem like very big players to a small, local community group. Representatives from small voluntary organizations tend to feel very vulnerable, not only when collaborating with statutory agencies but also when collaborating with more wealthy and institutionalized charities.

Collaborations involving voluntary organizations are relatively unusual compared to collaborations of public or private sector organizations, in the sense that the types of resources deployed may be quite different. For example, while a public agency may provide essential funding for the collaborative initiative and perhaps professional input, the role of a small community group in the collaboration may be to provide just as significant expertise, in the form of local knowledge. In these circumstances, the power to dictate what the collaboration does is often felt to be in the hands of those who hold the purse strings. It is hardly surprising therefore, that both volunteers and paid officers involved in community collaborations invariably report tensions between the voluntary and statutory agencies, and between the professional and the local people, involved (Barr and Huxham 1996).

If you are feeling vulnerable, it is worth remembering that the apparently powerful organizations would probably not be wanting to collaborate with you if you did not have something to offer over and above what they can provide themselves. If you can identify what this is, it can put you in a good negotiating position. On the other hand, if you are collaborating with organizations which are smaller than yours, it is worth remembering that they may be feeling much more vulnerable than you at first imagine. If you wish the partnership to be on roughly equal terms, you may need to find ways to demonstrate this to them. Paying attention to communication and especially to careful use of language is essential. The term **collaborative empowerment** has been used to describe a philosophy of empowering the community to manage its own future through collaboration (Himmelman 1992).

All of this leads to a conclusion that trust between participants in a collaboration is essential, though not necessarily easy to achieve. Differences in aims, culture, working practice, language and perceived power all mitigate against it. The people we have worked with stressed the need for respect and honesty and a recognition that it takes time to build trust. Trust can only be created as inter-organizational and inter-personal relationships develop and as the results of successful joint actions become evident. The problem often is that you do not feel inclined to commit to joint action unless you trust the other partners.

Getting started in a trusting relationship may mean committing yourself to taking a risk over a joint action. When possible, it is wise to start with smaller, less ambitious, projects to provide each party with the opportunity to get used to and learn their respective languages, cultures and working practices, and so create the basis for trust. Smaller, less ambitious projects also have a greater chance of succeeding and successful outcomes will in turn reinforce trusting attitudes and create the foundation for more substantial collaboration. This is sometimes called going for 'small wins' (Bryson 1988).

Determination, commitment and stamina

Most of the above considerations would tend to suggest that collaborating is not easy and that a great deal of time may need to be taken over ensuring mutual understanding and in negotiating ways forward that are mutually acceptable. For collaborations in which the members are not experienced in working together, the difficulty of achieving this is often too great and they flounder. To a casual observer it would be difficult to understand why the rate of work output of the collaborations is so low. We call this **collaborative inertia** (Huxham and Vangen 1994).

People involved in collaboration often feel that their lack of progress is due to lack of commitment from all members involved and that the solution is to gain somehow more commitment from all members. However, you need to recognize that commitment will vary from organization to organization depending on how closely their agendas match that of the collaboration. Individual commitment will also vary from one time to another depending on other demands made by their employer.

Despite varying commitment, members of collaborations who pay specific attention to how they work together as a team and who strive to keep up the continuity in their working seem to benefit. The people we have worked with argued that determination and stamina are **essential** to successful collaboration. You need to accept that it will take longer than you would normally anticipate, that it will be demanding on your time and that you need to be persistent and keep trying.

CONCLUSIONS – A SUMMARY OF CONCERNS AND SKILLS

In this chapter we have only been able to cover a part of the story of collaboration. Never the less it seems worth summarizing the management concerns and key skills needed by staff in VNPOs for working in collaborations. You need to be able:

- to manage the dilemma of how to bring all of the goals of the various organizations and individuals involved out into open discussion – the important thing is to be able to judge when you have enough agreement about broad aims and about detailed actions to allow the joint initiative to progress;
- to be willing to compromise against your own priorities for the collaboration for the sake of defining goals that are realistic for the collaboration as a whole;
- to see if you can find a way to discourage others from pushing their own agendas forward inappropriately;
- to try, where goals are made explicit, to ensure they are expressed in a task oriented and tangible form rather than in more grandiose terms;
- to try also to ensure that the breadth of remit that you set yourselves is neither too wide nor too narrow;
- to recognize that tasks that you feel ought to be trivial or routine matters to carry out can take a great deal of time and compromise to sort out to the satisfaction of all concerned, and to allow time for this;

- to examine your own use of language – imagine yourself in the shoes of the people with whom you are trying to work and ask yourself what might not be obvious to them;
- to think about how you can ask others to explain their terminology and jargon without being aggressive and while maintaining your own dignity – remember that you are probably not the only one who cannot understand;
- to pay careful attention to ensuring that you understand meaning as well as language (not the same thing!);
- to consider who are the stakeholders in your collaborative initiative and which of them should be internal and which external; to persuade those who you would like or need to be internal to join – but do not forget the external stakeholders, think about how you are going to manage them;
- to be conscious about recognizing the value of each contribution and ensuring that everyone gets credit for joint action;
- to understand the significance of sacrificing credit for your own organization or yourself, in the interests of democracy;
- to remember that the apparently powerful organizations would probably not be wanting to collaborate with you if you did not have something to offer over and above what they can provide themselves – if you can identify what this is, it can put you in a good negotiating position;
- to remember, if you are collaborating with organizations which are much smaller than yours, that they may be feeling much more vulnerable than you imagine – pay attention to communication, to careful use of language and to empowering them;
- to be prepared to take a risk in order to get started in a trusting relationship; and
- to be forever aware that collaborative initiatives will take longer than you would normally anticipate, will be demanding on your time and will require you to be persistent in keeping on trying.

Clearly the above list is not a panacea for collaboration. It does not provide clear rules for how to collaborate successfully. Collaboration is too complex for that. Through raising some of the key issues it does, however, provide a review of those things you need to have a conscious awareness about. Such an awareness is the starting point, not the conclusion, of successful collaboration.

REFERENCES

Barr, C. and Huxham, C. (1996) Collaboration for community development, in *Creating Collaborative Advantage* (ed C. Huxham) Sage, London.
Bryson, J. (1988) Strategic planning: big wins and small wins. *Public Money and Management* (Autumn).
Finn, C. (1996) Utilising stakeholder strategies to ensure positive outcomes in

collaborative processes, in *Creating Collaborative Advantage* (ed C. Huxham), Sage, London.

Himmelman, A. (1992) *Communities Working Collaboratively for a Change*, The Himmelman Consulting Group, Minneapolis.

Huxham, C. and Macdonald, D. (1992) Introducing collaborative advantage: achieving inter-organisational effectiveness through meta-strategy. *Management Decision*, **30**, pp. 50–6.

Huxham, G. and Vangen, S. (1994) *Naivety and Maturity, Inertia and Fatigue: Are Working Relationships between Public Organisations Doomed to Fail?* Paper presented at the Annual Employment Research Unit Conference, The Contract State: the Future of Public Management, University of Cardiff.

Landry, C. (1985) *What a Way to Run a Rail-road*, Comedia, London.

Leat, D. (1988) *Accountabilities*, NCVO, Worcester.

Stryjan, J. (1989) *Impossible Organizations*, Greenwood, New York.

Vangen, S., Huxham, C. and Eden, C. (1994) *Understanding Collaboration from the Perspective of a Goal System*, Paper presented at the International Workshop on Multi-organisational Partnerships, Brussels.

GUIDED READING

Bryson, J. and Crosby, B. (1992) *Leadership for the Common Good: Tackling Public Problems in a Shared-Power World*, Jossey Bass, San Francisco. This book explains the dynamics of change in a 'shared power' world. It is an extensive guide for community leaders in VNPOs, to tackling complex societal problems.

Gray, B. (1989) *Collaborating: Finding Common Ground for Multiparty Problems*, Jossey Bass, San Francisco. A classic work on collaboration. The book draws upon case case studies to demonstrate how collaboration can be used to solve shared problems and resolve conflict.

Gray, B. and Wood, D. (1991) Collaborative alliances: moving from practice to theory- part I. in a special issue of the *Journal of Applied Behavioural Science*, **27** (1). A collection of cases and theories about collaboration over social issues, such as education, the environment and the management of global common property.

Huxham, C (ed) (1996) *Creating Collaborative Advantage*, Sage, London. A collection of cases, insights and process for collaborative practice. Many of the authors have extensive experience in facilitating collaborative groups and the book describes a number of processes for aiding collaborative groups and processes.

Winer, M. and Ray, K. (1994) *Collaboration Handbook: Creating, Sustaining and Enjoying the Journey*, Amherst H. Wilder Foundation, Minnesota. A guide to help you do it. This book is by far the best of its type on the market. It contains many valuable insights about effective collaborative practice and a wealth of exercises which you can use directly to help you make progress.

ACKNOWLEDGEMENTS

Especial thanks are due to our colleagues Catherine Barr, who played a central role in the data collection and analysis with a number of groups we have referred to in the chapter, and to Colin Eden who facilitated the strategy workshops and who has been involved in the work and a source of inspiration in countless other ways. We should also like to thank Damian Killeen and Janet Muir of The Poverty Alliance, based in Glasgow, for working with us and allowing us to work with them over a good number of years. Thanks too to the many 'collaborators' who have been the source of the material discussed here. A part of the research which informs this chapter is funded by the Economic and Social Research Council, Grant number 000234450.

14 Performance and quality management in VNPOs

Stephen P. Osborne

INTRODUCTION

This chapter explores new frameworks for performance and quality management in voluntary and non-profit organizations (VNPOs). It is based upon research and consultancy work carried out by the author and his colleagues over the past five years with a range of VNPOs throughout Britain. By the end of this chapter you should

- be clear about the nature of performance and quality management;
- have thought about their importance to your organization and yourself; and
- have begun to think about how to implement or improve these systems within your own organization.

A basic starting point is to be clear about the difference between performance and quality management. This is not so much a question of a clear-cut differentiation, as one of balance and emphasis. Performance management is essentially an internal organizational tool, concerned with **the utilization of organizational resources** against a number of priorities and organizational objectives. Quality management is rather more externally focused. It concerns **the experience of your services by their beneficiaries and their impact upon them**. As suggested, these two perspectives are not entirely separate. As will be seen, there is a deal of overlap between the ideas of 'effectiveness' in the performance vocabulary and 'fitness for purpose' in the quality vocabulary. Nonetheless it is a useful starting point in deciding upon a way forward.

It is also important to think about why performance and quality management are important issues for managers in VNPOs. In recent years these management tools, particularly the former one, have received some bad press in both the voluntary and public sectors. Organizations and staff within them have complained variously that they are simply political devices for politicians to mask their own intentions with, that they are time-consuming to use and get in the way of the actual purposes and services of an agency and that they are negative and critical processes which de-motivate staff and concentrate upon blaming individuals for poor performance rather than praising them for good performance.

It is argued here that these criticisms are as much about the poor implementation of performance and quality management than about the tools themselves. Properly implemented, they offer a number of important gains to a VNPO. These include

- ensuring that scarce organizational resources are being used to their best advantage;
- being clear about how the activities of an organization relate to its purpose and objectives and their impact upon the lives of its beneficiaries;
- thinking about how to ensure that the way that the staff of the organization acts is congruent with what it is trying to achieve;
- recognizing good quality work and performance by individuals and groups in the organization and highlighting areas where these can be improved (and how); and
- being able to provide informed feedback to the stakeholders and funders of the organization about what it is doing.

PERFORMANCE MANAGEMENT IN VNPOs

The section will begin by reviewing briefly the component parts of performance management, as well as some common indicators of performance. It will situate these within the rationalist tradition of decision-making and summarize the main critiques of this tradition. Following on from this it will offer a revised model of performance assessment for VNPOs, which is situated within the rationalist model but which responds to the key points of these critiques. It will conclude by highlighting some positive principles of performance management for VNPOs.

The rational model approach to performance management

As a solution to the complexity of the task of performance management in multi-objective public programmes or VNPOs, the rational model of decision-making focuses on breaking down the decision-making process into simpler stages and sub-sets of decisions. The fundamental assumptions underlying this rationalist approach are the availability of relevant information, the ability of actors to access it and process it and a unitary organizational purpose which legitimates this approach (Simon 1957). This section explores the building blocks of performance assessment and management as viewed from within the rationalist perspective.

What is performance assessment?

According to the rationalist approach, performance assessment is the evaluative process by which a view is reached about the performance of a set of activities against the achievement of specified objectives. Five separate elements are contained within it:

1 *Performance appraisal* – the prior assessment of the degree to which proposed activities are likely to achieve their objectives, and the development of indicators and targets by which the performance of the activity or programme can be monitored and evaluated in the future.
2 *Performance monitoring* – the ongoing assessment of an activity, both in terms of its objectives and its process, often concentrating on the evaluation of the achievement of 'lower level' objectives, such as physical progress, meeting of deadlines and the keeping within budget guidelines.
3 *Performance (ex-post) evaluation* – the retrospective evaluation of a programme against its objectives.
4 *Performance indicators* – surrogates for the levels of performance. Often quantifiable indicators are utilized because of their ease of use, but qualitative indicators are also possible and indeed may be preferable.
5 *Performance management* – the process of ensuring that:

- performance assessment is an integral part of any organization/project from its outset;
- its component parts are understandable to those gathering the data on performance and to those analysing and using it;
- the results of performance assessment are used to inform all levels of organizational/project planning and implementation; and
- the performance assessment process is oriented toward enabling and improving performance in the future.

Why assess performance?

Performance assessment should not be viewed as an end in itself. Rather, it is a particular way of gathering and reporting information in order to alert managers to any potential problems or benefits from possible changes. It can also be a way to ensure accountability for the use of public money by both public and voluntary organizations (see the chapter in this book on accountability). This is a complex task. For each logically separate objective held by a VNPO, the rational model requires at least one performance indicator, developed from within a framework of the inputs and outputs of the organization.

Traditionally, there are four different conceptual dimensions of performance at which indicators are directed. These are economy, efficiency, effectiveness, and equity (Bovaird *et al.* 1988) though the rational model has tended to concentrate upon the first three (for example, Butt and Palmer 1985).

The measurement of **economy** is required to ensure that, for any given cost, **inputs** (the resources going into a service or organization) are maximized. Typical performance indicators would be comparisons of wage levels across an organization and/or over time or comparisons of the purchase price of materials. By contrast **efficiency** is concerned with the relationship between **inputs** and **outputs** (the actual services that an organization produces), such as the extent to which outputs are maximized for any given level of inputs. Typical indicators here are unit costs, levels of activities carried out and the productivity of staff.

The concept of **equity** is less generally applied. This requires that the **distribution of outputs** is consistent with the agreed policies of the VNPO, with regard to the distribution or redistribution of resources and services to the population as a whole. This requires the assessment of the degree to which a service provided is fairly distributed and accessible to the individuals/groups for whom it is intended. Typical indicators of this level of performance include the geographical distribution of users, the knowledge of availability of a service within the target beneficiary group, and the accessibility of a service to potential users (for example, wheelchair access for people with disabilities).

Finally, **effectiveness** is concerned with the achievement of **the strategic objectives of an organization**, such as the precise beneficiary group to be served **or the desired outcomes** (the short-term effects and/or longer term impacts upon the lives of this beneficiary group) for that group. It is the most important, but most difficult, dimension of performance to measure. Typical indicators can concern the targeting of organizational resources on its beneficiary group (this target group as a proportion of all users, for example) or the impact of an organization upon these users (such as changes in the well-being or welfare of users, user satisfaction with services and the achievement of agreed policy goals). The relationships between these four dimensions of performance indicators and the different parts of the service production process are illustrated in Figure 14.1, and the types of indicators linked to each dimension are explored further in Osborne *et al.* (1993).

At which level should performance be assessed, by whom, and how often?

The rational model requires that performance must frequently be assessed at multiple levels of any organizations. At each level the information gathered is expected to be useful both to those gathering it and to those above them. In most cases, it is expected that an organization will need to assess performance at three levels and in a form able to be aggregated to the next level:

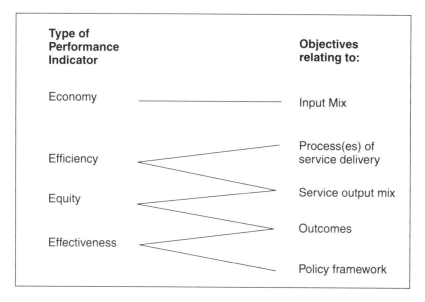

Figure 14.1 Performance indicators for different parts of the service process

1 **The project or team level.** Performance assessment needs to be able to help project or team managers and staff with the progress of their own objectives and motivate them to solve problems.
2 **The programme or departmental level.** Performance assessment needs to be able to help programme/departmental managers to utilize their resources appropriately and to ensure that their projects and teams are working to the priorities of the organization and to help them with medium-term decisions about resource acquisition and allocation.
3 **The strategic or organizational level.** Performance assessment needs to enable senior managers to ensure that the different components of the organization adhere to its overall aim and strategic plan and to make medium-to long-term decisions about resource acquisition and allocation.

The rationalist model thus views organizations as a collection of relatively discrete entities, with specific performance assessment measures required for each level, and concentrating largely upon the economistic concepts of inputs and outputs. Such an approach has been challenged in recent years by a number of alternative perspectives. These perspectives will now be outlined below, and their implications for performance management highlighted.

Alternative perspectives on performance management

'Political' models of performance assessment

Political science perspectives have always emphasized the differential access to information enjoyed by ruling groups. These models attack much government-funded performance assessment as fundamentally a public relations exercise, designed to praise politically popular programmes and to criticize programmes and agencies which politicians wish to cut (Pollitt 1993).

However, any analytical tool used by the ruling group can be appropriated by other groups to further their own causes. As an antidote to these dangers, the 'pluralist' political model proposes that all the key agencies be empowered to engage more effectively in the decision-making process, by enabling them to carry out performance asessment from their own perspectives. In this view, performance assessment is not an objective process, but a highly subjective and selective exercise, more akin to marketing than planning.

Organizational models of performance assessment

Two main strands of organizational theory conceptualize the role of performance assessment in organizational behaviour – theories of bounded rationality and of organizational excellence. The model of **bounded rationality** (March and Simon 1958) assumes that each participant in a decision has cognitive limitations and only has access to part of the information needed. This problem of information processing and flow is sufficient in itself to make the rational model of decision-making inapplicable in a bureaucratic environment as it involves the imposition of the information demands of one stakeholder upon other stakeholders by whom this information is perceived to be of little or no value.

The **organizational excellence** approach seeks to categorize the critical success factors which distinguish organizations which have performed well in the past and, it is hoped, are therefore likely to perform well into the future. Popularized by Peters and Waterman (1982) these approaches tend to emphasize the value of a strong corporate organizational culture, which produces and reproduces these critical factors of successful performance. However, much of this literature is anecdotal in its evidence gathering, carefully selective in the examples chosen, conceptually incoherent and even sometimes internally self-contradictory (though an exception to this is the rigorous work of Kotter and Heskett 1992).

Symbolic approaches to performance assessment

Recent writers have tended to assume that performance assessment is essential to public accountability. However, there are several models of public accountability which do not require performance assessment – for example, models based on the 'public choice' perspective (Lane 1993). Where such models of accountability are dominant, we might expect that performance assessment would be relatively unimportant. However, this ignores the possibility that performance assessment may have become important for organizations because of its symbolic role in a social and political context, rather than because of its perceived direct contribution to improved decision-making. From this stance it has been argued that, for VNPOs, the potent symbol of a performance orientation has helped to establish the 'myth' that they have a sense of strategic direction and an explicable rationale for their actions when in fact they exist in a world of uncertainty and ambiguity (Singh *et al.* 1991, Tucker *et al.* 1992). This sense is reinforced by the rituals of performance assessment, which also help to shape the image which the VNPO projects. The image of the organization embodies its claim to legitimacy in the eyes of its stake-holders, that is, the basis upon which it will be held accountable (Bovaird 1993).

Constitutive analysis of performance assessment

Townley (1992) has recently argued that performance assessment:

> . . . serves to render visible certain aspects of the functioning of the enterprise but in so doing it constructs a particular field of visibility . . . Its exercise creates the dimensions of 'reality' it is assumed to reveal . . . [Performance assessment] as an interactive and creative process contributes to the 'forming' of the organisation in making visible a particular order.

In this reading, particular approaches to making visible some aspects of an organization simultaneously make other aspects invisible. Thus, performance assessment 'can function so as to influence and eventually change the nature of the organizations'. Whilst such changes may be precisely what is desired, this perspective illustrates the danger of being overly mechanistic in setting up a performance assessment system. Such systems are, and will always remain, highly subjective procedures which provide a selective view of organizational 'reality' within chosen parameters. Which aspects of an organization are selected for evaluation, and within which parameters, is decided by those who control the assessment systems (Osborne 1988).

Developing an integrated model of performance assessment

The conclusions of these alternative approaches clearly threaten the dominant rationalist model of performance assessment for VNPOs. However, acknowledgement of their claims does not have to lead to complete rejection of this model. This tradition has built up robust performance assessment tools. The real challenge, therefore, is not to replace this rationalist hegemony with an alternative orthodoxy. Rather it is to integrate the lessons of the alternative perspectives with the rationalist one, to produce performance management systems which better respond to the needs of VNPOs, in a highly political world.

Linking performance monitoring to the organizational context

In recognition of the above critique, it is suggested that performance assessment cannot simply be used within a VNPO without recognizing the different levels of the organization and their needs. The model offered here specifies six different types of performance assessment processes which would be required to assess the overall performance of a VNPO:

1 Context monitoring. Involving examination of the extent to which the impacts which the organization is seeking to achieve are also being influenced by the activities of complementary or competing agencies, and by changing socio-economic and institutional circumstances.
2 Strategy monitoring. Involving the checking on a regular basis that the activities carried out, and the overall level of inputs and activities of an organization comply with its strategy, and specifically with its objectives targets and priorities. This is a basic need for any organization to ensure compliance with its strategy and resource allocation.
3 Progress monitoring. Involving ensuring that operational targets are being met on time. This is particularly important to maximize the use of resources, to control overspending and prevent underspending, and to highlight problems as they arise. Whilst financial control information is the commonest form of progress monitoring, physical progress on capital projects and achievement of tasks by key dates can also be used.
4 Activity monitoring. Involving a more detailed monitoring of the activities and numbers of projects and tasks in progress. It is the basis for efficiency reviews and particularly for comparisons of unit costs and productivity. It requires frequent recording but less frequent reporting and analysis than in the case of progress monitoring.
5 Impact monitoring. Involving the assesment of the achievement of the highest levels of organizational objectives, normally in terms of the impacts (outcomes) achieved on the targeted client population or organizations. It is difficult, and therefore generally occurs less frequently, though conversely it is one of the most significant forms of performance assessment. It is made much easier if expected impacts are clearly spelt out at the start in 'hierarchy of objectives' (Mallinson and Bovaird 1988) for the organization.
6 Catalysis monitoring. Involving the evaluation of the effect of an organization in influencing other important and influential organizations and

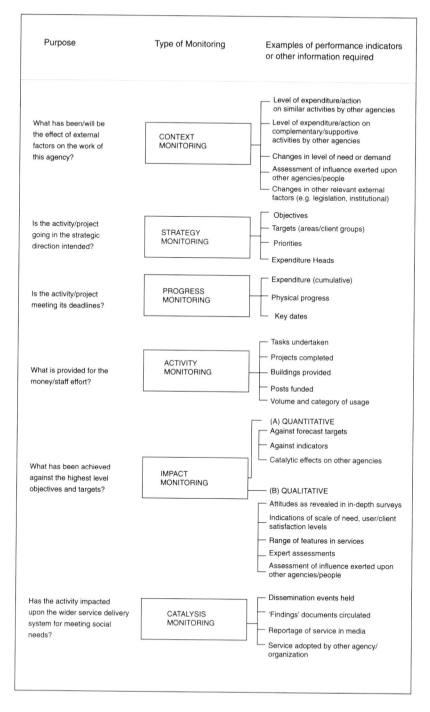

Figure 14.2 Performance monitoring (*Source*: Adapted from PSMRC 1992)

individuals in the provision of a service or the meeting of a strategic objective. It is required to assess the wider impact of the organization in meeting its key objectives.

Taken together with the three organizational levels identified previously (project, programme and strategic), this approach offers a matrix-framework for performance assessment. Not all of these six types would be required at each of these organizational levels, and some would be of more importance to one VNPO than to another. The precise mix would depend upon the needs of the organization in question. Further, performance systems themselves have costs, in terms of their implementation. These would need to be weighed against the sophistication of the performance management system required and a judgement made about the appropriate balance between costs and effectiveness for any particular VNPO.

Such a multi-dimensional approach acknowledges the complexity of the organizations that it is being used by, whilst also allowing different factors to be separated out for analysis and/or comparison. It also allows for recognition of the differing political view-points and constitutive perspectives upon performance assessment within different parts of an organization or programme. It does not solve these differences, but does provide a framework within which they may be resolved. A case study of the application of this framework to a government programme which used VNPOs to identify and respond to social needs in rural areas can be found in Osborne *et al.* (1995), whilst PSMRC (1992) gives more detailed examples of the performance indicators which could be used as part of such a framework.

Conclusions on performance management

This section of this chapter has reviewed the utility of the rationalist model of performance management for VNPOs as well as offering a critique of it. It has responded to this critique by presenting a revised model of performance management. This model has sought to embrace the political nature of performance management and to combine quantitative and qualitative approaches in a more sophisticated way than previously (see also Osborne and Tricker 1995). This section concludes by outlining some core components of a good performance management system and which would need to be addressed in the design and implementation of any such system by a VNPO. These are that:

1 Performance management needs to be an **integral part** of any VNPO, bringing benefit to all concerned. It is feasible to impose it from top down but then its reliability and impact is limited. Staff are unlikely to collect (or to collect accurately) information that they do not understand or see no use for (even if it is useful to other levels of management);

2 Performance indicators need to be set and agreed in a way which is understandable to all. It is no use designing a sophisticated set of indicators which defy staff attempts to implement them;

3 The meanings attached to performance indicators should be recognized to vary between shareholders just as their priorities vary. The reconciliation of meanings should be seen as a long-term, not an immediate, prospective, to be negotiated in the continuing process of performance management;

4 Performance management needs to concentrate on strengths and positive outcomes, as well as organizational weaknesses and shortfalls. If the evaluative process is perceived as too negative then, rightly or wrongly, staff will often find ways to sabotage it;

5 Performance management must integrate judgements of excellence relating to organizational performance, service system performance and the performance of the communities for whom the services are undertaken;

6 Performance management has a cost in terms of time and money. The cost of more elaborate and sophisticated systems needs to be measured against their potential gains and a balance should be struck; and

7 Performance management needs itself to be evaluated by the extent to which it has supported a performance enhancing culture and has enabled performance improvement within the organization. This must be kept firmly to the fore in designing the performance assessment system.

Finally, four points should be emphasized. First, performance management needs to be planned at the outset of a project or activity and form an integral part of it, not be added on at a later stage. Second, performance management should reflect the complexity of the phenomenon that it is measuring. It needs to be multi-layered and employ a range of different indicators of both a quantitative and qualitative nature. To do otherwise risks sophistry.

Third, performance assessment and performance indicators are tools to manage with, not a substitute for management. They aid decision-making, not take its place. Finally, performance management needs to be part of a wider package of service evaluation for VNPOs. Thus whilst performance assesment may measure what an organization achieves, it needs to be alongside a system to evaluate, for example, the quality of its services for its beneficiaries. It is to this issue that the rest of this chapter is now devoted.

QUALITY MANAGEMENT IN VNPOs

The first thing to understand about 'quality' is that it is not a thing but a concept; a way of thinking about things. It is not possible to see or touch quality and different people will often disagree about how much 'quality' a particular product or service possesses. Despite its elusive nature, quality is nonetheless crucially important for managers of VNPOs, because it represents an assessment of their services by their beneficiaries.

Quality covers both the **process** and **content** components of a service, and so can be defined in two ways. The first of these is what is called 'fitness for purpose' (FFP). To the industrial producer the measurement of this is relatively straightforward, usually by reference to the appropriate British Standard. This will specify the characteristics of a 'quality' product in an objective, if arbitrarily defined, manner. Thus, if a car engine part is not to within, say, 1/100 centimetre of the required standard, it is of poor quality, because the machine that it is intended for will not tolerate the divergence. That is, the component is not 'fit for its purpose'.

With manufactured products, FFP is relatively easy to define. This is not so with human services, however, where the output of such services are usually related to individually defined (i.e. subjective) needs. With a day service for adults with learning disabilities, for example there is also a question of who is its prime 'customer'. Is it the adults who attend to learn a range of practical and social skills, or is it their carers, who are able to have a break from their care whilst knowing that they are in a safe place? Depending on your answer, this could mean providing different things in order for the service to be 'fit for its purpose'. FFP therefore requires clarity over the organizational purpose to be established at the strategic level.

The second definition of quality is not to do with the purpose of a service, but the process of its delivery. This is even more subjective than FFP might be, because it needs the evaluation of the subjective experience of a service by its users. It is better to think of this characteristic of quality as to do with its 'excellence in experience' (EIE). To take an easy example, if you eat in a restaurant, no matter how good the quality of the food is (how 'fit for its purpose' it is), you might define this as a bad experience, because of the rude and poor service that you received. In terms of services, it is helpful to think about what Normann (1991) calls the '**moment of truth**'. This is where the whole of a service or organization is represented to its beneficiaries by the one person with which they are interacting (such as a child-care agency being represented to a single mother by the play worker that she is being supervised by). The EIE of a VNPO can result from many factors depending upon what the service is. The list below, although not exhaustive, lists some of the key factors:

- staff attitudes to their own roles and to their consumers;
- furnishings/decoration of buildings;
- state of buildings;
- experience of discrimination;
- explanations offered as to the purpose of a service;
- waiting times for services;
- reception upon arrival and punctuality of staff.

With regard to VNPOs, especially those providing public services, both these characteristics of quality are important. A service must be both fit for its purpose, in the sense of addressing identified needs (such as a home care service which is focused upon completing those tasks which enable an elderly person to continue living in their own home), and of excellent experience (in the aforementioned home care service, by ensuring not only that identified tasks are completed, but also that the service is provided in a friendly and companionly manner, and on time).

Why is quality important?

The easy answer would be that good managerial practice in VNPOs requires it. Unfortunately such good intentions have frequently not been able to produce good quality services. For service providers, though, quality is vital. If a service does not provide good quality for its users, then it is unlikely to survive. Existing and potential customers will go elsewhere. Once again, Normann has made plain the links between quality and survival for service producers.

Of course, if it were simply (!) a question of quality, then the task might be less daunting for VNPO managers. However, there is the additional complication of the costs and budget of a service. The question that such managers may have to ask is therefore not 'what quality of service should I be providing' but 'what quality of service should I be providing within my budget'. Purchasers of services will need to balance quality against cost in comparing alternatives, whilst service providers will need to decide what their users are prepared to pay for, in terms of quality, and what they will not pay for.

Turning to the issue as to why it is necessary to evaluate quality, a cynic, or ardent libertarian, might argue that there is no need to evaluate quality, as in this era of contracting for services, the market will always be its final arbiter. Whether this is true or not, such a terminal evaluation is of no use to a service provider, who requires to be one step in front of the market. It is of no use for a service manager to contemplate the lack of quality of their service once it has closed down, when ongoing quality evaluation could have enabled them to change the service and avoid the ultimate sanction of the market.

How to evaluate quality

Having decided that it is important for managers of VNPOs to evaluate their quality, it is necessary to move on to the key issue of how to do it. To start with, readers might consider their own agency. Does it have systems to evaluate quality and what are they? Do they cover both the characteristics of fitness for purpose and excellence identified earlier? How are their results used?

A common problem with evaluating quality, especially in human services, is the confusion over what is being measured – in particular whether it is the quality of service that is being evaluated, or the quality of life of its recipients. These concepts are not identical yet can be confused in practice. Thus, for example, it is possible for an adult with learning disabilities to receive a poor quality residential service, but to have a considerably higher quality of life because of their involvement in an excellent day occupation service.

Despite these problems, quality of life has nevertheless often been used as a way of evaluating the quality of service. There are many good reasons why not to do this, however. First, 'quality of life' is a complex subject, yet quite simple measures have often been used to try and evaluate it. Second, the supposed links between quality of life and quality of service are not made explicit. It is not sufficient merely to assert these links, they need to be demonstrated. Without this, one is left with the problem of whether a change in the quality of life was brought about by a change in the quality of a service, or by other factors. Third, the relationship between quality of life and of service may not be a constant one and may change over time. It can be misleading to measure over too short a time scale. To take a simple example, consider again a day service for adults with learning disabilities. A prime objective of this service could be to raise the expectations of its users as to their potential to achieve in life. Success in this could lead to a short-term lowering of personal satisfaction as service users strive, unsuccessfully, to fulfil their newly realized potential, but to a raising of it in the longer term. In this case, a good quality service could be indicated by a lowering of the perceived quality of life of its recipients in the short-term, in the expectation of an increased quality of life in the future.

Fourth, many evaluation tools have often been developed within research contexts. They are often time consuming to administer and may require expert skills to carry out. Even if they represent the most sophisticated developments in evaluation, their cost (in time and money) could outweigh their potential benefits. Fifth, many measures of quality rely upon its definition by 'experts', rather than by service users. Critics have for a long time argued that not only does this devalue the experience of the service users themselves (Ackoff 1976) but also reinforces their dependency upon external definitions of what makes a good service, rather than their own observations. In this respect, best business practice in the service industries is in advance of its non-profit counterpart, in the development of a customer based approach to quality (Hensel 1990). Finally, and perhaps most importantly, many of these quality evaluation systems are not integral to the service production process, but 'add-ons'. Because of this they are frequently experienced as an unnecessary intrusion by staff and consumers alike.

The most obvious approach is to steer clear of the issue of quality of life entirely, and to concentrate upon quality of service. It is what the service manager can influence most directly. It is useful to consider such quality of service in the context of the work of Ackoff mentioned above. He argues for service provision to be treated as a **system**, rather than as a series of separate problem-solving exercises. Thus, the key managerial role is not individual decision-making, but management of the system as a whole. Within this system, he argues, quality is best evaluated not by external experts with proxy measures, but by the direct participation of the service user. This participation will not only give the best evaluation of the quality of service, but also in itself contribute to this quality.

Designing a quality evaluation system

In order to do this, it is necessary to establish some clear rules for quality evaluation. Six principles are suggested here, based upon the reading at the end of this chapter. The overruling theme is that quality evaluation should be an **integral** and **participative** part of the service process, not an add-on. These principles are:

1 Any evaluative system must be an integral part of human service provision and not either a separate or an additional process.
2 Any evaluative system must fit the purpose for which it is intended and not simply gather that information which is most easily available.
3 Any evaluative system should build upon existing knowledge and skills. It should be simple to use and not require specialists for its implementation.
4 Any evaluative system should actively involve all participants in a service, not solely management. It must be demonstrably useful to these participants and not be perceived as a bureaucratic process imposed from the top down.
5 Any evaluative system must focus upon how to ensure that services fit the needs of their consumers and not vice-versa.
6 Any evaluative system must produce findings which are usable **and** are used.

The next stage of designing a quality management system is deciding when you are going to evaluate quality. Traditionally there are two approaches to this – **quality assurance** and **quality control**. The former usually occurs before service production and seeks to develop mechanisms to ensure that good quality services are being produced (such as charters, quality circles, and feed-back systems). The latter happens during and after the delivery of services. It is about ensuring that they come up to your standards (such as complaints systems).

It is a mistake to counter-pose these two approaches. A good quality evaluation system requires both. Quality assurance allows for the development of good quality services, rather than simply the correction of problems as they occur. Quality control allows you to pick up any problems which do occur, resolve them and then feed the issue back into the quality assurance system for the future.

CASE STUDY

A national child-care VNPO needed to develop a quality system for a regional service to support children with chronic life-threatening illnesses and their families. It would need to use existing information and allow it to modify its services both to satisfy the health authority with which it was contracted to provide the service and its beneficiaries. After taking advice from a consultant it designed a system with three stages, comprising a quality assurance stage and two quality control stages, which built upon existing frameworks and expertise.

Stage one was the quality assurance stage. It required a clear service philosophy and strategy which linked the identified needs which the service was addressing to its objectives and outputs (fitness for purpose). This was necessary in order to focus the service upon its targeted area of need. It also required a clear statement of the value base of the service both in terms of professional values and the centrality of the consumer. This was important in order to contribute to an organizational culture which positively promoted a responsive and participative service production process (excellence).

Both of these needed to be stated in a way which would allow their translation into objectives capable of being monitored in service production. An example of this is the way that the so-called 'five accomplishments' (community presence, choice, competence, respect, community participation) can be used to evaluate the achievement of an ordinary life in services for people with a learning difficulty, and hence implement the service philosophy of normalization (Leedham 1988). An alternative approach could have been that of the 'hierarchy of objectives' (Mallinson and Bovaird 1988).

Stage two was the first quality control stage. It was concerned with the process of service provision and service outputs. It required local managers of the VNPO to be informed about the local demography and pattern of potential consumers. This information could then be used to assess both the effectiveness of the service in reaching its target population and in providing the services it required and the extent to which that target population was covered. In this way, service outputs could be related to consumer needs (fitness for purpose). It also required the evaluation of the direct experience of the service process by consumers, through an abundance of feedback loops (suggestion boxes, questionnaires, quality circles, informal and formal meetings). No matter how 'effective' a service might be, it will not be experienced by consumers as a quality service if the process is not a good experience (excellence).

Stage three was the second quality control stage. It was concerned with the relationship between service outputs and consumer outcomes, both intermediate and final. Intermediate outcomes needed to be evaluated in terms of the relevance of the service (and its outputs) to identified needs and progress towards meeting them. A possible mechanism to do this existed in the participative planning system already used by this service (which was based on the idea of Individual Programme Planning). This allowed both regular (six monthly) assessment of individual progress toward the meeting of their needs, by measuring sub-objectives, and their aggregation for evaluation of the effectiveness of the service as a whole (Osborne 1991).

Final outcomes of the service required evaluation at longer intervals (say, two yearly) of its success in the reduction of identified welfare shortfalls. It is a mistake to expect easy mechanical formulae for this process. It required an integration of professional and consumer judgements and the negotiation of conflicts and dissonance. It also needed an understanding of the relationship between the service itself and the social environment which its consumers inhabited. However, it was clearly facilitated by reference to the agreed objectives of the service, and their specification with regard to the needs of individual consumers. This approach emphasized the point of viewing monitoring and evaluation as an ongoing and integral part of the service process, rather than an add-on, at a later stage (fitness for purpose). Stage three also required the periodic evaluation of the well-being of consumers and their life satisfaction in areas relevant to the service. A number of relatively straightforward instruments exist to measure this (for examples see George and Bearon 1980), which are appropriate for use by VNPOs in providing human services (excellence).

Taken together, these three stages provided a quality evaluative system which was based upon an understanding of the role and processes of human service production as a system, and which was integral to these processes and relevant to consumers, staff and managers (and built upon existing knowledge and skills). It is illustrated in Figure 14.3.

Designing your own quality management system

By now you should have a good understanding of what goes to make a good quality service and have thought about the ways in which to evaluate its quality. It is important to remember that there is no such thing as a 'ready-made' quality system which you can plug into any VNPO. Your quality system needs to be designed with the needs of your service and service users, uppermost in your mind. In order to design your own quality system, you should go through the following steps.

1 The starting point has to be the purpose(s) of your organization; start with the service that you want to provide and work backwards to where

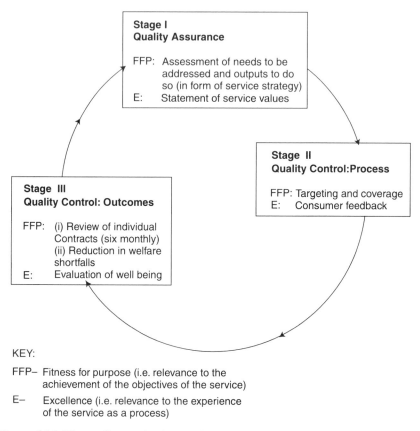

KEY:

FFP– Fitness for purpose (i.e. relevance to the achievement of the objectives of the service)

E– Excellence (i.e. relevance to the experience of the service as a process)

Figure 14.3 The quality evaluation cycle (adapted from Osborne 1992)

you are now, especially in terms of resources. You may not live up to your expectations (yet!), but you will be clear about where the gaps are, so that you can think about what you need to do to alleviate them. Consider the purpose(s) of your VNPO. Now think what needs to happen before a service is delivered in order to ensure its 'fitness for purpose'.

2 Having clarified the sort of service that you want to provide, you now need to develop quality assurance (QA) mechanisms to ensure that this happens. Ask yourself what you need to do to ensure the type of service that you want to provide is realized in practice.

3 Now you need to decide what quality control (QC) mechanisms you are going to use to check on the quality of your services. Remember here that you need to measure both the ongoing process of service delivery and the outcomes for your service users. Remember also that, like with performance management, your mechanisms need to be easily under-stood by those who use them, be seen to have purpose and produce

results which are used and highlight positive as well as any negative aspects of the service.

4 Finally,you will need a review mechanism for correcting deficiencies in the service noted by your QC system and integrate the lessons learned into your QA system, to prevent this problem arising again.

Above all, remember to be realistic. It is no use designing a sophisticated quality management system which is beyond the resources or ability of your service to implement. It is far better to start off with limited goals and expand gradually, building upon your success. Your beneficiaries and colleagues are more likely to subscribe to a system which has shown its worth, rather than an ambitious plan which is unproven.

REFERENCES

Ackoff, R. (1976) Does quality of life have to be quantified? *Operational Research Quarterly*, **27** pp. 289–303.

Bovaird, T. (1993) *Current Approaches to Performance Assessment in the Public Sector: Pure Symbolism, Limited Learning Systems in the Beginnings of TQM?* Paper presented to Public Productivity Working Group, International Institute of Administrative Sciences, Leuven.

Bovaird, T., Gregory, D. and Martin, S. (1988) Performance measurement in urban economic development. *Public Money and Management*, **8** (4), pp. 17–22.

Butt, H. and Palmer, B. (1985) *Value for Money in the Public Sector*, Blackwell, Oxford.

George, L. and Bearon, L. (1980) *Quality of Life in Older Persons*, Human Sciences Press, New York.

Hensel, J. (1990) Service quality improvement and control: a customer based approach. *Journal of Business Research*, **20**, pp. 430–54.

Kotter, J. and Heskett, J. (1992) *Corporate Culture and Performance*, Free Press, New York.

Lane, J. (1993) *The Public Sector*, Sage, London.

Leedham, I. (1988) *Research Methodology with Special Reference to Services for People with Learning Difficulties* PSSRU Discussion Paper, University of Kent.

Mallinson, I. and Bovaird, T. (1988) Setting objectives and measuring achievement in social care. *British Journal of Social Work*, **18**, pp. 309–24.

March, B. and Simon, H. (1958) *Organizations*, Wiley, New York.

Normann, R. (1991) *Service Management: Strategy and Leadership in Service Businesses*, Wiley, Chichester.

Osborne, S. (1988) Performance review: the 'Yorkie Bar' model. *Insight*, (June), pp. 16–17.

Osborne, S. (1991) The management of need. *Local Government Studies*, **20**, (3) pp. 5–12.

Osborne, S. (1992) The quality dimension. Evaluating quality of service and quality of life in human services. *British Journal of Social Work*, **22**, pp. 437–53.

Osborne, S., Bovaird, T., Tricker, M. and Waterston, P. (1993) *Performance Management in Complex Public Programmes*, PSMRC Working Paper 21, University of Aston.

Osborne, S., Bovaird, T., Martin, S., Tricker, M. and Waterston, P. (1995) Performance management and accountability in complex public programmes. *Financial Accountability and Management*, **11**, (1), pp. 19–37.

Osborne, S. and Tricker, M. (1995) Researching non-profit effectiveness. *Voluntas*, **6**, (1), pp. 93–100.

Peters, T. and Waterman, R. (1982) *In Search of Excellence*, Harper & Row, New York.

Pollitt, C. (1993) *Managerialism and the Public Services*, Basil Blackwell, Oxford.

Public Sector Management Research Centre (PSMRC) (1992) *Performance Assessment and Performance Indicators*, PSMRC, University of Aston.

Simon, H. (1957) *Models of Man*, Wiley, New York.

Singh, J., Tucker, D. and Meinhard, A. (1991) Institutional change and ecological dynamics, in *The New Institutionalism in Organizational Analysis* (eds W. Powell and P. DiMaggio), University of Chicago Press, Chicago, pp. 390–422.

Townley, B. (1992) In the eye of the gaze, in *Managing Organisations in the 1990s* (eds P. Barker and C. Cooper), Routledge, London.

Tucker, D., Baum, J. and Singh, J. (1992) The institutional ecology of human service organizations, in *Human Services as Complex Organizations* (ed. Y. Hasenfeld), Haworth Press, New York, pp. 47–72.

GUIDED READING

Normann, R. (1991) *Service management*, Wiley, Chichester. The best background study of the need for quality and performance management and their links to organizational survival.

Bovaird, T., Gregory, D. and Martin, S. (1988). Performance measurement in urban economic development, *Public Money and Management*, **8** (4), pp. 17–22. A useful guide to the components of performance management.

George, L. and Bearon, L. (1980) *Quality of Life in Older Persons*, Human Sciences Press, New York. A hand-book of psychological measures of quality of life.

Martin, E. (1986) Consumer evaluation of human services, *Social Policy and Administration*, **20** (3), pp. 185–200. Excellent guide to the issues of involving users in service evaluation.

Ward, L. (ed.) (1987) *Getting Better All the Time?* Kings Fund, London. A range of practical examples of quality systems for human services.

Cassam, E. and Gupta, H. (1992) *Quality Assurance for Social Care Agencies*, Longman, London. A practical guide to implementing quality systems.

Rossi, P. and Freeman, H. (1991) *Evaluation*, Sage, Beverly Hills. Good review and guide to evaluation systems for all sorts of organizations and projects.

15 Accountability. What is it and do we need it?

Sarabajaya Kumar

INTRODUCTION

The origin of concern with questions of accountability can probably be traced back as far as the 'Athenian state' (Day and Klein 1987), over 2000 years ago. Although the issue is well established, it is no less contentious today. This is particularly true of Britain and Europe, given the rapid growth in government and voluntary sector activities. In the UK alone the statistics speak for themselves. The VNPO sector has an estimated total income of £9.1 billion, over 400,000 employees and contributes to around 1.38% of GDP (Osborne and Hems 1995). VNPOs are now key public agencies, delivering mainstream public services in the fields of education, health care, welfare and housing. In accountability terms this is potentially problematic. During the days of grant aid, VNPOs acted as 'watchdogs on the State holding it and others to account' (Taylor 1995). Now they will be expected to be accountable for their own role, so who will 'watch the watchdogs?'

In attempting to unravel the complex concept of accountability in the voluntary sector you need to consider a number of perplexing questions. By the end of this chapter you should be able to:

- say what accountability is and why it is important for VNPOs;
- understand to whom and for what are voluntary sector staff and board members accountable;
- appreciate what management concerns accountability raises; and
- understand how contracting has affected accountability.

THE 'ESCHER FACTOR' IN ACCOUNTABILITY

Accountability characteristically evades any simple definition. It is an ambivalent and elusive concept that has been described as a 'chameleon word' (Day and Klein 1987) and 'difficult to grapple with . . . (due to the) lack of agreement about its meaning' (Kramer 1989). For Simey (1985) accountability is a 'moral principle . . . whose purpose is to govern the relationship between those who delegate authority and those who receive it.' At its simplest, to be accountable means to 'account for that for which one is responsible, and to those to whom one is responsible' (Wadsworth 1991). These latter two definitions of accountability acknowledge two important aspects of the concept. First, that accountability is a relationship between people where 'one is always accountable to someone (or groups), never in the abstract.' Second, that it refers to patterns of behaviour. I will return to these points later, in the section about why accountability is important for VNPOs.

To help get some idea of the complexity of accountability relationships, it is helpful to think of the lithograph called *Relativity*, by Escher. In this lithgoraph,

> . . . the three forces of gravity are working perpendicularly to one another. Three earth planes cut across each other at right angles, and human beings are living on each of them. It is impossible for the inhabitants of different worlds to walk, sit, or stand on the same floor, because they have differing conceptions of what is horizontal and what is vertical. Yet they may well share use of the same staircase.
>
> (*Escher 1990*)

In this lithograph, when you focus on one part of the picture you are able to see the figures acting quite naturally within their environment. However, every time you look at a different part of the picture, the reference point for what is up and what is down changes. The distinct elements that appear ordered and logical within their own context reveal a more convoluted representation when examined as a whole. The same can be said of accountability.

Just as the inhabitants of such a world of relativity have differing conceptions of gravity and space, so recent research on the accountability of small voluntary organizations found that there appeared to be many and various definitions, meanings and levels at which accountability operated. This ambiguity and lack of agreement in perceptions is inherent to the whole notion of accountability. It is what I refer to as the **Escher factor** in accountability.

WHAT IS ACCOUNTABILITY?

In general terms accountability is closely bound up in the wider philosophical debate, where issues about the preservation of appropriately placed trust, democracy, responsibility and participation are thrust together. Questions of power, balancing vested interests and control are at the kernel of such relationships, given the informal and formal linkages that exist between any organization and its many stakeholders.

Obligation is a key element of accountability. In the practical application of the concept, accountability refers to the often unequal, yet complimentary, relationship between individuals, organizations and sectors, where one is obliged to render account for performance to another. It also involves those being accounted to having the knowledge, time and expertise to ensure accountability. In addition, according to Leat (1988) 'proper accountability' involves the right to 'impose sanctions if the account is inadequate'.

At the organizational level, there are four dimensions of accountability, where those with delegated authority (the providers) are answerable to those who control the resources (the enablers) for tasks that they are carrying out (Kramer 1989; Day and Klein 1987). This is what I refer to as 'management accountability'.

Robinson (1971) refers to three areas of management accountability: 'fiscal', 'programme' and 'process'. A fourth type linked to the fiscal form is 'legal accountability'. **Fiscal accountability** involves being able to match up the intended and actual expenditure of funds (to demonstrate that funds have been spent where they were intended to be spent). There are three methods by which to do this: post audit, line item budget and pre audit. These fiscal issues are discussed in more detail in the chapter in this book on financial accounting. **Legal accountability** is about ensuring that the actions of organizations or individuals comply with statutory provisions and regulations in the relevant legislation. The other two dimensions, programme and process accountability, are to a large extent subjective and qualitative, not susceptible to the types of statistical analysis found in accounting systems. **Programme accountability** refers to the effectiveness of a programme in achieving its intended objectives, whilst **process accountability** is concerned with the process of implementation and the level of efficiency with which a programme is managed within its financial limitations. For instance, if an organization is involved in service delivery, process accountability will be concerned with whether services have been delivered according to agreed policies and procedures and whether value for money has been achieved. These issues are addressed in more detail in the chapter in this book on performance and quality management.

Forms of accountability

According to Leat (1988) there are three forms of accountability which frequently occur in VNPOs – explanatory, responsive and accountability with sanctions. These three forms illustrate that the right to demand accountability with formal sanctions attached is not equally, universally available to all, but that there may be informal sanctions which can often be as powerful.

Accountability with sanctions

For many this is 'real' accountability. It is not only characterized by the fact that the VNPO is obliged to account for performance to a stakeholder, but this is backed up by the power and ability of the one who is accounted to, to apply sanctions, for example through the withdrawal of financial resources.

Explanatory accountability

This form requires the account giver to explain and give an account of their actions through either verbal, written or formal means. However, as in the case of many watch-dog bodies, although criticism of this account may be expressed, there is no subsequent right to impose sanctions.

Responsive accountability

This form requires the VNPO to take into account the views of those to whom they are accountable. However, as is the case with explanatory accountability, there are no formal sanctions available to guarantee or ensure that these views are not disregarded. Public consultation is governed by this form.

WHY IS ACCOUNTABILITY IMPORTANT FOR VNPOS?

In the 1990s, shifting trends and developments are raising various concerns about the nature of accountability. The rapid growth of the voluntary sector, increased public support and contributions, changes in government policy and legislation (such as the *NHS and Community Care Act 1990* and the *Charities Act 1992*), the introduction of the Citizens' Charter and its offshoots, and the shift in the government role from 'provider' to 'purchaser' of services, have all thrown into focus such concerns and challenged existing perceptions of accountability. In particular, the development of the 'contract state' has 'transformed the way in which the Welfare State is organized: (from a) . . . Provider State into the Regulatory State' (Day 1992). Within the context of the developments illustrated above, VNPOs have moved from a peripheral to a central role in the delivery of some essential public services. This has prompted the development of new accountability relationships between the voluntary and non-profit, and the statutory sectors. Through the process of drawing up contracts and/or service level agreements, both parties have had to be more explicit about what is being purchased. According to Lipsky (1978):

> Only if a pattern of behaviour exists can predictability and therefore accountability exist. In practical terms this means that efforts to change

or improve accountability cannot succeed unless patterns of behaviour (exist).

Accountability relationships between the government and voluntary sectors

Government departments and agencies work with VNPOs as service providers, yet they remain accountable for the achievement of policy objectives using public money. This is a complex task and requires a sophisticated approach by both government agencies and voluntary organizations. (See Osborne *et al.* 1995). A central dilemma faced by the government sector, therefore, is how to ensure congruence between public policy and its implementation, whilst keeping the balance between independence, accountability and control required, when it delegates power outside itself (Perrow 1976; Smith and Hague 1971).

In contrast, of fundamental concern for VNPOs when dealing with questions of organizational autonomy and dependence, competition and co-operation with other organizations, is how to balance their multiple and possibly conflicting (and at times ambiguous) accountabilities to their various stakeholders. Although the possibility of 'goal displacement' (Pifer 1967) for VNPOs has always been an issue, the starker relationships and increased accountability requirements involved in a contractual setting has thrown this concern into greater relief. Increasingly, accountability has come to be seen not just as holding an organization responsible for exercising delegated power, but also as the means by which the actions and policies of the organization are validated in the first place. It is bound together with the concept of **legitimacy** for a VNPO.

The new **welfare pluralism**, together with the withdrawal of grant aid and the growing participation of VNPOs in wider fora for social and political decision-making, has meant that they are being expected increasingly to be bound by the sort of public accountability that underpins, in theory at least, the actions of statutory organizations. This expectation involves pressure for VNPOs to have certain standards of openness, such as those required of local government. This can include, for example, a register of members' interests, all relevant agendas, background papers and minutes and meetings, open to the public (with exceptions for confidential business), and obligations to publish auditors' criticisms and performance indicators.

Without such forms of visible public accountability, the credibility and legitimacy of VNPOs managing and implementing public programmes may well be called into question. Balancing this with their independence, autonomy and organizational missions is a testing challenge for the modern manager and/or chair of a VNPO.

TO WHOM AND FOR WHAT ARE VOLUNTARY SECTOR STAFF AND BOARD MEMBERS ACCOUNTABLE? HOW HAS CONTRACTING AFFECTED ACCOUNTABILITY?

In attempting to answer the above questions and to clarify the interactive accountability relationships between trustees, paid staff and the many stakeholders of VNPOs within the complex contracting state, I have developed a conceptual framework. This is represented in Figure 15.1, in which a variety of accountabilities are illustrated: public, end user, legal, delegated and contractual (with various sub-divisions).

At the bottom of the figure, the box labelled 'key' indicates that there are two types of accountability. The thick lines represent **external** account-

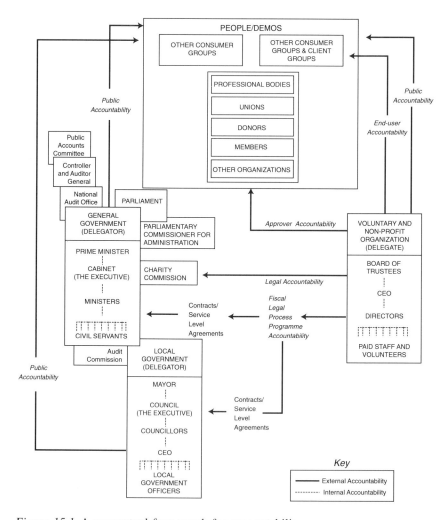

Figure 15.1 A conceptual framework for accountability

ability. This means that the VNPO is obliged to account for its policies and practices to individuals, groups or organizations both outside of itself and linked to it. The thin dotted line represents **internal** accountability within the organizational structure itself. Leat (1988) refers to this latter feature as 'structural accountability'.

Approvers and approver accountability

Extending from the top of the box labelled *Voluntary and Non-Profit Organization* towards the top of the diagram, there is another line of external accountability labelled 'approver accountability'. This consists of accountability to a range of individuals, groups or stakeholders (approvers) comprising professional bodies, unions, donors, members and other organizations or collaborators which the VNPO needs to carry with it, but to whom it has no direct accountability. Mutual approbation rather than formal resource exchange characterizes these relationships, and securing such approval is a basic task of the trustees.

In this sense approval has close links with the concept of legitimacy but it is also wider than that. **Approval accountability** helps to explain much of the way in which VNPOs seek to project themselves to the outside world. In order to gain approval, they may well find that they have to be accountable to their approvers in some specific ways and though this may not be as strong as formal power-based accountability, it may never the less be an important element of the considerations of the trustees in juggling the variety of accountabilities with which they are concerned.

These 'approvers' may simply accept things as they are and seek to sustain the VNPO giving their approval, or they may seek change in its mission and practice, so that the VNPO conforms more closely to their own values. Such approval is more than just giving a VNPO 'a pat on the head'. Approvers legitimate the mission and practice of the organization. VNPOs cannot ignore approvers as they control resources which the organization needs, such as donations and workers (Lansley and Kumar 1995).

VNPOs

In the box labelled VNPO, internal accountability within the organization commences with the volunteers and paid staff, extends through the management structure and chief executive officer or equivalent post holder, to the volunteer board of trustees. This board is legally responsible under the governing document of the VNPO for 'supervising and controlling the work of the officers'. They are legally externally accountable to the Charity Commission (represented by the thick line extending from the VNPO to the box labelled *Charity Commission*), for the 'solvency and continuing effectiveness of the charity and the preservation of its endowments' (Charity Commissioners 1993). The roles and relationships of governing bodies have been addressed elsewhere in this book. Finally, the VNPO is publicly accountable through an annual report and a set of accounts.

The Charity Commission

In turn, the Commission is internally 'structurally' accountable through its organizational hierarchy to central government, the executive and Parliament, which in turn is accountable to the people (depicted by the thick line labelled *public accountability*) through democratic elections.

Parliament

The Public Accounts Committee (PAC), an all party select committee, scrutinizes the annual report of the Comptroller and Auditor General on departmental expenditures, which includes the Charity Commission and any bodies that have been funded with public monies. This ensures that ultimate fiscal accountability is to Parliament. The Parliamentary Commissioner for Administration is appointed by the Crown but at the service of Parliament. The Commissioner acts on the request of an MP and can ask for oral or written evidence and can examine files. If the complaint is seen to be justified, the department responds by rectifying the situation which then puts an end to the matter. If the matter is not satisfactorily resolved at this stage, the Commissioner reports to Parliament which has established a select Committee to consider complaints further (Birch 1990). In local government the Ombudsman plays a similar role to the Parliamentary Commissioner.

Central and local government

When VNPOs enter contracts or service level agreements with central or local government departments, the line of external accountability to government and the public follows a similar path to the one described in the above example of the Charity Commission. The main difference is that the types of accountability required are those of provider to purchaser or, as in principal-agent theory, those of agent to principal and which I referred to earlier as management accountability. The contractor or agent employed to act on behalf of the principal will be required to provide fiscal, legal, programme and process accountability, in terms of their delegated activities. In this model, the contract or service level agreement therefore has a new and pivotal role in the processes of policy implementation, as any agreements made by an agent are regarded as entered into by the principal. As a rule the principal is bound by them.

As has always been the case, government, central or local, is internally accountable through its organizational hierarchy to its executive (i.e. the cabinet or the council), which in turn is accountable to the public, through the elections. Elected representatives must remain answerable for the policy making and implementation process, whether providers are governmental, VNPOs or private institutions. Accountability from this perspective cannot be separated from democratic processes. Because elected politicians are directly responsible for delivering services, this is seen, in theory at least, as guaranteeing in itself accountability.

It is important that organizations acting on behalf of government are accountable for the use of public monies. The implications of the accountability of politicians to the public for services delivered through increasingly fragmented systems can mean that if the provider account is judged to be inadequate, VNPOs may face penalties and even termination of the contract or service level agreement. In practice this is the 'nub of the accountability problem' (Day 1992). The theory takes as given that there are effective links between politicians, professionals and managers across the sectors and that managing accountability is unproblematic. Reality can be far more messy and problematic.

Accountability within organizations and performance measurement

The development of performance management systems are critical for ensuring accountability within organizations because if they do not know how to measure performance, employees cannot be held accountable for their performance, nor can the efficient and/or effective use of resources be ensured. These issues are addressed in detail in the chapter in this book on performance and quality management.

Client accountability

A further route of external accountability reaches from the VNPO to the 'client group', variously called the 'service user', 'service beneficiary', 'end user' or 'customer'. I have called this **end-user accountability**. Government rationales for contracting with the voluntary sector include perceptions about their characteristics, such as 'representing the needs of users', 'being responsive to local need', and 'being flexible and providing an advocacy role for marginalized client groups'. Implicit in this perception is also the expectation that each client will be treated as an individual who requires a response tailored to their particular needs. If the client wishes to make a complaint to the VNPO, there should be a clear, independent, user friendly, well publicized complaints procedure in place.

VNPOs thus have diverse obligations to a wide variety of interests although these can be at differing levels. **Multiple accountability** arises because of the expectation that an organization is simultaneously accountable to all stakeholders. Some may see this plurality of accountabilities as a strength and an opportunity to take into account perspectives of a range of interested parties and as another route for the organization to ensure public accountability. However, tension may arise where one or more of these accountabilities conflict. Being accountable to the client may not always be possible in some instances, particularly those where the use of education, health and welfare services may not be voluntary and the client is being required to receive a service (such as for families within the child protection system or an adult receiving compulsory treatment for a mental health problem). Further complications occur if accountability to one set of service users conflicts with of another set or with any of the other internal or external stakeholders; for instance, if compliance with the conditions of a contract clashes with internal management policies set by the trustees.

WHAT MANAGEMENT CONCERNS DOES ACCOUNTABILITY RAISE?

Accountability as an holistic concept raises many management concerns within organizations, as it touches on and involves the evaluation of every aspect of organizational life and activity, from financial to service delivery aspects. Handy defines accountability in terms of 'Type 1' and 'Type 2' errors:

> . . . a Type 1 error . . . means getting it wrong and a Type 2 error in effect means not getting it right, or as right as it could have been. There is an important difference. A Type 2 error means that the full possibilities of the situation have not been exploited or developed . . . errors of omission not commission . . . which could have made a difference . . . to have been better than expected.

> *(Handy 1994)*

The management concerns that accountability raises are linked to the disjunction between formal **systems** and informal **networks**, through which a VNPO is held accountable. VNPOs may find their activities are monitored and evaluated via Type 1 (fiscal and legal) and/or Type 2 (programme and process) accountabilities by two or more stakeholders, through two or more sets of formal systems and informal networks. The pull in terms of accountability is likely to concentrate on the activities which are formally measured, through one kind of (often quantitative) data, by the dominant actor who has strong 'voice' and 'exit' opportunities.

As organizations creak under increased formal, quantitative, accountability requirements due to the 'audit explosion' (Power 1994) of recent years, there has been an increase in ritual accounting and game playing. VNPOs have been encouraged to become accountable **to the measure**, rather than accountable **for the service**. This in turn gives rise to the criticism that an emphasis on increased accountability has more of a symbolic role and is a public relations exercise.

Managing multiple accountability, of both Types 1 and 2, is in practice primarily a question of how VNPO trustees and managers develop their policies and practices, whilst balancing the various tensions, conflicts and dilemmas outlined above. In this situation it is up to the VNPO to decide which type should take priority in order for them to be 'really accountable'.

In this context, trust, time, expertise and the judgement to ask the 'right' questions are all essential components of any accountability relationship. It is important that trust exists between the organizational stakeholders at all levels (i.e. volunteers, paid staff, service users, managers, trustees, delegators/purchasers and donors); it needs to be earned and kept between the various groups, individuals and organizations that the VNPO has relationships with. Time, expertise and judgement are required to deliver, monitor and evaluate the service effectively in order to ensure accountability. It is important for all the individuals working in the VNPO to identify which meanings and levels of accountability are, or should be, in play between organizations, agencies and their other stakeholders who may have diverse and sometimes overlapping interests. The best way of beginning to address the crucial question of what concerns accountability raises, is for all those working in VNPOs to consider three simple questions in relation to all aspects of their organization:

- **how** is the organization accountable?
- **to whom** is it accountable? and
- **for what** is it accountable?

Some of the accountability questions that can be posed for VNPOs can be illustrated best through the following case study. It is an example of how a critical incident can give rise to a number of accountability issues and conflicts which a small organization (which is part of a national one) is then forced to consider.

CASE STUDY

I visited a welfare service to talk to some service users (parents of children with a range of special needs) about accountability. The service, one of a number offered by the local VNPO, was in part funded by the local authority. It had its own management committee on which the users were represented.

On the whole, the service users I interviewed felt that the project co-ordinator encouraged their participation in decision-making and service delivery and they were very happy with the way in which the services were developing, largely due to their involvement. However, a recent issue had caused alarm for many of the stakeholders of the organization, particularly for the service users, the project co-ordinator, the local authority project officer, the Director of Social Services of the local authority that part-funded the services, and the Director and the Chair of trustees of the local VNPO.

The project provided a meeting place for parents and children with special needs. It was located within a business community, on an industrial estate away from any public transport routes. As the project became more well known, more parents came with their children. More recently this had caused intermittent problems, as there was not enough car and minibus parking space to meet the growing need. There was, however, plenty of car spacing space available in the surrounding business unit car parks, which the project co-ordinator and parents noticed were hardly ever used. As the businesses had expressed their support publicly through high profile dona-tions and local newspaper advertisements, the parents and the co-ordinator thought that the businesses would not mind accommodating them until they moved to bigger premises with ample car parking, later in the year.

However, their assumption was incorrect. Some of the businesses did mind and they decided that a representative of one of the organizations should contact the local VNPO and voice their concerns. A managing director of one of the companies telephoned the director of the VNPO with whom he played golf and said that because of his accountability to his shareholders, he had a duty not to put off prospective customers. He felt that unfortunate as this may be, the businesses may withdraw any potential future donations should the parents continue to park on their premises.

The VNPO director, fearing the loss of voluntary income, telephoned the project co-ordinator to tell her that as they had an accountability to their donors, he was therefore planning to write to users to advise them that the services would be withdrawn should they park there again. The co-ordinator vehemently protested and asked the director to whom he thought the VNPO was being accountable, to its service users or to its donors? She also questioned the accountability of the local businesses to the service users. Why, for example, did not the businesses themselves confront the users, perhaps even threaten to clamp their vehicles, if they were so concerned about the issue. The director informed her that during the conversation the representative of the businesses had explained that they felt uneasy about complaining to the users, in part because they recognized the difficulty about parking and also because their children had disabilities. They did not wish to appear heartless, but they were concerned that the continued use of the parking spaces might affect their custom.

The co-ordinator proposed that she would ask the users for their sugges-tions in dealing with the parking problem, since she did not believe in merely paying 'lip service' to user participation in decision-making. She also argued that if the agency withdrew services, this would not only bring its accountability to its clients in question, but would also break the terms and conditions of its contract with the local authority. As a consequence, the project would lose some of the current, and any future, statutory funding and their relationship would be jeopardized.

Concerned that her protestations fell on deaf ears, the project co-ordinator discussed these anxieties with her colleague, the monitoring officer at the local authority, who in turn voiced her own concerns to the director of the VNPO. The VNPO director subsequently telephoned the director of Social Services, who confirmed that the contract would be broken if he wrote to users threatening to withdraw any services.

News travelled about this matter to the chair of the VNPO, and to the Chief Executive and the trustees at the national headquarters, who have subsequently all become involved in the matter. To date, however, the matter has still not been resolved.

Discussion

This case poses some important accountability questions.

1   **In financial terms, to whom is the VNPO accountable?** The VNPO is accountable to the individuals and organizations who donated money to it. In this case this is the local authority, business donors, individual donors and taxpaying members of the public.
2   **How is it accountable to those who finance it?** The accountability issue here is about which demands should take priority: accountability to business donors, individual donors or to the local authority (in its role as purchaser or as surrogate client). The organization should also be accountable to its users (for its programme and processes), whether they finance its activities directly (through donations or fees), indirectly (as taxpayers) or not at all.
3   **Different people prioritize accountability in different ways to different parties**. The project co-ordinator saw accountability to users (for process) and to purchasers (for fiscal, legal, programme and process accountability) as being of a higher priority, than accountability to the business community for current and future donations (fiscal). She also felt that the VNPO had a wider accountability (moral) to children and parents of children with disabilities, and a responsibility to educate donors, in this case the local business community, about disability issues. She felt that this conflict presented an opportunity, in a small way, to challenge the views of the donors. The VNPO director, on the other hand, prioritized fiscal accountability to the business community first, although for him this impacted indirectly on accountability to users of services, since without the donations the voluntary income of the agency would dip (probably substantially) and they would not be able to finance any future services. This was followed by accountability to the statutory authority and then to the users who were the ostensible cause of the conflict. In contrast, the local authority monitoring officer and Director of Social Services were concerned about the contractual accountability (fiscal, legal, programme and process) of the VNPO to themselves, since they as purchasers were accountable to the public for taxpayers monies and to the service users, having purchased services on

their behalf. As all of the service users were or had been taxpayers they were concerned, as members of the public, about how the organization (which as a charity received tax relief) was accountable to them. Finally, the businesses were concerned about the accountability of the VNPO and its users to them. They felt that the users were trespassing, but were uneasy about confronting them because they had children with disabilities. They also assumed that this usage was off-putting for their customers. Their accountability to their shareholders and customers was primary.

4 **Can the VNPO afford to accept or refuse money from certain donors – individuals, other organizations or statutory sources?** Since it accepted money from individuals, the local business community and the local authority, and wished to continue to accept from all sources, the VNPO needs to consider what this implies in terms of its financial and political independence. Indeed, is it possible to continue to be responsive to such a wide constituency of donors?

CONCLUSIONS

In the above case study, the locally based project had a democratic/participative management style. However, the rest of the VNPO had a hierarchical structure and authoritarian style. Thus there was a conflict of different accountability structures and styles in different levels of the VNPO. Users were represented in decision-making at a policy level on the management committee of the project, but not of the VNPO and they were not consulted about this issue. This raises two fundamental questions for VNPOs. Who should they be primarily accountable to; and if being accountable to their service users conflicts with being accountable to their donor(s), which accountability should take priority? There is no easy or ready resolution of such complex issues for VNPOs with multiple accountabilities.

Because VNPOs have no clear-cut 'owners', accountability in VNPOs is a stakeholder driven activity. Both organizations and their stakeholders have implicit, non-formalized goals which makes the activity of 'accounting for' very complex, due to the sheer volume of information travelling, being received, passed on and assimilated throughout the organization, whatever its size. In order to operate accountably, organizations need to provide a forum where stakeholders can negotiate.

Ultimately, human judgement is involved in ensuring accountability. Kanter recommends:

> . . . the development of more informed human judges, more accountability of the measures themselves to various constituencies and more

open discussion of larger purpose and meanings whenever organisational effectiveness is to be assessed.

(Kanter 1979)

This takes us back to Simey (1985) for whom accountability is a 'moral principle' where organizations cannot look at the issue of accountability without considering ethical questions about the appropriateness of what they are doing in the first place. There are no right answers, only what Day (1992) calls 'tin opening questions' that organizations can ask themselves in this dilemma ridden area.

REFERENCES

Birch, A. (1990) *The British System of Government* Unwin Hyman, London.

Charity Commission (1993) *Responsibilities of Charity Trustees*, HMSO, London.

Day, P. (1992) *Accountability*. Paper to the Rowntree Symposium, University of Birmingham.

Day, P. and Klein, R. (1987) *Accountabilities*, Tavistock Publications, London.

Escher, M. (1990) *The Graphic Work*, Benedikt Taschen, Germany.

Etzioni, A. (1968) *The Active Society* Columbia University Press, New York.

Everitt, A. (1995) Monitoring and Evaluation: A Culture of Lying? Paper presented to the Researching the Voluntary Sector NCVO and Non Profit Studies Conference, London, 7–8 September.

Handy, C. (1994) *The Empty Raincoat*, Arrow, London.

Kanter, R. (1979) *The Measurement of Organisational Effectiveness, Productivity, Performance and Success. Issues and Dilemmas in Service and Non Profit Organisations*, Institution for Social and Policy Studies, Yale University.

Kramer, R. (1989) From voluntarism to vendorism: an organisational perspective on contracting, in *Services for Sale* (eds H. W. Demone and M. Gibelman) Rutgers University Press, New Jersey.

Lansley, J. and Kumar, S. (1995) *Approvers and Accountability*. Paper presented to NCVO Conference, Researching the Voluntary Sector, London.

Leat, D. (1988) *Voluntary Organisations and Accountability*, NCVO, Worcester.

Lipsky, M. (1978) The assault on human services: street level bureaucrats, accountability and the fiscal crisis, in *Accountability in Urban Society*, (eds S. Greer, R. Hedlund and J. Gibson) Sage, Beverly Hills.

Osborne, S., Bovaird, T., Martin, S., Tricker, M. and Waterson, P. (1995) Performance management and accountability in complex public programmes. *Financial Accountability and Management*, **11** (1).

Osborne, S. and Hems, L. (1995) The economic structure of the British charitable sector. *Voluntary and Nonprofit Sector Quarterly*, **24** (4), pp. 321–36.

Pifer, A. (1967) *Quasi Non Governmental Organisations*, Carnagie Corporation, New York.

Perrow, C. (1976) *Control in Organisations: The Centralised and Decentralised Bureaucracy*. Paper presented at the Annual Meeting of the American Sociological Association.

Power, M. (1994) *The Audit Explosion*, DEMOS, London.

Robinson, D. (1971) Government contracting for academic research; accountability in the American experience, in *The Dilemma of Accountability in Modern Government: Independence versus Control* (eds B. Smith and D. Hague) Macmillan, London.

Simey, M. (1985) *Government by Consent: The Principles and Practice of Accountability in Local Government* Bedford Square Press, London.

Smith, B. and Hague, D. (eds) (1971) *The Dilemma of Accountability in Modern Government: Independence versus Control* Macmillan, New York.

Stewart, J., Lewis, N. and Longley, N. (1992) *Accountability to the Public*. Paper presented at the European Policy Forum Conference, London.

Taylor, M. (1995) *Between Public and Private*, Paper presented to NCVO Conference, Researching the Voluntary Sector, London.

Wadsworth, Y. (1991) *Everyday Evaluation on the Run*, Action Research Issues Centre, Melbourne.

GUIDED READING

Three books provide the best way into this complex issue.

Day, P. and Klein, R. (1987) *Accountabilities*, Tavistock Publications, London. The best guide to the theory of accountability and its application, though its context is limited to local government.

Leat, D. (1988) *Voluntary Organisations and Accountability*, NCVO, Worcester. Possibly dating slightly now, particularly about the implications of the 'contract state'. Still the classic text, none the less.

Simey, M. (1985) *Government by Consent: The Principles and Practice of Accountability in Local Government*, Bedford Square Press, London. Again, slightly limited by its local government content, but a fascinating account of the perils and pitfalls of public accountability from the inside.

The chapter in this book on relationships with governing bodies is also useful.

16 Financial reporting and accounting for the voluntary and non-profit manager

Paul Palmer

INTRODUCTION

In this chapter we explore the distinct differences of the financial reporting of VNPOs, compared to commercial companies, illustrated by examples of financial issues for them. We explore further the importance of financial planning with different budgetary techniques. Finally we look at budgetary and accounting control systems.

By the end of the chapter you should be able to:

- understand the principal characteristics of VNPO financial accounting;
- relate these to specific organizations, through the numerous examples; and
- be fully briefed on the importance of financial accounting, planning and control.

First a short introductory word on the language of accounting and financial management. Accounting can be said to be a tool to support the aims and activities of an organization. It is the end product of the accounting system and produces financial information from which management can make decisions.

Accounting can be traditionally divided between **financial accounting**, which is reporting on the transactions of the organization, and **management accounting**, which is the assembly of information for assessing and making future decisions. The role of financial management and of the finance manager in all organizations is to ensure that funds are made available at the right time, for the right length of time and are obtained at the lowest cost in the most effective way.

Auditing can be divided between **internal** auditing, concerned with the accuracy and integrity of internal systems, and **external** auditing, which is closely allied to financial accounting. External auditing is a statutory requirement on companies of a certain size. It was introduced on larger charities in 1995 by regulation, following the *Charities Act 1992*. External auditing is carried out by registered firms of auditors which are appointed by the 'owners' of the organization. For VNPOs this is the responsibility of the trustees. There are now a number of firms of accountants who have specialist 'charity' departments. As we explore in this chapter, the special financial characteristics of VNPOs should mean that trustees should take great care in appointing their auditors. It is worth remembering that auditors are providing services like everyone else and therefore should be providing the charity with a keen price and professional service. It is well worth every few years putting the audit out to competitive tender.

PRINCIPAL DIFFERENCES BETWEEN COMMERCIAL ORGANIZATIONS AND VNPOs

There are a number of features which distinguish VNPOs from commercial organizations. These are summarized in Table 16.1.

In the category of planning it is evident that most commercial organizations are primarily influenced by internal policy (with the clear exception of technology). Occasionally policy decisions may be influenced by external considerations, notably government direct financial aid (incentives), tax

Table 16.1 Differences between commecial organizations and VNPOs

Characteristic	Commercial Organizations	VNPOs
Motivation:	Profit earning.	Altruistic with charitable classification of permitted activities.
Ownership:	Partners/shareholders.	Members (no financial benefit).
Management Control:	Partners or Board of Directors.	Trustees (unpaid).
Capital Structure:	Fixed-interest loans/equity shares.	Voluntary funds.
Borrowing Capacity:	Mortgages.	Fixed Interest loans.
Sources of income:	Sales/provision of services. Investments.	Voluntary funds. Grants (statutory and non statutory). Fees/charges. Investments.
Performance Measurement:	Profitability. Dividend growth/Capital growth.	Quality and economy of service. Outcomes.
Planning decisions based on:	Technological improvements. Expansion of activity. Quality enhancement. Diversification. Plant replacement.	Expansion/contraction of activities. Impact of statutory changes affecting work; funding changes. Research findings.

(concessions) and where the company is supplying to one specific market (for example to the NHS and therefore can be subject to changes in reorganization by government). In these specific cases the characteristics of the commercial companies are more closely allied to VNPOs, except of course that the rationale for the expansion is driven by either retaining profit/market share or by the opportunities to increase profit. For a VNPO these should not be the first criteria for expansion, though for survival and opportunity reasons VNPOs will inevitably be interested in expansion. A word of caution is necessary here. In seeking expansion, the VNPO should consider the effect this can have on its financial structure and ultimately the independence of the organization. If the organization becomes too heavily dependent on one financial source then who is really directing the organization? How would the voluntary organization survive if this one source disappeared? This can be an especial problem if a VNPO becomes over dependent upon governmental funding for its income.

SPECIFIC FINANCIAL PROBLEMS FOR VNPOS

VNPOs, particularly those which are client-oriented, are perhaps more susceptible to change within the community – and particularly those receiving government assistance. This is because government-dependent charities can become victim to 'flavour of the month' policies. For example, a charity running a project for unemployed young people may find that funding from the Employment Department is being reduced, so it looks at perhaps focusing its work at the Education Department, where funds may be available, but where project criteria may be different.

It is not just government-dependent VNPOs which see very large variances in their yearly income, though. Some well-known charities who receive most of their funds from the public have seen their incomes rise and fall from year to year; for example War on Want and Action Aid in overseas aid, and Childline and Shelter on domestic issues have all faced financial crisis in recent years due to falls in income from previous years.

VNPOs are constrained to a greater extent than commercial agencies by financial availability since there is no financial 'return' on which capital borrowing can be justified and serviced. A forward capital programme of a charity is therefore more at risk from unforeseen reductions in the estimated cash flow. This contrast can be seen most starkly when it is compared with the ability of successful commercial enterprises to respond to market needs and to satisfy increasing demand by increasing short-term or long-term borrowing using bank facilities, issuing loan or debenture stock or by a rights issue. In contrast, for VNPOs the problem is in deciding priorities between competing client needs, as there are never the sufficient financial resources to satisfy all the demands made upon its resources. It is because of this that the level of reserves and cash flow are the most important operational considerations for the financial manager of the VNPO.

We illustrate the importance of establishing clarity in these areas with the following three case examples of three very different types of VNPOs.

A grant making trust

It is wrong to believe that a VNPO which has substantial reserves and whose purpose is to award grants to other charities does not have a cash flow issue. The ability of a grant maker is dependent on ensuring that it is maximizing returns on its investments. Except for the occasional 'blip' it has been evident over the last forty years from financial statistics on investment performance that longer term investments will always outperform short-term investments.

The problem for the financial manager of a trust is twofold. The first relates to their responsibility to the VNPO they are funding. The second is to ensure the trust itself is suitably diversified. Charitable trusts, particularly funding smaller VNPOs, should ensure they pay their grants on time, if not (as some government departments do) in advance to ensure the small agency is not incurring bank charges. To resolve this problem of prompt payment but also maximizing investment requires balancing timing differences: if too much is held in short-term investments then the return for the trust will be less than it could have been; however, if the trust has insufficient cash to meet its grant liabilities then it will either have to borrow or sell longer term investments, maybe at a loss.

The second issue for charitable trusts is to ensure that they are suitably diversified with their long term investments and cash. This is a complicated area requiring detailed professional advice and could also involve issues of the original charitable endowment (see Harrison in the guided reading). The general rule, however, is to ensure that long-term investments are diversified across a wide range of company shares and not all held in one company. The recent Baring Foundation loss was where the majority of the trust's money, some £309m. out of £359m., was all held in one company. The Nuffield Foundation in the 1960s suffered a similar fate with considerable historic investment in the old British Motor Corporation.

The over-reserved VNPO

This has caused considerable publicity in recent years (Harrison 1993; Hind 1993; Framjee 1994), with some charities being perceived to have too great financial reserves. The problem for those in this situation is usually that they have become victims of their own fundraising success. This may have been due not to current fundraising but to campaigns of many years ago. Legacies for many major VNPOs may have been determined before the Second World War, whilst VNPOs with well-known names and fundraising departments cannot turn public donations on and off like a tap.

It is recommended that a VNPO sets what it believes is its appropriate reserve level. This would be probably within a range covering revenue expenditure and appropriate capital equipments less any designated or restricted funds for these purposes. The VNPO, in determining that reserve level, should be able to publicly defend why it has been set in that range. If it exceeds or goes below its target range then it should adjust over a reasonable period its expenditure/income. If a VNPO is established as being over reserved and it is meeting its stated aims then in the last resort it should consider requesting the Charity Commission to extend its objectives through what is called a 'Cy pres' scheme so it can spend its surplus funds. Specific advice from the Charity Commission on this issue was due in 1996.

The 'committed' charity

Many charities enter into long-term commitments. This may be a capital project, a new building for example or to fund a long-term commitment (such as an overseas aid charity with a five year literacy programme). The most conservative financial plan would be to have all the necessary funds before embarking on the project. How practical is this? There is no one or easy answer. There are some guidelines we can suggest as well as obvious legal control safeguards. You will need:

1 A clear indication of how the total funds will be raised with clear performance dates.
2 A reserves policy for the project.
3 A contingency plan at stages if the plan is not being achieved.

ACCOUNTING ISSUES

There is no specific accounting standard for VNPOs, but specific regulations on accounts for registered charities are being developed. Charities will be asked to follow a recommended practice, called a SORP (Statement of Recommended Practice), which itself is advisory but which has formed the basis of regulations to be issued by the Home Office. These regulations are mandatory on charities. SORP is in practice, however, mandatory only on charities with incomes greater than £250,000 as they will require a professional audit. Those with incomes below £250,000 but above £10,000 will have what is termed an **independent examination** by someone suitably qualified. The new accounting regulations reflect the intention for charity accounts to be consistent with each other, allowing for ease of understanding and comparison.

It is impossible within the restrictions of one chapter to cover the statutory accounting regulations and the SORP. The Charity Commission issues free guidance and there will be numerous specific books on this one subject. The important concept to note is that the SORP and the regulations recognize a distinction from normal commercial accounting. The principal of **Fund Accounting** for VNPOs, based upon restrictions about what they can do with their funds, is at the core of these requirements. VNPOs with restricted funds (which are funds subject to specific conditions imposed by the donor or by the specific terms of the charity appeal and binding on the trustees) may only use these funds for that purpose. They cannot 'lump together' all their funds. In recognition the old **Income and Expenditure Account** has been amalgamated with the **Movement of Funds Account**, to produce a new accounting statement called a **Statement of Financial Activities** or **SOFA**. The main purpose of the SOFA is to bring together all transactions in a single statement so as to present a complete picture of its financial affairs. This statement is radical for accountants in that it brings together both revenue and capital transactions. Traditionally in commercial accounting these are kept separate. Charity accounting has therefore some important variations from commercial accounts and specific guidance and training is essential.

THE BALANCE SHEET

This is applicable to both registered charities and other VNPOs. It tends to be ignored in favour of the Income and Expenditure Account, in part because by the time it is produced it is quite dated and because it involves understanding some specialist financial accounting practice. The balance sheet, however, is a very important financial statement as it reflects the financial stability of the organization and how it is financed. It does not have to always be a historic document. In preparing forward plans you can also forecast a balance sheet to a future date. Let us now in detail look at and explain a **balance sheet**.

The balance sheet is often described as a photograph of what an organization owns (assets) with what it owes (creditors) and what resources (funds) it has available. A typical balance sheet for a VNPO is shown in Figure 16.1. We have only shown one set of figures but you would normally have comparative figures from a previous period, usually the last year. It comprises the following:

Assets

These are items owned by the VNPO which have a monetary value. They are sub-divided into two categories: fixed assets which are tangible in nature and will certainly last for more than one year (for example a building or a computer), and less 'tangible' assets such as long-term

	£(000)	£(000)
Fixed assets		350
Current assets	450	
Less: Creditors – amounts falling due within one year	300	
Net Current assets		150
Sub total		**500**
Less: Creditors – amounts falling due after one year		(200)
Net assets		**300**
General Funds		
Accumulated fund		100
Designated fund		50
Restricted funds		50
Permanent endowment fund		100
Total funds		**300**

Figure 16.1 Balance sheet of a VNPO at 31 December 19XX

investments like shares in a company. The more tangible the assets, the less liquid (the less the ease of its disposal for cash) it is. Fixed assets are traditionally shown in the balance sheet at what they cost or what they were valued at when acquired, less depreciation to date. **Depreciation** is the term used to describe the process of writing off the value of the assets over the years it has been used. A motor vehicle purchased for £10,000 will not be worth the same amount two years later. There are many methods of depreciation. The simplest is called straight line. In the example of the motor vehicle you may decide to 'write it off' over five years. You would divide the £10,000 by five and reduce the asset on the balance sheet by £2,000 each year.

This process would continue until the asset had no nominal value. Some assets (such as investments) can increase in value. Here the opposite of depreciation occurs. It is revalued upwards and the amount on the balance sheet increases.

Current assets are items like stationary, which are very liquid or will be realized within one year. Debtors are those who owe the VNPO money and they are current assets if they are due to repay this sum within the following year.

Creditors within one year

These are liabilities to pay others and are the opposite to debtors. **Creditors** can be bank overdrafts or loans, organizations or people who you have contracted to, to provide a service or equipment. **Accruals** are expenses incurred during the period covered by the accounts which remain unpaid at the end of the accounting period (for example, telephone and electricity bills). **Deferred income** is income which has been received before the balance sheet date but has been prepaid in advance for the next period, for example a government grant received in March for expenses for the following April to June. If the VNPO was to close down, then this grant would be repayable. **Provisions** are also creditors. A provision can be an order for equipment or service that has been charged to the current income and expenditure account but which at that time cannot be exactly calculated.

Net current assets

These are the current assets minus the creditors and indicate how **liquid** or solvent the organization is. Trustees must be extremely careful if this is a negative figure, for it means that the long-term assets of the organization are having to be used to support it. If the only asset is the building that the VNPO uses for its work there would be very serious problems if the building had to be sold.

Creditors – amounts falling due after one year

These are **long-term liabilities**, including contractual commitments which do not have to be paid in the forthcoming year (for example, the balance on a long-term loan or a mortgage). A lease arrangement would also be a long-term liability.

Net assets

The net asset figure is the balance after deducting all the liabilities from all the long-and short-term assets. If this is a negative figure then the question has to be asked: who is financing the VNPO?

Funds

The funds section of the balance sheet indicates how the assets have been provided. For VNPOs they are divided between **general funds** which include designated funds, and **restricted funds** which include permanent endowment funds and money given for specific purposes.

Unrestricted or general funds are funds which, as the name suggests, are not subject to special restrictions. For registered charities, however, they must be used in pursuance of its objectives and in a way which is consistent with its charitable status. A designated fund is a particular form of unrestricted fund, consisting of amounts of unrestricted funds which the organization itself has allocated or designated for specific purposes. Examples would be for a new building, staff redundancy, or a grant making charity ensuring it had funds to meet a specific long-term commitment. Designated funds can be 'undesignated' if the trustees so decide.

Restricted funds are subject to specific conditions imposed by the donor and binding on the VNPO. It may only incur expenditure for that purpose. It cannot 'mix' or shift such funds to other purposes. VNPOs must ensure that they have specific assets that can find this specific liability. If the fund is supported by cash, while a separate bank account is not necessary the VNPO must ensure that it has sufficient cash within its balances to meet the restricted funds. Restricted funds are being 'held in trust' and the organization must not assume that they are part of their general reserves and funds. A permanent endowment is a special form of restricted fund. The capital of the fund must be held permanently, although the asset which makes up the capital may be changed from time to time. Only the income earned on the capital may be spent.

The balance sheet is thus a very important accounting statement, but it only shows the financial position at one point in time. It should not be relied upon in isolation to assess an ability to fund current operations. This can be done only by proper **cashflow forecasting and budgeting**.

CASHFLOW FORECASTING, FINANCIAL PLANNING AND BUDGETING

There are four key terms that need to be understood here:

- **budget** – a forward plan for a prescribed period, usually expressed in financial terms, against which actual performance may be monitored;
- **forecast** – a realistic assessment of a likely outcome during the course of a financial period, based on actual results to date and the likely pattern of events in the remainder of the period;
- **estimate** – an informed view of a likely outcome in the absence of firm data or historic evidence;
- **target** – a goal set for an individual or team as an incentive to achievement.

It is essential to realize that, whereas targets, estimates and forecasts may be changed in the light of altered circumstances, the essence of a budget is that **it is fixed for the period and is a benchmark against which actual results may be measured**. We shall look at this in more detail in the section on budgetary control reports below. Many of the general issues of budgeting were also covered in the earlier chapter on financial management.

There are some planning principles that are specific to registered charities. These are:

1 Check that all proposed projects fall within charitable objectives – this is particularly important on more specific projects when 'funds' of the charity are being used.
2 Agree priorities and forward planning periods with the trustees. The legal liability is with the trustees who must formally approve the plan/budget of the charity.
3 Pay particular attention to sources and levels of expected income. Prudent realistic assumptions about these must inevitably rule. On 'voluntary fundraising' in particular constant re-evaluation and control is required.

Budget setting

Once a VNPO has clarified its objectives and produced a variety of action plans to achieve them, the next stage is to put them in to money terms. There are two parts to setting a budget. The first is **to translate plans into monetary terms**. This is composed of two steps: deciding how quantities will change with the plan, and deciding how prices will change. For example, a special school for mentally handicapped children plans to increase its intake by 20% next year. There may be implications here for changes in the number of teachers, classrooms, laboratories, sports equipment, school buses and administration. The exact changes will be clarified by the detailed action plans. In addition to these changes, the budget for the school must include an allowance for the likely changes in the price of relevant items during the budget period, such as teachers' salaries.

Thinking about such numbers and prices in detail is also a test of co-ordination. If you have the resources to increase your number of classrooms, are you also able to recruit the number of special teachers required to utilize them? In commercial manufacturing organizations, production has a maximum level after which it can no longer produce an item. This is called **the limiting factor**. Many assume that finance is the limiting factor for voluntary activity, but this is not necessarily so. In the early 1980s, when the author was a finance director of a drug rehabilitation charity, finance from government was not a problem. Instead, it was suitable sites and buildings in the relevant geographic areas and the acquisition of trained staff.

The second part of the process is allotting responsibility. The planning process will have helped to clarify who has the power to affect various parts of the budget. As far as possible, action plans should have been provided by those who carry responsibility for delivering the service, and the ideal approach is to devolve the financial authority down to that level (for example, to the person who has responsibility for incurring the expenditure). However, your trustees may not always favour such an approach.

In charities the trustees should always express clearly who has authority according to the planning and budgetary process. A word of warning is necessary here. It is a common mistake that a budget represents an authority to spend. As we shall see with control reports, this has to be tempered by actual performance throughout the budget for the **whole period**. (For example, if an activity has been budgeted for at one level and in reality the activity is at a lower level, then you cannot continue to authorize expenditure at this lower activity.) To understand this concept requires an understanding of **cost behaviour**.

Where we can quantify expenditure, we call this cost. The basic principal of cost behaviour is that as a level of activity rises, so costs will usually rise. If someone works for five hours they will expect more pay than if they work for four hours. This is simple enough. The problem is, in what way do costs rise and by how much, as the level of output increases. The answer is to divide costs into their fixed and variable components. However, whilst such definitions are easily agreed, in reality costs are not so easily identified as being purely fixed or purely variable. In considering telephone allocation, a VNPO may make or receive so many calls that a second telephone line is needed. Here the fixed cost has increased rather like a **step**. Similarly, for salaries there may be a fixed element and an overtime element. These are called semi-fixed costs, or **mixed costs**. These issues were raised previously, in the chapter on financial management.

Breakeven analysis

Many VNPOs enter into a project on the basis that the project should not make either a profit or a loss – that the income and expenditure should 'breakeven'. To use breakeven analysis, you must understand the concept of **contribution**. This is where, if the planned activity is to be financed not purely by a fixed grant but rather in part or wholly financed by fees (a variable income), then you must find out how much of variable income, less variable expenditure, is required to cover the fixed costs.

For example, a day centre is financed by fees from the local authority of £100 per user. The centre has certain fixed costs. In preparing the budget, it would be useful to know at what point does the variable income (less variable expenditure) cover the fixed costs. The annual fixed costs are £462,500.00, and the variable cost per client is £7.50. Here the contribution per client is £100 minus £7.50, or £92.50. The breakeven point is therefore £462,500 divided by £92.50, or 5,000 clients. If you were receiving a grant then, depending on the grant conditions, you would deduct this figure from the fixed costs before calculation.

Budgetary control reports

The term 'control' is used to describe the complete process of monitoring actual performance, comparing it with the plan and responding appropriately to differences between the two. It therefore starts by comparing actual revenues and expenditures with the intended budget. This is not to suggest that other, non-financial measures of performance (as discussed in the chapter on performance management) are to be ignored, but that they have to be understood alongside this financial information. Actual performance reports are, therefore, not necessarily restricted to financial measures. The point of a performance report is to enable the budget holders to determine whether they are achieving their agreed targets and to tell them in time for them to take useful action. This means that there is a wide variation in the levels of frequency and detail required by different budget holders and the trustees of a VNPO.

Comparing actual revenues and expenditures with the budget will show up differences (**variances**). Small variances are obviously to be expected and do not require special comment. Indeed to avoid overwhelming managers and trustees with unnecessary information, it may be appropriate to provide **exception reports**, that is, reports which show only large variances (for example, in a large charity above a certain percentage amount, and in a smaller charity a cash amount). Any such variance needs investigation to determine its cause and to decide what action might be taken to get the organization back to the plan. One important distinction to make is whether the variance is **controllable**, in other words due to factors within the VNPO which can be rectified, or **non-controllable** and due to factors outside the control of the VNPO. Large non-controllable variances may require a rethink of the plan. Although budget holders may be required to account for why a variance has occurred, it is not necessarily their actions which have caused it. The point of the control process should be **to facilitate appropriate action, not find someone to blame**.

Flexible budgets

The term **fixed budget** has become synonymous with the voluntary sector. A common misconception is that once set it cannot be changed. Clearly, however, if required, revisions have to be made. Rather, a 'fixed' budget means that the budget has been prepared on **one estimate of income and expenditure at one level of activity** (such as, a hostel will have ten residents). No plans are made therefore which show the resulting effect on expenditure if the numbers are higher or lower than this. For control purposes you can imagine the problem if your project is based on one level of activity and it is actually 20% more or less. **A flexible budget** recognizes both the existence of these problems and the different behaviour of fixed and variable costs. It therefore allows you to relate your input to your output levels for a matching activity in the same period.

The advantage of flexible budget planning is that you can identify problems in advance and have an action strategy available if they do arise. Imagine a totally subsidized meals facility, based on providing 4,000 set meals a week. Budgeted unit costs are compiled into a total budget which is then compared against actual performance with a variance report indicating adverse and favourable variances. Scrutiny of the individual variances could show that labour costs were considerably higher than expected but this had been outweighed by a lower than expected cost for provisions. However, in making such an analysis it would be important to ensure that 4,000 meals had actually been provided. If this were not so then you would need to rework the figures. It is essential to analyse variance on actual output.

Virement

This is a mechanism by which managers may be given authority to re-allocate monies from one budget heading to another, where it is believed that by the end of the period the former would be underspent and the latter overspent; so that an imbalance may be corrected. Many see this as a good way to devolve financial decision-making to an appropriate level. However, it can be argued that such a process undermines the whole concept of budgeting. Virement needs to be closely monitored, therefore, as it can hide poor management which may have incurred a deficit.

Cost codes

Any accounting system must be designed to facilitate budgetary control. It is essential for budgetary control that a cost code system is introduced. To ensure that there is consistency in recording financial information, converting that information into management reports and then comparing actual and budgeted income and expenditure, it is essential to introduce a set of cost codes so that every item of income or expense will be allocated systematically as indicated by the appropriate manager. Depending upon the sophistication of your accounting procedure, this manager will be responsible for placing the appropriate code on the income or expense voucher before passing the documentation for processing. Cost codes are necessary whether a manual or computerized system is being operated, and properly operated should reduce the propensity for error which could otherwise exist.

Most small or medium sized VNPOs will use a simple numeric code with four to six digits. For ease of operation the cost codes should be established logically, using the first part of the code to indicate the area or type of activity (type of income, project expenditure, core costs, asset or liability) and the second part of the code to donate the class of income, expense asset or liability.

For example, a VNPO running a number of residential homes could operate a four digit code where the first two digits denote respectively fundraising items (10–19), project items (homes) (20–29), core items (30–39), assets (40–49), liabilities (50–59), or control accounts (60–69). The last two digits would indicate respectively income (00–19), salary related costs (20–29), property related costs (30–49) administration costs (50–69), or capital expenditure (70–79). Thus, the first home would be allocated code 20, a second home 21 and so on. The final two digits denoting salary related costs could include the code 20 for gross salary and 23 for staff pension contributions. At the end of the period when costs are allocated to individual cost centres, the salaries of staff at the first home would be coded 2020 and their pension contribution 2023; for the second home the equivalent codes would be 2120 and 2123. (In the guided reading section below, the book by Manley develops cost codes in detail).

Periodic reporting

The VNPO needs to determine both the method and frequency of the financial reports comparing actual results with budgets. For most medium and large sized VNPOs a monthly system is recommended, as this usually fits in well with other accounting cycles.

Many grants are paid quarterly and for smaller VNPOs quarterly reports may be sufficient, if supplemented by other information such as regular cash in hand or bank reporting. However, for some functions or at certain times of the year more intensive reporting may be required. For example, a charity shop may well be subject to weekly or even daily reports of cash takings to compare with budget expectations. Where there is a large volume of cash and cheque transactions the bank position will need to be monitored daily to take the best advantage of surplus cash which may be placed in the overnight or very short-term money market.

Setting up and approving control systems

In setting up an effective accounting control system the normal principle of **internal check** should be used. This may be somewhat difficult for the smaller VNPO where inevitably full control may be exercised by one or two key individuals. In such cases it is prudent for the honorary treasurer to be more actively involved on a regular basis, which should be determined by the volume and importance of particular transactions.

The trustees should ensure that there are clear written instructions concerning:

1 authority for recruitment, exercising disciplinary action and the dismissal of staff;
2 authority for placing orders and signing contracts. (These may be tiered, with different limits in a larger VNPO); and
3 bank mandates (authorization) and responsibility for operating cash **imprests**.

FINANCIAL REPORTS FOR THE TRUSTEES/MANAGEMENT COMMITTEE

Trustees/management committees must receive the financial information they require, to ensure the proper stewardship of the organizational funds, in as comprehensive yet succinct form as possible. These issues are discussed in more detail in Palmer and Harrow in the Guided Reading. Where there is a finance employee and honorary treasurer they should consult together on this aspect. It will usually suffice for the financial statements to be produced in summarized form on one sheet of A4. This may take the form of either a cash flow summary where a cash accounting basis has been adopted, or an income and expenditure summary where full accounts are prepared.

The summarized income report should include all the main sources of income on a functional basis, similar to that adopted for the strategic plan and financial budget. Expenditure may also be shown either on a functional basis by project, cost centre or unit of activity (again conforming to the strategic planning/budget form of presentation), or simply by main items of expense (salaries or rent for example).

The trustees, given the importance of liquidity, particularly in smaller VNPOs, should also have information about bank and cash deposits, or a full balance sheet. Finally, a brief report should accompany the financial statements to the trustees commenting on the main events or features of significance during the financial period, giving a brief explanation of the reasons for the main variances and providing an early warning of information which has been received which may affect the VNPO over the remainder of the budget period. It is important for trustees to receive timely information and where monthly reporting is being operated, the aim should be for trustees to have their financial report by the third week of the following month.

REFERENCES

Framjee, P. (1994) Charity reserves – counting the cost of commitment. *NGO Finance Magazine*, **4**, (5).
Harrison, J. (1993) Financial reserves – too much of a good thing?' *NGO Finance Magazine*, **3**, (13).

Hind, A. (1993) Financial reserves – time for charities to grasp the nettle. *NGO Finance Magazine*, **3**, (13).

GUIDED READING

The books below all provide good introductions to the key aspects of financial reporting and accounting.

Bruce, I. (1984) *Meeting Need: Successful Charity Marketing*, ICSA Publishing, London.

Harrison, J. (1984) *Managing Charitable Investments*, ICSA Publishing, London.

Manley, K. (1984) *Financial Management for Charities and Voluntary Organisations*, ICSA Publishing, London.

Mullin, R. (1985) *Foundations for Fundraising*, ICSA Publishing, London.

Palmer, P. and Harrow, J. (1984) *Rethinking Charity Trusteeship*, ICSA Publishing, London.

17 Conclusions: developing your managerial skills further

Stephen P. Osborne

INTRODUCTION

The intentions of this book were to help you to develop both your understanding of the key managerial challenges facing contemporary VNPOs and your skills with which you could deal with these challenges. With regard to the former intention, this book has, for example:

- helped you to understand what is 'voluntary' about VNPOs and their changing context;
- discussed the key roles and values of VNPOs; and
- reviewed the changing financial structure of the sector.

Similarly, with regard to the latter intention, this book has:

- suggested ways in which you might develop a marketing and/or business plan for your organization;
- talked about how to develop performance and quality management systems; and
- offered you a number of approaches for the strategic management of your organization.

These ideas and skills will be immensely useful to you in your role as a manager. However, it would be unrealistic to expect one book alone to meet all your development needs. This would belie the complexity of the tasks which confront you. You therefore need to consider where you go now, with regard to your future development.

A good place to start would be to conduct an audit of your strengths and weaknesses as a manager and to highlight areas which you think that you need to develop in order to increase your managerial effectiveness.
Look at the list produced by this audit and consider:

- have you been able to meet all your needs whilst studying this book?
- if not, which ones have you not yet addressed, or addressed only in part?
- do you need to prioritize these outstanding needs in any way?

Your answers to these questions will depend upon your own personal and work experience and expectations. Each reader is likely to have a different set of answers. However, it would be very surprising indeed if you did not list some unmet needs.

How you choose to meet these needs will vary with your own circumstances. It would be rash indeed for me to suggest one way forward for everyone. However, in this concluding section I list briefly some of the possible ways in which you might tackle your developmental needs in the future. These suggestions are made with the training and development resources available in Britain in mind. However, similar resources are often available in other parts of the world, so these ideas can easily be transferred to your own national context.

Having reviewed your needs, and considered your options, your next step should be to discuss your future plans with your line manager, your staff development officer or management committee. Inevitably, training has its own costs (for your organization and/or yourself) and these need to be considered as part of your personal plan.

AVENUES FOR FUTURE LEARNING AND DEVELOPMENT

Further reading

Undoubtedly the simplest way forward is further reading by yourself, perhaps guided initially by the 'guided reading' sections at the end of each of the chapters in this book. This is certainly the cheapest way forward and one that you can pursue at your own pace. The disadvantages are that it may lack any overall coherence and that you will have no one to resort to for advice if you are finding a particular issue or skill difficult to grasp. None the less there are a range of excellent texts available, ranging from the introductory to the advanced, and they offer a relatively cheap accessible source of further learning.

Short courses

Another easily accessible form of training is through short courses. These may be provided either as part of 'in-house' programme by your organization, or through one of the many external providers of managerial training (these include technical colleges, independent consultants and professional associations). These are an excellent route to further development, if you have identified a specific skill that you want to develop (such as recruitment techniques or stress management). They may also be the only option available to you with your present organization, because of the cost of other forms of training.

A traditional problem with short courses was that they stood alone and were not integrated with one another, and did not build into recognized

qualifications. This problem has, at least potentially, been rec
development in Britain of the system of National Vocational C
(NVQs). These focus upon your ability to demonstrate the pos
key competencies that are deemed necessary for you to carry
They allow you to build up to recognized qualifications using short courses
and they also recognize your prior development (this is known as the
Accreditation of Prior Learning, or APL). The NVQ framework is an
important one for the voluntary sector (Garner 1992) and may be an
advantageous one for you, but it does have two drawbacks. First, it is
still developing and does not yet cover all jobs, levels and roles. Second, it
has been criticized by some as allowing employers to provide training on
the cheap, rather than upon the basis of identified needs (Abse 1993). It is
therefore important for you to discover what you can about the NVQ
framework for your area of work, and then to discuss the alternatives
with your staff development officer or management committee. Your
local Training and Enterprise Council (TEC) would be a good starting
point for this process.

Advanced practice courses

It may well be that your needs lie in a particular area of practice which
faces some very special managerial challenges. If this is the case then you
may want to consider a specialist course in this area. These are offered at
both further and higher educational establishments. Examples include
Master's level courses in the Management of Community Care Services,
in Social and Community Development, and in Health Care.

The advantages of such courses are that they will be tailored to your
managerial needs as they are now defined. The drawbacks are that, if you
do change your organization or role in the future, then you may find that
there is limited transferability of these courses to other settings.

Formal management training

The final option, and in many ways the most complete, is to undertake a
course of formal management training. This is now available on a full, part-
time (usually one day a week) and modular basis, though not all these
options are available everywhere in the country. There are also a growing
number of courses based upon distance-learning materials. Such courses
can lead to the award of:

● Certificates and Diplomas in Management Studies, with the emphasis
   upon practical skill development; and
● Masters (MScs and MBAs) in Management. These courses concentrate
   upon understanding the managerial task, as well as equipping you with
   the skills that you need to carry out the role. They are now available as

generic courses in Management and also as specialist courses in such areas as **Public Services** or **Voluntary Sector Management**. You will need to think carefully about whether your needs will best be met by a generic or tailored course. Both provide different challenges and meet different needs. Aston University, for example provides both generic management courses and specialist public services ones; participants from the voluntary sector are found upon both courses. You need to decide which will most effectively meet your needs. For many senior managerial posts, in both the public and voluntary sectors, the possession of such an advanced level qualification is nowadays becoming an essential prerequisite to appointment.

There are a range of sources for such training, including technical colleges, universities and also professional institutes. Not surprisingly, this is the most expensive option for your development, though also the one most likely to enhance your career prospects. You may find that your organization will be prepared to second you onto one of these courses, and pay your fees, in return for a promise to return to work for them for a specified period afterwards. A number of professional training organizations (such as the Central Council for the Training and Qualification of Social Workers) also provide bursaries through regional consortia for the fees of recognized courses. Finally, you may be able to secure financial support, possibly in the form of an interest-free loan from your local TEC or from one of a number of independent sources of training support (such as a charitable foundation).

Clearly, undertaking such a course is no light matter and you will need to think through all the implications for yourself. Ultimately, though, it is the one that you may find both most satisfying and most useful in your career development.

The first step will be to get as much information as you can on the courses available in your area and about possible sources of support. Unfortunately there is no one source for this information, but you could try your TEC or local 'umbrella' organization for voluntary organizations. NCVO has also produced a directory of management training courses (NCVO 1993).

No one solution is going to be right for everyone. You need to be clear about your needs and choose the option that is right for you. The one thing worse than no training is to find that you have picked the wrong sort for yourself – especially if you are paying for it!

In conclusion, I would emphasize three points:

- do not think of your development as a manager as a 'once and for all' exercise. Your needs will change over time, as will the skills and understanding required for managing in the voluntary and non-profit sector;

- do be open to new ideas, whatever their source. The rapidly changing nature and context of VNPOs requires this; and
- do be clear about your learning and developmental needs for the future, and plan to meet them.

The voluntary and non-profit sector is an important part of contemporary society and managing in it is a complex and demanding, but ultimately rewarding, task. I hope that this book has helped to enhance your approach to this.

REFERENCES

Abse, D. (1993) The great NVQ swindle. *Voluntary Voice* (November), p. 11.
Garner, G. (1992) NVQs and the voluntary sector. *Voluntary Voice* (October), pp. 12–14.
NCVO (1993) *Voluntary Sector Management Qualifications*, NCVO, London.

GUIDED READING

Hems, L., Waterston, P., Osborne, S. and McCabe, A. (1995) *Training for the Voluntary Sector*, NCVO, London. This report reviews some of the strategic issues in providing training for the voluntary sector and questions whether a lead body is required. A good background to your own needs.
Osborne, S. (1996a) Management education for managers of public services. *Challenge Magazine*, **1**, pp. 28–9. This brief article rehearses some of the arguments for and against generic and specialist management training courses. Although written with the civil service in mind, the issues are highly germane to the voluntary sector.
Osborne, S. (1996b) What kind of training does the voluntary sector need?' in *Voluntary Agencies* (eds D. Billis and M. Harris) Macmillan, London, pp. 200–221. This paper reviews existing research and knowledge about the training needs of staff and managers in the voluntary sector. It considers options to meet these needs.
Pedler, M., Burgoyne, J. and Boydell, T. (1992) *A Manager's Guide to Self Development*, McGraw Hill, Maidenhead. An excellent guide to structuring the independent learning process for managers.

INDEX